CADWALLADER COLDEN

"Portrait of Cadwallader Colden by John Wollaston (The Younger) dated 1749–1752. Oil on Canvas." Courtesy of The Metropolitan Museum of Art, Bequest of Grace Wilkes, 1922 (22.45.6).

CADWALLADER COLDEN

A Figure of the American Enlightenment

ALFRED R. HOERMANN

Contributions in American History, Number 195
Jon L. Wakelyn, Series Editor

GREENWOOD PRESS
Westport, Connecticut • London

Library of Congress Cataloging-in-Publication Data

Hoermann, Alfred R., 1937–
      Cadwallader Colden : a figure of the American Enlightenment / Alfred R. Hoermann.
          p. cm. — (Contributions in American history, ISSN 0084–9219 ; no. 195)
      Includes bibliographical references and index.
      ISBN 0–313–32159–0 (alk. paper)
      1. Colden, Cadwallader, 1688–1776. 2. Lieutenant governors—New York
(State)—Biography. 3. New York (State)—History—Colonial period, ca. 1600–1775. 4.
New York (State)—Intellectual life—18th century. 5. United States—Intellectual life—18th
century. 6. Intellectuals—United States—Biography. 7. Scientists—United
States—Biography. I. Title. II. Series.
      F122.C683 2002
      973.2'092—dc21   2001040592
      [B]

British Library Cataloguing in Publication Data is available.

Copyright © 2002 by Alfred R. Hoermann

Library of Congress Catalog Card Number: 2001040592
ISBN: 0–313–32159–0
ISSN: 0084–9219

First published in 2002

Greenwood Press, 88 Post Road West, Westport, CT 06881
An imprint of Greenwood Publishing Group, Inc.
www.greenwood.com

Printed in the United States of America

The paper used in this book complies with the
Permanent Paper Standard issued by the National
Information Standards Organization (Z39.48–1984).

10 9 8 7 6 5 4 3 2 1

CONTENTS

A photographic essay appears following page 108.

ACKNOWLEDGMENTS

Research for this book has involved consulting the repositories of numerous institutions.

I am particularly grateful for the use of materials primarily obtained from the following: The New-York Historical Society; The New York Public Library; The New York Academy of Medicine; The Museum of the City of New York; The Historical Society of Pennsylvania; The Rosenbach Museum and Library (Philadelphia); and Edinburgh University Library.

For providing several illustrations, I want to thank the New-York Historical Society; the New York Public Library; the Metropolitan Museum of Art; and especially Mr. Steve Scoppetta, of the New York City Partnership and Chamber of Commerce, for his valued assistance in locating and making available a portrait of Colden in their possession.

I am also indebted to Ms. Sandra Kissam, President of SPARC (Stewart Park and Reserve Coalition), for arranging an extended tour of Coldengham, located near Newburgh, as well as such members of SPARC as Mr. Bob Monell, for providing an original map designating the Coldengham property and its vicinity, as well as several others of this group for newspaper articles and useful material relating to the site.

Finally, I especially wish to note my personal gratitude to Kathryn Baker for her interest and encouragement during all that time that was required to bring this extended work to completion.

INTRODUCTION

Although considerable attention has been given to Cadwallader Colden's political career, so that he is more commonly known as the Tory lieutenant governor of New York, he has not achieved comparable recognition for his extensive scientific and philosophical interests in the American colonies of the eighteenth century. It seems probable, however, that if Colden had had any choice in the matter, he would undoubtedly have preferred to be remembered more for his scientific than his political activities.

His political career was attended with no small measure of conflict and dissension, as the adverse remarks on his public career testify.[1] Again, his increasing involvement with several events that led to the American Revolution could not but render him generally unpopular.[2] This involvement may not have been without its repercussions with regard to his scientific and literary reputation. Benjamin Franklin—with whom Colden corresponded on botany, medicine, electricity, and natural philosophy—made no mention of Colden in his *Autobiography*, begun in the 1770s. At this stage, it may have been difficult to separate Colden's private and public careers but, had he been more magnanimous, it is quite probable that Colden would have been given earlier recognition for some of his more notable endeavors and accomplishments.

In any case, Colden's intellectual and scientific achievements have been neglected for an unduly long time. For over a century after his death, only oblique references were made to his work in some of these areas and these were usually contained in abbreviated biographies. Indeed, it was not until the beginning of the twentieth century that an attempt was made to identify

Colden's philosophical contributions. One of the first to recognize Colden as a "philosopher scientist" was I. Woodbridge Riley. In his *American Philosophy: The Early Schools* (1907), he regarded the entire subject of colonial philosophy—and Colden's relationship thereto—as little studied and imperfectly understood.[3] Coincidentally, a political biography of Colden's career in government also appeared at the same time. In her work, *Cadwallader Colden: A Representative Eighteenth-Century Official*, Alice M. Keys devoted only one chapter to Colden's cultural contributions; yet she described Colden as an individual "the vigor and breadth of whose intellectual life was nothing less than astonishing."[4]

Nothing, however, was more important in enhancing Colden's reputation than the publication of his letters and papers, begun in 1917, by the New-York Historical Society. These materials had been donated to the society in the nineteenth century by a great-grandson of Cadwallader Colden. The first published series comprised a total of seven volumes. These were later supplemented by an additional two volumes.[5] Even so, numerous letters, papers, and smaller treatises are still available only in manuscript form. Both the published and unpublished papers reveal the extensive scientific and intellectual activities that Colden pursued and certainly justify Alice Keys' interpretation. If any further confirmation of this were required, the preface to the first volume of these papers states: "One cannot read the correspondence of Cadwallader Colden and peruse his philosophical and scientific papers without realizing what a genius he was and wondering why he did not achieve greatness in the country he had served so faithfully during a long life . . . [it appears that] his wonderful range of knowledge has been quite lost sight of."[6]

In an article entitled "Cadwallader Colden, as Scientist and Philosopher," another writer evidently still felt that the "distorted picture" of Colden as primarily the Tory lieutenant governor of New York required correction, for he urged that Colden be seen in his "true light," as one who had made contributions to both philosophy and such sciences as botany, physics, and astronomy. He concluded: "As one of the small group of liberals who were touched by the currents of enlightenment in eighteenth century Europe, Cadwallader Colden left a marked impress on early colonial cultural life. Scientist and scholar, patron of learning, contemporary of the leading intellectual men of his time—this was the true Colden."[7] Finally, one of the early historians of the city of New York would describe Colden as "the first New Yorker to achieve a trans-Atlantic reputation," and a current work on the city cites Colden as "New York's answer, as it were, to Benjamin Franklin."[8]

Except for an article dealing with Colden's natural philosophy, not much has been written on specific aspects of Colden's intellectual interests.[9] There is still the need for a "detailed examination" of Colden's system, for a "new technical criticism" of his philosophy, as one author has argued.[10] More recently has come a recommendation for a biography of Colden, described as "a giant by reason of his virtuosity . . . [as] historian, philosopher, scientist, physician, engineer, and savant."[11]

Cadwallader Colden's varied contributions in these fields can perhaps be best understood within the broader framework of the trans-Atlantic repercussions of the Enlightenment of the eighteenth century. The Enlightenment exercised a major role in stimulating and, to a great degree, unifying many of the intellectual and scientific aspirations of the age. It was within this context that Colden found much of the guidance for his own activities and hoped to achieve a measure of fame and remembrance.

NOTES

1. *William Smith Diary*, MS, Vol. 5, October 30, 1776. Quoted in part in Paul M. Hamlin, "He Is Gone and Peace to His Shade," *The New-York Historical Society Quarterly*, 36 (1952), 171.

2. A discussion of Colden's role in this development can be found in Carl Becker's *History of the Political Parties in the Province of New York, 1760–1776* (Madison, Wis., 1960), 29–34.

3. Vincent Buranelli, "Colonial Philosophy," *William and Mary Quarterly*, 16 (1959), 347.

4. Alice M. Keys, *Cadwallader Colden: A Representative Eighteenth-Century Official* (New York, 1906), 1.

5. *The Letters and Papers of Cadwallader Colden*, 9 Vols. New-York Historical Society, *Collections*, 50–56 (1917–1923); 67–68 (1934–1935), hereafter cited as *Colden Papers*, with volume and page number. The society had previously published *The Colden Letter Books*, Vol. I (1876); and Vol. II (1877). The latter covered the period 1760–1775.

6. *The Letters and Papers of Cadwallader Colden*, I, *i*.

7. Louis Leonard Gitin, "Cadwallader Colden as Scientist and Philosopher," *New York History*, 16 (1935), 177.

8. Martha J. Lamb, *History of the City of New York, Its Origin, Rise and Progress*, 2 Vols. (New York, 1877); I, 55, E. Burrows and M. Wallace, *Gotham: A History of New York City* (New York, 1999), 133.

9. Brooke Hindle, "Cadwallader Colden's Extension of the Newtonian Principles," *William and Mary Quarterly*, 13 (1956), 459–475.

10. Buranelli, 36.

11. Milton M. Klein, "Politics and Personalities in Colonial New York," *New York History*, 47 (1966), 12.

Chapter 1
COMING TO AMERICA

> When I first came to America, I was very young and though I had some
> knowledge of books, I was absolutely a stranger to the World. The en-
> couragement to a meer Scholar is very small in any part of North America.

After several years as an undergraduate meandering the winding streets of
the ancient university town of Edinburgh and, thereafter, as a medical student caught up in the teeming life of London, choosing colonial Philadelphia as a place in which to establish a medical practice must have proved
challenging for a newly trained physician. At twenty-two years of age, Cadwallader Colden disembarked from an Atlantic voyage of some five weeks
to settle in a city perhaps best described in the early eighteenth century as
a raw frontier village with scarcely 2,500 inhabitants.

Founded by William Penn on the upper reaches of the Delaware River in
1681, Philadelphia was soon settled primarily by shopkeepers, artisans, and
merchants. Largely due to its religious toleration, it would increasingly attract a heterogeneous group of Quaker, Anglican, Presbyterian, and Baptist
religionists, while the rich agricultural hinterland was dominated by Swedish,
Dutch, and English farmers. In time, it was to be the massive Scotch-Irish
and German immigration that would transform and enlarge the city
throughout the first half of the eighteenth century. Indeed, Philadelphia
would remain the principal port of entry for immigration from England and
Europe throughout the American colonial period.

For Colden, the choice of settling in Philadelphia was not entirely fortuitous. He had an aunt living in Philadelphia, a widowed and childless sister of his mother, whose reports on the city may have attracted Colden's attention and possible interest. More to the point, after completing his medical training he realized that he lacked sufficient capital to start a medical practice in London, as he had originally hoped, and that opportunities might be sought elsewhere. If so, it exemplifies the dictum that, throughout much of their history, the Scots have been a nation of emigrants. This became especially pronounced with the Act of Union in 1707, when Scots could more freely immigrate to the American colonies, expand their trading and commercial activities throughout the British Empire, and serve in the British military or imperial administration. Over time, this would enhance the connection between the American colonies and both Scotland and England. It would also furnish an informal network that was to serve as a background to Colden's subsequent scientific pursuits and political career.

Colden was raised in the close-knit family of a Scottish parson. His father, having obtained an M.A. degree from the University of Edinburgh in 1675, was ordained as a Presbyterian minister in 1683. That same year, he received a parish in Enniscorthy, County Wexford, Ireland, remaining there until 1689, when he was transferred to the Presbytery of Dunse, Scotland. Cadwallader Colden was born in Ireland the year preceding this move, in February 1688.[1] Like his father, Colden was also destined to attend the University of Edinburgh, graduating with the degree of M.A. in 1705.

Unlike his father, however, who apparently had hoped his son would follow in his footsteps and become a cleric in the Presbyterian Church, Cadwallader decided to pursue a medical career. Rather than accepting a secure tenure in the church, which his father might have procured, he opted for a profession more closely related to the sciences. Perhaps that decision was due to a certain independence of mind or to an appreciation of the presumed social and economic benefits of a career in medicine. More generally, it may have been influenced by Colden's undergraduate curriculum, with the emphasis on scientific investigation that was a notable feature in Scottish universities—particularly in terms of its practical or social applications—or by a shift in emphasis and values as expressed in the nascent Enlightenment of the eighteenth century.

Upon arrival in Philadelphia, in 1710, as Colden later mentioned to a correspondent, he soon became inquisitive about American plants.[2] It is a statement that reflects his early commitment to some kind of scientific investigation into the flora found in the New World. An education which he felt had not fully prepared him to study botany "from my books" and the unfamiliarity of the local environment led him to ruefully remark, however, that he "was soon discouraged in that study." For a physician such as Colden, the investigation of plant forms proved challenging not only due to his initial scientific curiosity, but also because of the prospect of their medicinal applications.

By this time, botany had already been introduced as an academic discipline to various universities and was also aided by the establishment of several botanical gardens. In England, for example, the Society of Apothecaries developed a garden at Chelsea in the 1670s that became, in time, an important center for botanical teaching and research.[3] That apothecaries would undertake the task of developing a garden reveals the close relationship between botany and medicine at that time. In the 1680s, Robert Morrison developed a botanical garden and taught botany at Oxford.[4] In 1724, Cambridge established a chair for botany; in the American colonies, botany was taught at Harvard as early as the seventeenth century.[5] Again, the evident connection between botany and medicine at the University of Edinburgh is attested by the recommendation made by the Town Council, in 1676, that "considering the usefulness and necessity of encouragement of the art of Botany and planting of medicinal herbs, and that it were for the better flourishing of the College that the said profession be joined to the other professions . . . they unite, annex, and adjoin the said Profession to the rest of the Liberal sciences taught in the College, and recommend the Treasurer of the College to provide a convenient room in the College for keeping books and seeds relative to the said Profession."[6] Equally important was the increasing participation of the physicians of Edinburgh in the teaching of botany when, following the example of the surgeons, they established two "Physic Gardens"—one at Holyrood and another at Trinity Hospital—in the latter part of the seventeenth century.[7] Thereafter, botany and anatomy were confirmed as important prerequisites for the student who intended to enter the medical profession.

In one of his all too brief autobiographies, Colden acknowledged that he had taken undergraduate courses in botany from Charles Preston, who succeeded James Sutherland, the original intendant of the Town's Garden at Trinity Hospital, and who himself had been appointed professor of botany in 1676 and had, in 1693, published his *Hortus Medicus Edinburgensis.*[8] A later holder of this post, Charles Alston, not only communicated on botany with another member of Colden's family, but taught botany to both Alexander Garden and John Mitchell, two physicians who became active in the pursuit of botanical studies after they, too, migrated to the American colonies.[9] Both later were also correspondents of Colden on botanical topics.

While expectations subsequently outran actual remedies, it is not difficult to understand why "Europeans quickly came to believe . . . that America might have medicines to cure all of man's ills."[10] Even the eminent Dr. John Morgan, a notable eighteenth-century colonial physician, would claim: "This part of the world may be looked upon as offering the richest mines of natural knowledge yet unrifled, sufficient to gratify the laudable thirst of glory in young inquirers into nature. The discovery must greatly enrich medical science. . . . How many plants are there, natives of this soil, possessed of peculiar virtue?"[11]

On a more informal basis, private gardens also became quite popular throughout the eighteenth century with the result that there was a continuing demand for new and especially rare plants. Here, indeed, the colonists often had unprecedented and unique opportunities to aid their English and European counterparts in contributing to the collection and study of various plant specimens.

While in Philadelphia, Colden not only put his initial botanical pursuits aside, but also apparently began to realize that the medical profession was neither as socially nor as financially gratifying as he might have been led to expect. Indeed, the benefits of living in Philadelphia according to the city's propagandists included its having few physicians or lawyers—obviously, neither were required nor much desired at that time.[12] Another ongoing reality—especially for a university-educated physician such as Colden—was the plethora of "empirics" who dispensed various nostrums, in addition to perhaps some native American drugs, and generally practiced a kind of "folk medicine" acceptable to their patients.

To supplement his income, Colden imported and dispensed drugs, and even dabbled in merchandising various goods, primarily those channeled through the West Indian trade. The principal goods for export were usually agricultural products, including meat, grain, flour, and lumber. The usual arrangement was for a group of merchants to enter into some kind of speculative venture and hire a factor to sell the cargo to West Indian planters.[13] In return, sugar or rum was imported or, preferably, bills of exchange were remitted that were used to purchase manufactured goods from Great Britain. In 1711, Colden himself made a trip to Jamaica for commercial purposes, while also acting as an agent for another Philadelphia merchant; in 1713, he sailed to both Antigua and Barbados.[14] He made reports of goods sold—such as pork, dry goods, limejuice, wine, herring, and even some tobacco obtained from South Carolina—and prepared copies of invoices and bills of lading. He would note that, at times, there were problems with an oversupply of goods, due to several other merchant ships with similar cargoes that had also arrived in harbor, or with goods that were often spoiled while in transit.

On at least one of these excursions, Colden observed a curious phenomenon that would be recalled many years later at the instigation of Benjamin Franklin. Writing to Colden at one time, Franklin mentioned his experiments with electricity, particularly with lightning and its relationship to atmospheric conditions, which stimulated an interest in meteorological events. A topic that especially intrigued him was the appearance of water spouts at sea. He first broached his views on this phenomenon to Colden and opined that it was apparently caused by water being sucked up from the sea. In response, Colden recalled that he had observed such spouts some forty years previously while on a voyage to the West Indies and "it made so strong an impression on me that I very distinctly remember it." He described the water spout as shaped in the form of an inverted cone, with its apex about eight feet above the surface of the sea. He added:

I could plainly observe that a violent stream of Wind issued from the spout which made a hollow of about six feet Diameter in the Surface of the Water & raised the Water in a circular uneven ring round the hollow in the same Manner that a strong blast from a pair of bellows would do when the pipe is placed perpendicular to the surface of the Water & we plainly heard the same kind of hissing noise which such a blast of wind must produce on the Water. I am very sure there was nothing like the sucking of Water from the sea into the spout, unless the spray which was raised in a ring to a small height could be mistaken for a raising of Water.[15]

This induced Colden to reject Franklin's argument and, as an alternative, assign the cause to "an intestine motion like a violent fermentation." He thereby reasoned that its force could be dissipated by firing a cannonball through it so that "a horizontal vent is given to the wind." Franklin remained skeptical regarding Colden's explanation, if not his suggestion for dealing with the phenomenon.[16] Nevertheless, it was Colden's analysis that proved the correct scientific version.

Another imponderable that Franklin brought to Colden's attention was the shorter time required for ships to travel from North America to Europe, as compared to the return voyage. At first, Franklin believed that the diurnal motion of the earth was responsible, on the supposition that it might complement the "velocity" of the ship. Having had insufficient mathematical training in this regard, he deferred to Colden to determine to what extent the weight, dimensions, or shape of the vessel would have to be taken into account in resolving this matter.[17] Colden regarded the resistance of the water as a negligible factor and assumed that it would be either the frequent westerly winds or the tides, perhaps both, that could explain such differences.[18] This time, however, it was Franklin who eventually came up with the right answer, namely, the Gulf Stream.

Aside from his trips to the West Indies, and another to Portugal while enroute to England, it was Colden's first and last return visit to Scotland in 1715 that would mark a significant change in his life. Not far distant from where his father had resettled to administer a Scots parish, in 1700, Colden renewed a personal friendship with a former classmate from the University of Edinburgh, James Chrystie, in the neighboring town of Kelso. The two had continued to exchange letters after Colden had immigrated to the American colonies.[19] Through his friend, Colden was now introduced to James' sister, Alice, two years younger than Colden; after a relatively brief courtship, they were married in November 1715. The previous October, Colden had been requested by a member of the Scottish nobility, who had also been a childhood acquaintance, to raise a contingent of about seventy volunteers to thwart the advance of the Jacobite rebels near Kelso. However, no immediate military action resulted and Colden and his men were advised to disperse.[20] That winter, Colden traveled to London where he had previously submitted to the Royal Society a paper he had prepared on "Animal Secretions."[21] It was subsequently read before the society's members, although Colden most likely was not present at the time.

While Colden and his new wife were still in London, arranging for a vessel to take them back to America early the following spring, Alice's mother in Scotland hastened to send off a reply to a letter from her daughter, intended to reach her before the couple's departure. The letter itself conveys something of the pietistic values of a clerical family and the somber sentiments of a mother losing her daughter and the vain hope (as it turned out) of ever seeing her again.

Kelso, Scotland, February 2, 1716

I received your ever welcome letter with very great Joyfulness of heart, for since God in his Providence is thought fit to remove you at so great a distance from me, the way only for mitigating my great grief for parting with such a dutiful daughter which I was in good hopes should have been the holder up of my head and the light of my old age and years (you my dear child). You might easily know the great pleasure I always took in your refreshing company to me, would not be easily forgot with me, and nothing keeps my spirits at ease, but some hopes you give me in a joyful meeting you was in hopes to have with us all, which joyful meeting come often in my heart, and I hope it shall not be over much out of yours. I hope you will not forget your Mother in law has good hopes and advice she gave you, that she hoped that going to Philadelphia would be a means in bringing home her sister, and if once she would come over, there would be no fear of your husband and your return any more there again, whose coming would be a great means to both your father in law's family, and your father and me to renew our old age again like the days (whose wings if I had our joyful meeting should not be long deferred), but now since it is so failing out of your great absence and must of need be greater, there is nothing new will be so desirable to me as the good news of your happy arrival at your journey's end. And I recommend you to the protection and care of the almighty God (who is had a special care of you ever since you came into the world); that he may send his holy angels to guard your dear husband and you, and all your concerns wherever you shall go, by sea or by land, for he is a God by sea as well as by land. And I am hopeful daughter you will not forget to call upon Him (when you shall see his wonders in the deep).

Now, I must take my leave of you with my blessing and prayers unto you (and God grant that you may be fruitful as Leah and be beloved as Rachel) and that you may be a faithful wife to your husband, is ever the desire of your,

Loving Mother.[22]

Correspondence between family members in the New World and their relations in Scotland often took several months to reach its destination and was sometimes likely to be lost or misdirected in transit. Consequently, years could often pass before letters were exchanged. In 1721, for example, Colden's brother-in-law, David Chrystie, wrote to complain that "I have not seen a word from you these several years; I am as great a stranger to your way of living as the person that never knew you," and asked: "Why should we be dead to one another before the time[?]"[23]

Chrystie used the occasion to inform Colden and his wife that he now had three children, with another on the way. One of them was a daughter who, he said, reminded them of their deceased mother, for she had died in 1720. Apparently, Colden must have chided him while he was in Scotland for being a bachelor, perhaps at Colden's own wedding, and, in jest, suggested that it might be due to the rigors of a cold climate. With several children, however, he now could tell Colden, "You see our spirit can be as lively to get children in our cold rocky country, after we begin to it, as perhaps the most of people in your hot and fine country," and, to the allegation that the cold climate might have "immuned his spirits," he responded, "No, no, therein he was mistaken."

By this time, Philadelphia itself was gradually being transformed from a frontier outpost on the edge of the wilderness to an expanding city that was to prove most receptive to the ideas that constituted the eighteenth-century Enlightenment and, indeed, would eventually become the center of intellectual life in the American colonies.[24] The individual most notably associated with this early transformation was James Logan, who would dominate the political and cultural life of the city for almost half a century.[25] Born in 1674 in Ireland, the son of an impoverished Scottish Anglican clergyman who later became a Quaker, Logan would describe his childhood as a time of tribulation, due to Catholics who raided his home and destroyed crops. He later recalled, "In the days which should have been my gayest, I knew nothing out of school but terror and horror."[26]

He took refuge in learning. He taught himself Latin, Greek, Hebrew, French, and Italian, as well as mathematics, and began to collect an extensive library. In 1699, William Penn invited him to be his secretary and Logan left with him to settle in Philadelphia. Thereafter, Penn appointed Logan commissioner of property and receiver general of Pennsylvania. Logan went on to become a member of the governor's council and served for varying periods in such offices as mayor of Philadelphia, justice of the Supreme Court, Indian agent, and acting governor.[27] As a merchant, he engaged in the fur trade and eventually amassed large landholdings in both Pennsylvania and New Jersey.[28]

While mathematics may have been Logan's primary avocation, which he applied in such scientific pursuits as calculating astronomical observations, it was in such fields as botany and optics that he gained greater public recognition. He experimented, for example, with the hybridization of corn, a report on which was subsequently published in the *Philosophical Transactions*, wrote a paper on his revision of Huygens' method for finding the refraction of a lens, and also wrote a paper on spherical aberration, both of which were printed in European journals.[29] Working in relative isolation, he maintained a correspondence with noted scientists in Europe and, in the American colonies, aided and encouraged the scientific aspirations and work of others. In this way, he established the nucleus of a scientific community in Philadelphia.

Logan's singular status as an early proponent of scientific investigation in the Quaker colony and his widening contacts with like-minded individuals were soon to prove useful, once again, in the subsequent career of Cadwallader Colden. Colden would certainly have had a basis for a personal friendship with Logan who was his wife's cousin. He would have also been given access to Logan's extensive library located on the latter's estate, Stenton. Logan was probably the earliest colonial American to obtain, in 1708, the first edition of Isaac Newton's *Principia Mathematica*. He was also able to obtain the next two editions, as well as the first edition of Newton's *Opticks*. In time, his library contained the most complete collection of Newton's works in the colonies, as well as works by such diverse authors as Plato, Aristotle, Seneca, Boethius, Descartes, Spinoza, Locke, Hobbes, Harrington, Boyle, Harvey, and others.[30] Logan also wrote a treatise, *The Duties of Man Deduced from Nature*, based on the writings of Shaftesbury, Clarke, Wollaston, and Francis Hutcheson.

As part of a cooperative venture, Logan invited Colden, in 1717, to assist him in using a recently imported telescope to observe an eclipse of the sun. Such "readings" were not only useful in themselves, but they could also serve as a basis for comparative observations made by astronomers in England and Europe. Again, in a quest to find individuals who shared his scientific aspirations and to compensate for his relative isolation in Philadelphia, Logan would at times initiate a correspondence with others in the colonies. In September 1712, for example, Logan wrote to the governor of New York, Robert Hunter, telling him that he had learned from friends in England that Hunter was "not only famed for his great Abilities & exact Justice," but that he was someone interested in the pursuit of knowledge.[31]

Hunter was, indeed, one of those rare administrative appointees to the American colonies in the eighteenth century who brought an exceptional background to his post. A Scot, he had been born into relative poverty. After working as an apothecary, he joined the military and eventually rose through the ranks to attain a commission as brigadier. He was both a poet and a playwright. He knew—and his own work was highly regarded by—such literary luminaries of the age as Jonathan Swift, Joseph Addison, and Richard Steele. He also had a reputation as a classical scholar, a linguist, and an amateur scientist.[32] He became a member of the Royal Society and was personally acquainted with many of the political elite in Great Britain at that time.

Logan's overtures to Hunter met with a positive response, although their relationship would become more literary than scientific. They discussed, for example, the relative merits of various English poets and when, in 1716, Hunter sent Logan a copy of a Latin ode he had composed, Logan translated it into Greek. In 1717, they collaborated on translating the work of an English poet into Italian.[33] At one time, Hunter was even induced to visit Logan at Philadelphia.

Colden himself apparently was not given the opportunity to meet with Hunter while in Philadelphia, but he would certainly have known, through Logan, something of Hunter's scientific interests. Whether this encouraged Colden to make a brief excursion to New York City or whether the trip was related primarily to his merchandising activities is not known. As it happened, Colden took advantage of a trip to New York City, in the summer of 1718, to introduce himself to Governor Hunter at his residence at Fort George. The meeting proved so agreeable to Hunter that Colden was invited to extend his visit, and he returned again the next day with an invitation to stay for dinner. At the conclusion of Colden's visit, Hunter, sufficiently impressed, discussed with Colden and would subsequently confirm the offer of an administrative position in the colony. Colden moved with his family to the city of New York that same year. This relocation was to become the proverbial "sea change" in his life and fortunes.

Cadwallader Colden arrived at a time when the city's population has been generally estimated as numbering approximately 7,000 inhabitants, almost all of them concentrated south of Wall Street.[34] Except for some expanding farm holdings outside this area, the rest of Manhattan Island was still a virtual wilderness. A map completed several years later would show the several wards into which the city had been divided and the construction of numerous slips, wharves, and piers, principally along the East River, where ships were now able to directly unload their cargoes.[35]

After 1713, with the conclusion of Queen Anne's War, the colony prospered economically and began to compete with Philadelphia in the shipment of grains and foodstuffs to the West Indies. New York was a major port for the British navy, and also notable for privateers. A visitor to the city, early in the eighteenth century, remarked on its physical appearance and its inhabitants' social behavior:

The City of New York is a pleasant, well-compacted place, situated on a commodious river which is a fine harbor for shipping. The buildings [are] brick, generally very stately and high. . . . The inside of them are neat to admiration, the wooden work, for only the walls are plastered. . . . They are generally of the Church of England . . . and have a very fine church set out with all customary requisites. There are also a Dutch and divers Conventicles, as they call them, viz. Baptist, Quakers, etc. They are not strict in keeping their Sabbath, as in Boston and other places. . . . They are sociable to one another and courteous and civil to strangers, and fare well in their houses.[36]

Logan would certainly have been reluctant to see Colden and his family leave Philadelphia for New York City. Colden had also formed a professional relationship with several physicians in that city, and hereafter had to rely on correspondence to discuss medical diagnosis and treatments with his several colleagues.[37] In leaving Philadelphia for New York, Colden was also moving away from a social and cultural setting that might have been somewhat more amenable to his later scientific and intellectual interests. There seems to be a general unanimity among students of the period that the denizens of New York were primarily devoted to business concerns, with little time or concern for the arts or sciences. One writer, for example, succinctly notes that "New York was fundamentally a commercial city . . . with but a limited intellectual curiosity in regard to nature."[38]

There was, obviously, no lack of wealth, as the growing number of merchants, lawyers, and large landowners would testify, and as suggested by the mansions that were increasingly being built in the more fashionable sections of the city. The relative lack of interest in science, compared to that of their counterparts elsewhere in the colonies, may also explain some of the city's cultural deficiencies. This was a situation that did not appreciably change, if at all, until the 1750s.[39] No inhabitant of the province of New York, for example, was ever elected to the Royal Society throughout the colonial period. The example of the Massachusetts Bay Colony, which had nine fellows accepted into this prestigious association, may not be an apt comparison. However, while Pennsylvania was represented by three fellows, even Rhode Island and the Carolinas managed to have at least one of their inhabitants elected.[40]

Whatever relevance this might have had for Colden, it was really the political landscape in the province of New York that was to prove the more fundamental reality in his public career. Hunter had induced Colden to move to New York with the promise that he would appoint him surveyor general of the province, pending approval from London. In the interim, several minor positions were given to Colden, including that of weighmaster of the Port of New York, granted in May 1718, and ranger of Ulster County, north of the city, in July 1719. Colden was also appointed as master in Chancery, a court that Hunter himself had instituted in the province.

While Hunter would relinquish his post by 1720 and return to England, the eight years that he spent in the province were sufficient for him to form strong opinions on the problems of an executive who had to deal with the various factions, shifting alliances, and competing interests within the province, which was largely under the domination of a political elite made up of large landowners and wealthy merchants who were often interrelated through marriage. Their forum became primarily the provincial assembly. Although the governor had broad prerogatives, in theory, and was to apply these within the confines of imperial policies, it was the assembly, in fact, that had been granted control of revenue, including the governor's salary.

The exercise of such powers usually forced some compromise on the part of the governor and, over time, the gradual diminution of the executive's prerogatives. Hunter, for example, was prescient enough to predict that, if continued, it would lead to a general rebellion in the colonies against the mother country.

Such views must have influenced Hunter's protégé, Colden, with whom he privately shared his considered opinion that "People think it is a fine thing to be a governor. A governor by ——— a Tom Turdman's is a better office than to rake in the dunghill of these people's vile affections."[41] Years later, with some experience of dealing with the assembly, Colden would note to his son that "Assemblies in North America consist generally of a low rank, or people who have no generous principles. But it was much worse at that time [1719]. Several of the Assembly were Dutch boors, grossly ignorant and rude, who could neither write or read nor speak English."[42]

Colden, of course, continued to think highly of Hunter, a fellow Scot, not only as a man of culture and letters, but as a governor who had "extraordinary abilities both natural and acquired and had every qualification requisit in a Governor."[43] Colden may not only have imbibed Hunter's imperial outlook but, with regard to the assembly, he may increasingly have shared in the view that, contrary to its claims, it was guided in its political objectives more by factional interests and personal ambitions than by any overt principles.

Upon his return to England, Hunter was able to secure for Colden the post of surveyor general of the province of New York in April 1720, although Colden did not take up the position until 1722.[44] Hunter also had a hand in choosing his successor as governor, William Burnet. Within his social circle, Hunter had become friendly both with Burnet and his father, the Scots bishop and historian, Gilbert Burnet. The son also had the distinct advantage of being the godson of King William and Queen Mary.

Hunter must have advised Burnet on some of the key personalities and general political developments in the province before his departure. Burnet however, lacked some of Hunter's abilities to compromise and to ingratiate himself with the various factions. Arriving in New York in September 1720, Burnet would soon initiate policies that, in conjunction with those of his successors, would largely set the subsequent tenor and direction of provincial politics. Against the advice of Hunter, for example, he removed several potential opponents—largely representing mercantile interests—from the provincial council and replaced them with people he regarded as his political allies. A direct beneficiary of this move was Cadwallader Colden, who was appointed as a member of the provincial council in 1721.

The council itself was composed of twelve members and, while nominally independent, was chosen by the governor to serve "at will." Among its various functions, which were enlarged over time, it was expected to advise the governor as a kind of privy council or perhaps quasi-cabinet, to sit with the governor as the colony's highest appellate court, and to serve as a body that approved bills. Next to that of the governor, it became the highest colonial office in the province. As such, it conferred a certain social prestige on its members and, moreover, could exercise some political patronage and preferment.[45] The latter would become particularly relevant to an issue that was central to much of provincial politics of the eighteenth century: land distribution and ownership. Hereafter—both as surveyor general and as a member of the provincial council—Colden would invariably become drawn into such contentious issues. The office of president of the council was usually retained for the eldest of its members; in the absence of the governor, for example, the president of the council would assume the office of lieutenant governor of the province. Over time, with his continuing tenure on the council and with his advancing age, Colden would be thrust on several occasions into this office, as well as serving as acting governor, with its myriad political ramifications.

Another individual appointed to the council by William Burnet was James Alexander, a Scot who had arrived in the colonies in 1716. He was to become one of Colden's closest associates in the province and a lifelong friend. Alexander had received a mathematical education at the University of Glasgow and later studied law in London. A supporter of the Stuart pretender when he landed in Scotland in 1715, Alexander was subsequently forced into exile. Through a Scottish patron, he arrived in New York with a letter of recommendation to Hunter and was subsequently appointed to several offices, including that of receiver general of New Jersey and surveyor general of that province. Subsequently, he also served as deputy secretary and chief justice of the province of New York. He remained active in legal affairs and, in this capacity, was perhaps best known for his role in the notable trial of Peter Zenger, the publisher of the *New York Weekly Journal*, in 1735.

Burnet's continuing administrative problems with the provincial assembly led to his transfer in 1728 from New York to Massachusetts, where he died a year later. The next two governors, John Montgomerie, a Scot (1728–1731), and William Cosby (1732–1736), were largely placeholders who viewed their offices as a means of gaining wealth prior to returning to Britain. This, of course, was not unusual for appointees, who often thought of their office as a kind of temporary assignment and one which was generally bestowed through political influence, although Cosby was widely regarded as especially grasping. A later governor, George Clinton, who arrived in the 1740s, was so financially impecunious that he had pleaded with the Privy Council on several occasions to be appointed as governor of New York. His situation before arriving was so dire that, to escape his creditors, he had to leave his house early in the morning and return only to it late at night.

Both Montgomerie's and Cosby's administrations were apt to favor New York's mercantile interests, rather than the interests of the large landowners who provided much of the support for the policies of both Hunter and

Burnet. While Colden retained his seat on the council, the members of the group he was informally allied with now found themselves increasingly out of favor. These included James Alexander, who, as noted, was instrumental in the Zenger case, which was directed against Governor Cosby. By the time that Governor George Clarke arrived in 1736, Colden must have thought it wise to take a more circumspect position and possibly distance himself from provincial politics. Colden generally regarded politics, especially provincial politics, with a certain *hauteur*, and always hoped to free himself from a "servile dependence on publick employments."[46]

Such freedom as he could attain from the "dunghill of men's passions," as he termed politics, would come primarily through his retreat to a tract of land north of the city.[47] In spite of his early and rapid advance, Colden might have felt that his life in the city was often distracting and restrictive. He may also have found it difficult, with a growing family, to meet the expenses of living in the city or somewhat onerous to attend the various social functions to which he was invited by the governor. In any case, Colden regarded the urban environment as inherently "unnatural," and as one that also might offer "temptation to vices" (as he would later term it) that, as *paterfamilias*, he may have also wanted to avert for his children.[48] The city was noted for its numerous taverns and brothels, primarily frequented by sailors from merchant ships and the Royal Navy while in port. Areas in lower Manhattan and the ramparts around the fort itself were particularly notable for prostitution. A visitor to the city in mid-century was advised by a local individual that "to walk out after dusk . . . was a good way for a stranger to fit himself with a courtesan, for that place was the general rendezvous of the fair sex of that profession after the sun set. He told me there was a good choice of pretty lasses among them, both Dutch and English."[49]

It was probably Colden's appointment as ranger of Ulster County that led him to petition for a grant of land in that county, although his surveying activities would take him through much of the province, including the Catskill Mountains and the Mohawk Valley, as well as on various boundary surveys in Connecticut and New England. In 1719, he received a grant to a patent of 2,000 acres of land and, with the addition of further 1,000 acres to the original property in 1727, he moved his family to this rural setting in 1728. At this time, he already had several children, including Alexander, born in 1716, David, who died in infancy, Elizabeth (born in 1719); Cadwallader, Jr. (1722), Jane (1724), Alice (1725), and Sarah (1727), who also failed to survive childhood. Following the move, three more children would be born: John (1729), Catharine (1731), and David (1733). Of all his children, it seems that Colden was most solicitous toward his youngest son, David, perhaps due to the fact that an earlier son with the same name had died in infancy, or possibly because of a serious physical deformity that David developed in his early adolescence.

The location Colden had chosen was in a remote and relatively sparsely settled area, with only distant neighbors, approximately sixty miles north of New York City and a scant few miles from the Hudson River, near present-day Newburgh, in the townships of New Windsor and Montgomery. During the years between his acquisition of the original property and his final re-location with his family, Colden surveyed and cleared much of the under-growth, felled trees, laid out lines for buildings, fields, and pastures, and prepared cisterns, ponds, and wells. Livestock was introduced, gardens were prepared, and trees and plants were cultivated.

Using primarily local building materials, Colden built a commodious house with a thick slab stone exterior, in the construction of which Scottish stonemasons would be particularly adept, with floors made of sizable wooden beams and planking. The interior was divided into several large rooms, each containing a fireplace to provide light and warmth throughout the long winter months. Paneling was installed using the wood of local hardwood trees. Pathways and gardens were established as part of the land-scaping, and a road constructed that would provide direct access to the nearby Hudson River. At the river's edge, Colden had a wharf and store-house built. He kept a record of his "improvements" in a "Farm Journal" and, by 1727, he was able to write:

On the 15th of August, we sowed 4$\frac{1}{10}$ bushels of rye upon a summer fallow after Indian corn. The ground was very mellow. Sow'd under furrow about 3 acres. At the same time, sowed some spinage in the Garden. . . . On the 13th of September, we pulled our seed hemp. The same day I throw'd small quantities of hop Clover behind the house. . . . The 20th of Oct'r I put a parcel of Haws into hole in the ground in the second trench from the fence behind the house at the end next [to] the cow pen to be sown next fall. About that time I pail'd the Garden. The Posts & rails of Chestnut made of trees fell'd about 3 or 4 years & the Clapboards or pails of white oak from trees fell'd about the 10th of this month. The rails of the 5th and 7th panels from the Garden door next [to] the brook were of red oak rails that had been cut 6 or 7 years.[50]

As befitted a property comparable to the great estates that were becoming prevalent in the province or, more realistically perhaps, one retained by a country gentleman, Colden bequeathed the name of "Coldengham" to his rural property. The name itself may have simply been an extension of his surname or possibly inspired as a variant on the Bay of Coldingham in Ber-wickshire, Scotland. Colden soon told a correspondent that it was on his estate that he now hoped to raise his family and find that retreat in nature that would offer "quiet and innocent pleasures" for one involved in the passions of public affairs.[51]

One of the more unusual innovations on the estate was the construction of a canal which would allow shallow-draft vessels or barges to transport building materials, peat, or other goods on a natural stream that ran through his property. The canal itself originated in a marshy swamp, for which Colden also had a local pond enlarged and enclosed with sufficient stonework to collect and retain any run-off that could serve as an additional feeder for the canal. Remnants of that stonework, including the pond and canal, are still visible, as well as a small cemetery on the property—now with numerous headstones and enclosed behind a low brick wall—that may have been set aside at Coldengham as a local burial plot for the family.

As practical as it was, the building of the canal may have been visionary in another context. In some of the maps that he drew and later in his various reports on the geography of the province, Colden would suggest how its rivers and waterways could be connected to form a natural linkage with the interior of North America. In a report prepared for the Lords of Trade, for example, Colden expressed an imperial vision when he noted that, due to the length of the Hudson River, access was provided northward to Lake Champlain and Quebec, as well as westward to the Susquehanna River where "I am told that the passage through the Mountains to the Branches of the Mississippi which issues from the West side of these Mountains, is neither long nor difficult; by which means an Inland Navigation may be made to the Bay of Mexico." He also pointed out that it would be feasible to connect the Mohawk River to routes that would provide a direct link to the Cadarackui Lake (Lake Ontario) at Oswego, and thence to all of the other "Inland seas," and concluded: "By which means of these Lakes & the Rivers which fall into them, Commerce may be carried from New York, through a vast Tract of Land, more easily than from any other maritime town in North America."[52]

It is conceivable, therefore, that DeWitt Clinton, nephew of a later governor of New York, George Clinton, may have gotten his inspiration for the building of the New York State Erie Canal in the nineteenth century from viewing Colden's canal, since he grew up in the vicinity of Coldengham. Coincidentally, Colden's grandson, Cadwallader David Colden, was a member of the New York State Legislature at that time and lent his invaluable support to the proposal for the construction of the Erie Canal.[53]

Colden's quest for philosophic solitude and a retreat in nature may have been prompted by an attempt to distance himself both from the urban milieu as well as the ongoing political factiousness that dominated the province, but it was also broadly related to classical themes that were revived in the eighteenth century and were reflected in the works of other colonists of the period. Classical literature and language, as noted, were promoted by Governor Hunter, while his correspondent in Philadelphia, James Logan, collected works by various classical writers and translated such texts as Cato's *Moral Distichs* (1735) and *De Senectute* (1744). At the age of twenty-five, in 1747, William Livingston, a member of a prominent provincial family, would write an essay on " 'Philosophic Solitude,' or The Choice of a Rural Life" that gave expression to the Augustan ideal of a contemplative life in a rural setting.[54] Colden's "retreat" into the wilderness would be viewed not only as an extension of civilization, but as "civilizing" the wilderness. As he wrote: "I have made a small spot of the World, which when I first entered it, was the habitation only of wolves and bears and other wild animals, [but] now no unfit habitation for a civilized family."[55]

A large estate in a remote location had to be largely self-supporting to meet its various needs. Except for a few imported items, all the food had to be locally grown, and Colden's reference to "seed hemp" probably reflects the use of hemp for clothing. Finer fabrics would have been imported from England. Colden also attempted to distill rum, but found other distillers in the colonies reluctant to share any information on their methods.[56] The system of production required the participation of family members and often the assistance of temporary hired labor, perhaps even local tenants on the estate. Also, it often mandated the use of Negro slaves, given the scarcity of labor during much of the colonial period. Introduced by the Dutch as early as 1626, slaves eventually became an important component of the province's economy and were particularly valuable to owners of large estates in the Hudson Valley.[57] Wills of the period confirm that they were equally part of the estate of small farmers and might be inherited, sold or, from time to time, given their freedom. Again, slaves were also found in the city where they served in such varied occupations as cooks, butlers, and liverymen.

Colden must have already owned at least one slave, a female, while he was still in Philadelphia. In 1717, for example, he included her and one of her children as part of a consignment on a ship bound for Barbados, informing his correspondent that "She is a good house Negro, understands the work of the Kitchen perfectly & washes well." From the proceeds of the sale, he requested that he be sent the "Best & Whitest Muscavado Sugar you can get. It is for my own use & therefore do not mind the price & the rest in Rum."[58] Later, in New York, he wrote to accept an offer to purchase some slaves on his behalf: "Please to buy me two Negro men about eighteen years of age. I design them for labor & would have them strong and well made. Please likewise to buy me a Negro girl of about thirteen years old[.] My wife has told you that she designs her chiefly to keep the children & therefore would have her Likely [likable] & one that appears to be good natured."[59]

Living on a remote estate meant that education remained largely a family responsibility. While tutors were sometimes employed, it is more likely that Colden and his wife—who was also raised in a Scottish parsonage—made it their task to instruct the children in such basic subjects as reading and mathematics, while the sons might also receive some instruction in classical languages, such as Latin, in which Colden had apparently been instructed by his own father. Again, David would have acquired some of his scientific interests and training through assisting his father with astronomical observations and calculations. He later noted, with some pride, that he had never seen the inside of a school classroom.[60] Finally, all of the children would have had access to a modest library that Colden had furnished by importing books from England and continental Europe.

While Colden would have assumed the ongoing administrative responsibilities of managing the estate, his wife was equally obligated to take on such tasks while he was away for varying periods attending council meetings in the city, on surveying expeditions, or on various boundary commissions. Colden's apprehension about placing his wife in such a situation is evident when he wrote to tell her, "There is not a day passes without anxious reflections on the solitariness and difficulties you must be uneasy under in my absence."[61] Yet, she was just as apt to assume some of these duties to provide Colden with the necessary time and leisure to engage in his scientific and philosophical pursuits while on his estate and, for the same reason, can be credited with a major share in the education of her children. It was one of Colden's descendants in the nineteenth century who would recollect some of the stories that had been passed down to her and provide this account:

The virtues of [Colden's] wife cannot be better described than by the following lines from a valued relative who is now no more, in presenting me a family ring.

In the remote situation of Coldengham . . . she performed the duties of a wife, mother and mistress with peculiar propriety. The management of every part of her family was initiated and admired by all who had just ideas and were similarly situated. . . . this was fortunate for my Grandfather, whose superior genius for politics and philosophical pursuits rendered him indifferent to the management of household concerns—how happy was it for a man of his turn to be so connected: I never saw more proofs of the proper ascendancy of a husband, blended with esteem and love, than I have observed in this venerable Grand Mother, and I have often experienced how delightful it was to be an object of her affection. I have frequently heard those who have visited at the house observe, that the useful and agreeable qualities that should prevail everywhere, were by her judicious attentions very remarkably exhibited in those over which she had the direction, and when our intelligent progenitor, was called to preside over the government of New York, she did honor to his station by her conduct in every instance.[62]

One of Colden's earliest correspondents on botanical matters in the colonies was Dr. William Douglass of Boston. Douglass had been a student at the University of Edinburgh with Colden; both graduated in 1705. Thereafter, Douglass attended various medical colleges in Europe, including those of Paris, Leyden, and the University of Utrecht, from which he received his M.D. degree in 1712. He returned to establish a practice in Bristol, England, but left to settle in Boston in 1718. He began to investigate local botanical specimens and was soon able to inform Colden that he had collected over seven hundred plants within a four or five mile radius of Boston and indicated that he intended to extend his search to ten or more miles from Boston.[63] After the outbreak of a smallpox epidemic in Boston in 1721, he had to ruefully confess that he no longer had the time to continue with his botanical work. Even after the epidemic had passed, however, Douglass suggested that botany was a "rural amusement" more suitable for Colden's "Country retirement."[64]

Colden may well have been disappointed that Douglass had not done more to further botanical knowledge of the New World, particularly since there was no one to take up where Douglass had left off, but there certainly was no problem in finding other subjects of interest. Medical topics remained a continuing theme in the correspondence between Colden and Douglass and they could also turn to discussing such events as lunar eclipses and earthquakes. When Colden considered, at one point, that he might like to make a correct map of North America, Douglass promptly wrote that he would send Colden some "hints" that would assist him in making a map far more exact than any that had been published to date.[65] He warned Colden that if the map were to prove useful, Colden would have to revise the current boundaries between the provinces since they were no longer the same as those established by previous charters and grants. He then provided Colden with a series of observations and information on the latitudes of various cities in the New England colonies. At one time, he provided Colden with a detailed "History of the Winds and Weather in Boston" which he had collected for a year, but then had to confess, "I know of no Thermometer or Barometer in this place."[66]

Colden never completed his map. He later complained that although he had obtained numerous surveys from several colonies and had made astronomical calculations at his own cost while serving as surveyor general of New York and on various boundary commissions, he had not received any support in his endeavors from the British government. He added: "I was too inconsiderable to draw their attention to a work which must be attended with a large expense, however useful it may be of itself."[67] Douglass, however, continued with his own project, which resulted in a map published posthumously as *Plan of the British Dominions of New England* (London, 1753). It was subsequently used as a source for Thomas Jeffrey and John Green's *Map of the Most Inhabited Part of New England* (London, 1755) and in Lewis Evans's *General Map of the Middle British Colonies, in America* (Philadelphia, 1755).

Douglass's admonition to Colden that "botanical amusements" were more suitable for someone in a rural setting was made when Colden had recently settled at Coldengham and more than a decade before he became acquainted with the work of the greatest botanist of the age, Carolus Linnaeus. In the interim, Colden evidently must have instigated some botanical investigations on his own but—particularly in light of Douglass's remark—may have despaired of finding someone with whom to share those interests. His rural isolation, even in regard to finding like-minded individuals in the colonies, led him to tell Douglass at one point that "we are so made that our pleasure is but half finished till we can tell a friend how much we are pleased, and till we can if possible give him a share with us, and in a solitary life we lose all that share of Pleasure which a friend communicates."[68]

Colden evidently realized that such isolation or a "solitary life" also acted to retard the scientific progress that could only be attained by the fullest participation of all those committed to a particular discipline. He tried to compensate for this by suggesting to Douglass the formation of a society where scientific matters could be discussed and scientific information disseminated. Even after he had become acquainted with Linnaeus's work—and prior to the formation of a botanical circle in the colonies—he expressed a measure of despair in seeing any improvement in this science in the colonies, telling a correspondent that the colonists were "very poor in knowledge & very needy of assistance," adding that "few in America have any taste of botany."[69]

When the rather ambitious proposal for a book on American plants was suggested to Colden as one means of collating botanical information, Colden responded that sufficient information on American plants could never be collected until botanical gardens became as common in the colonies as they were in Scotland and England. He added, primarily in regard to such a book, "I may positively assert that not one in America has both the power and the will for such a performance."[70] Colden even considered the possibility of writing a natural history of the province of New York at one time but—as was the case with his proposal for a colonial map—the project was never realized, largely due to financial constraints.[71]

Colden's own reputation as a colonial botanist rests on his examination and classification of plants found on his estate at Coldengham during a relatively short period of two to three years. As he would recount later to a correspondent at the University of Edinburgh, "About the year 1742, a student from Leiden gave me the perusal of Dr. Linnaeus Character of Plants. As his Method was new to me and appeared exceedingly curious and his characters more accurate than any I had seen, it excited my curiosity to examine the plants which grew about my house. I put my observations in writing."[72] Colden had probably obtained the 1737 edition of the *Genera Plantarum*, in which Linnaeus had applied his binomial method of classification into genera and species based on the sexual characteristics of plants, that is, the number of pistils and stamens. Colden subsequently sent the results of his "observations" to John Frederick Gronovius of Leyden, primarily because of the latter's publication of the *Flora Virginia*.[73] That work was itself based on a manuscript and plant specimens supplied by John Clayton of Virginia.[74] Clayton's own interest in botany was probably due to his friendship with Mark Catesby, the artist and naturalist. When Catesby returned to England, Clayton continued to provide local plants and seeds to Catesby who, in turn, passed them on to Gronovius. Linnaeus examined and classified many of Clayton's specimens and incorporated them into an early work, *Hortus Cliffortianus* (1738).

An important intermediary in England between the colonists and their European counterparts was the London merchant Peter Collinson. With his brother, James, he inherited his father's business as a haberdasher and mercer.[75] Their commercial transactions soon brought them into contact with merchants and others in the American colonies and the West Indies. Peter Collinson's love of plants and gardening, apparently instilled in him by his Quaker background, motivated his search for like-minded men in the colonies. As Collinson expressed it, "My love for new and rare plants put me often in soliciting [American colonists] for seeds or plants from new countries." After 1728, when Collinson was chosen as a member of the Royal Society, he also forwarded to the colonists requests for the scientific information sought by that Association. Thus, his love for botany, his responsibilities as a member of the Royal Society, and his business interests all combined to promote Collinson's continuing interest in the American colonies. Collinson probably became acquainted with Linnaeus when the latter visited England in 1736.[76] Thereafter, he also acted as a *via media* between American botanists and Linnaeus.

Collinson confirmed the importance of Colden's achievement by telling him, "my valuable friend Doc Gronovius let me know what a fine present you have made him. The good man is in raptures."[77] Linnaeus, in turn, was pleased to learn what an apt pupil he had in Colden, the first American colonist to collect and classify plants according to his method. This was, indeed, a significant attainment since, unlike Clayton, Colden did not submit plant specimens to Europe in order to obtain an indication of their scientific status, but had been able to pursue and present this work on his own. Collinson joined the chorus of praise when he wrote that "it is a remarkable instance what leisure and application, assisted with a great genius can attain to" and added, "I could not have imagined it [the Linnaean method] had reach'd in so short a time to the remote parts of North America."[78]

Linnaeus included Colden's botanical descriptions under "Plantae Coldenhamiae" in the *Acta Upsaliensi* for 1743, and named a plant, a genus of borginaceous herb of the tribe *Ehreticoe* after him (Coldenia).[79] In addition, he honored Colden with the title of *Summus Perfectus*, which led Colden to reply with due humility, "I must inform you that the title of *Summus Perfectus* in no way belongs to me. I know not what has led you into this mistake."[80] Contained in these generous acts by Linnaeus was some small measure of that recognition that Colden sought for his scientific endeavors. As Franklin commented: "I congratulate you on the Immortality conferr'd upon you by the learned Naturalists of Europe. No species or Genus or Plants was ever lost, or ever will be while the World continues, and therefore your Name, now annext to one of them, will last forever."[81]

In spite of Colden's evident admiration for the Linnaean method of botanical classification, he did not accept it uncritically. He expressed his reservations concerning the Linnaean system both to Linnaeus and at greater length to Gronovius at the University of Leyden. To the latter, he stated his view that all systems of classification must remain incomplete until they can be made to conform more closely to nature, or a natural method of classification; otherwise, we can "so easily fall into mistakes of dividing & confounding what should be join'd or separated as we are tempted to do for the sake of a favourite system."[82] In addition, Colden suggested certain changes in the Linnaean method of classification. While some of these concerned the status of certain flora within a particular genus, a more general problem, Colden argued, was Linnaeus's predisposition to multiply classes unnecessarily.

Colden assumed that Linnaeus may have been forced to do so in order to prevent any one class from being too crowded; to remedy this, he proposed that botanists should revert to using some aspects of a more natural system as exemplified by the English botanist, John Ray (*Methodus plantarum emendata et aucta*, 1703). Too many botanical classes, Colden argued, violated that continuity in nature that should be the touchstone for any system of classification. He exemplified his views by telling Gronovius: "Indeed my opinion is that the Natural Gradation from the lowest class to the highest is by such small & imperceptible steps, that it is very difficult to distinguish every the [*sic*] next step either upwards or downwards tho' at some distance the distinction be very remarkable[.] For this reason, any system in botany would give me strong prejudice in its favor, where there appears such a gradation from one class to another & from one Genus to another through the several species, that the step from one to the other becomes almost imperceptible. When ever this system shall be discover'd, I shall conclude it to be the natural system."[83] Subsequently, French critics of the Linnaean system would raise much the same objections.

Nevertheless, the quest for a natural system of classification would have to remain more of an ideal, at least for the time being, for Colden realized that pragmatic as well as aesthetic and scientific concerns had to be considered in the creation of any method of classification. As an alternative, and largely for didactic reasons, Colden suggested that plants should initially be collected without any preconceived method and thereafter might be divided into such "artificial" systems as would best serve novices or those ignorant of botanical matters. Colden evidently viewed this approach as serving educational purposes, for he concluded by telling Gronovius, "I cannot forbear to wish you would try this method in a new edition of your American plants for my sake & other unskillful Philo-Botanists in America."[84]

Although Colden may have been the first to apply the Linnaean system of botanical classification to native plants in America, there were soon others who would contribute to this endeavor and provide the nucleus of an emerging botanical circle in the colonies that later also extended to various associates in England and Europe. In this way, botany together with other sciences soon served to create that Atlantic community which sustained numerous intellectual and cultural exchanges throughout the eighteenth century between the Old World and the New.

Although scattered throughout the colonies and possessing varying skills, two individuals who visited with Colden on his estate and would also achieve recognition for their botanical endeavors were Dr. Alexander Garden of Charleston, South Carolina, and John Bartram from Philadelphia. Colden also found a correspondent in Dr. John Mitchell of Urbanna, Virginia, who arrived in the colonies in 1735 and remained there for little more than a decade. Mitchell had two of his papers on botany published, the *Dissertation Brevis de Principiis Botanicum et Zoologorum*, and the *Nova Genera Plantarum*, in 1748.[85] While Mitchell corresponded for a time with Colden, it was primarily on medical and, to a lesser extent, political rather than botanical matters.

Garden was a graduate of the University of Edinburgh and arrived in the American colonies to settle in Charleston in the early 1750s, whereupon he almost immediately tried to undertake the study of plants in the area. The result was confusion and frustration due to the competing and incomplete systems of classification that he tried to apply to plant forms. As in Colden's case, it was not until Garden had been introduced to the writings of Linnaeus that he was able to renew his studies with greater satisfaction and enthusiasm. If Colden could credit the "excellency" of the Linnaean method for giving him "new lights," Garden could also tell Linnaeus that his books "Have first introduced into botany the science of demonstration, founded upon mathematical principles, and at the same time a sound, as well as easy mode of classification. . . . Such neatness! Such regularity! So clear and supremely ingenious a system, undoubtedly never appeared before in the botanical world."[86]

Garden's admiration for Linnaeus made him quite indignant with all those who could not appreciate his mentor's contributions and status in botanical science.[87] Yet this did not inhibit him from making several suggestions, like Colden, for revising aspects of the Linnaean scheme. Linnaeus welcomed such criticisms, sometimes incorporating them in subsequent editions of his works.

Garden became more fully acquainted with Linnaeus's books during the summer of 1754. Due to an illness that could only be aggravated by the inescapable heat and humidity in the south, he decided to take a trip to the northern colonies. There, he was given the opportunity to meet both Cadwallader Colden and John Bartram for the first time. Colden proved especially helpful to this fledgling botanist. He showed Garden the Linnaean literature in his own library, including both the *Systema Naturae* and the *Critica Botanica*, in addition to the letters that had passed between Linnaeus and Colden. This measurably broadened Garden's knowledge of the Linnaean method and inspired him, once he returned to Charleston, to begin the work of finding those plants that were unknown in the more northerly colonies. He wrote to tell Linnaeus that his trip was the inducement to initiate a correspondence with the eminent botanist and, while he felt that he might not be able to match the achievements of his host in New York, he was determined to do his part, and added: "I will not yield to them in my ardent desire to imbibe true science from the same source, and to quench my thirst at so pure a spring."[88]

After Garden returned to South Carolina, he instigated this plan although now, more than ever, he too felt isolated in "a horrid country, where there is not a living soul who knows the least *iota* of Natural History." His rewarding excursion to New York and Pennsylvania, where he also visited Bartram, led him to exclaim: "How grateful was such a meeting to me! And how unusual in this part of the world! What congratulations and salutations passed between us! How happy I should be to pass my life with men so distinguished by genius, botanical learning and experience!—men in whom the greatest knowledge and skills are united to the most amiable candour."[89]

Perhaps somewhat to his surprise, however, Linnaeus was less responsive to Garden's suggestion of looking for plants indigenous to the Carolinas, and more interested in having him obtain specimens of the fish, reptiles, and insects of the region. At first, this may have struck Garden as quite surprising and might have made Garden wonder how appreciative Linnaeus was regarding the botanical efforts of his disciples in the New World, especially since Garden had to wait nearly four years for a reply. Others also experienced the procrastination and unresponsiveness that Linnaeus sometimes exhibited. Collinson, for example, once advised Linnaeus, "It is a general complaint that Dr. Linnaeus receives all, and returns nothing. This I tell you as a friend, and as such I hope you will receive it in friendship."[90]

Garden graciously accepted his new instructions from Linnaeus and, while he admitted that he had never paid any attention to fishes, quickly added, "all your wishes are commands to me." Garden's success in meeting and surpassing the requirements of this task, whose results Linnaeus planned to use as a basis for comparison with the descriptions in Mark Catesby's *Natural History of Carolina, Florida, and the Bahama Islands, 1731–1743,* finally prompted Linnaeus to encourage Garden in his original proposal. In the end, it must have gratified Garden that Linnaeus included his descriptions of several new fishes as well as plants that he had collected in the twelfth edition of the *Systema Naturae* (1766–1768). In addition, Garden had a plant (*Gardenia*) named after him. After his election, in 1763, to the Royal Society of Uppsala, Garden was also honored by his election, ten years later, to the Royal Society of London.[91]

One colonial botanist who did not limit his botanical investigations to the immediate vicinity of his home outside Philadelphia and, indeed, made

botany itself a lifelong avocation, was John Bartram. His initial enthusiasm
for botany grew out of his profound fascination with a daisy. His charming
account recalls that moment of revelation:

One day I was very busy in holding my plough (for thou seest that I am but a
ploughman), and being weary, I ran under a tree to repose myself. I cast my eyes on
a daisy; I plucked it mechanically and viewed it with more curiosity than common
country farmers are wont to do, and observed therein very many distinct parts, some
perpendicular, some horizontal. "What a shame," said my mind, "that thee shouldst
have employed thy mind so many years in tilling the earth and destroying so many
flowers and plants without being acquainted with their structures and their uses." I
thought about it continually, at supper, in bed, and wherever I went.[92]

This event changed the course of Bartram's life for he soon developed a
passionate interest in flowers and plants. In time, he traveled extensively to
New England and Canada, as well as to Florida, in search of plants, seeds,
and information relative to the physical environment in which they were
found. The result of these travels was the publication of his *Observations on
the Inhabitants, Climate, Soil, Rivers, Productions, Animals, and other Matters worthy of Notice. Made by Mr. John Bartram, in His Travels from Pennsylvania to Onandago, Oswego, and the Lake Ontario, in Canada.*[93]

Largely self-taught, Bartram was at some considerable disadvantage in not
being able to classify all that he encountered on his excursions into the
backwoods of America. This did not dampen his enthusiasm nor does it
make his botanical contributions less impressive. Bartram was quite content
to collect various specimens and seedlings and send them off to England.
The English friends who came to rely upon him to furnish such specimens
later financed Bartram's botanical work.[94] In 1765, Bartram was rewarded
with an appointment as botanist to the King. Thereafter, Bartram took a
trip to Florida and subsequently published his *Description of East Florida,
with a Journal Kept by John Bartram, of Philadelphia* (1766).[95]

It was Peter Collinson who assumed much of the responsibility for guiding Bartram in his botanical excursions. Unlike Colden or Garden, Bartram
had no professional duties that might distract him from his search for plants
and he was often quite content to meet the constant demand for information
and specimens that Collinson placed upon him. It was primarily due to
Bartram's diligent labors that Collinson was able to build up a list of sub-
scribers who wished to import seeds and plants, which confirms that botany
and gardening were a favorite preoccupation of the upper classes in Great
Britain. As Collinson informed Bartram, "There is a [great] spirit and [love
of gardening and planting] amongst the nobility and gentry, and the pleasure and profit that attend it will render it a lasting delight."[96]

Every so often Bartram would submit a plant which Collinson would
consider so rare that it could only be reserved for study by the great Lin-

naeus. Bartram's self-esteem must have been substantially gratified when Collinson informed him, "All Botanists will join me in thanking my dear John for his unwearied pains to gratify every inquisitive genius. I have sent Linnaeus a specimen and one leaf of TIPITIWITCHET SENSITIVE, only to him would I spare such a jewel. Linnaeus will be in rapture at the sight of it."[97]

It may have been Peter Collinson who was responsible for introducing his Quaker friend to Cadwallader Colden. In one of his letters to Bartram, Collinson told him that he was enclosing a letter to Doctor Colden which was, in effect, a letter of introduction.[98] Collinson evidently believed that Colden, in his capacity as surveyor general, would know where to direct Bartram in his botanical excursions. Bartram missed seeing Colden on his trip but the next year, after a similar excursion, could report that "This hath been a happy Journey: and I met with our friend, Doctor Colden, who received me with all the demonstrations of civility and respect that were convenient."[99] Thereafter, Colden and Bartram were in constant touch with each other for several years.

In 1743, Bartram mentioned to Collinson that Colden had received a new edition of the *Characteres Plantarum* [*sic*] and had advised him to ask Gronovius for a personal copy of the same work. Bartram recognized the importance of this work, telling Collinson "by it he [Colden] hath attained to the greatest knowledge in Botany, of any I have discoursed with." Yet, it was too optimistic on Colden's part to expect Bartram to be able to read and use this book. Classification using Latin terminology was not Bartram's *forte*. Colden probably realized this when, sometime later, he had to translate from Latin into English Gronovius's reply to Bartram.[100]

Colden continued to show an ongoing interest in Bartram's progress, and Bartram certainly appreciated all the assistance this noted Linnaean botanist might provide. Bartram, who also dispensed medicine among his poorer neighbors, often requested and obtained information on suitable medical treatments from Colden.[101] In 1744, while on an excursion to Philadelphia, Colden visited Bartram at his home and later invited him to stop by at Coldengham on one of his "Rambles" to the Catskill Mountains, which Bartram did in 1753. While these two men may have had little else in common, their mutual devotion to botany proved sufficient to sustain a relationship that both men valued. Colden could tell Bartram, "It gives me much pleasure to think that your name and mine may continue together in remembrance of our Friendship," whereas Bartram would describe Colden as "a worthy gentleman, of pleasant and agreeable conversation, and great humanity."[102]

John Bartram can also be credited with creating the first authentic botanical garden in colonial America, begun in 1728 and completed about 1735. On his return trip from New York, Alexander Garden stopped by to visit with Bartram in Pennsylvania, and has left a revealing description of Bartram as reflected in his botanical garden, in a letter to Colden:

His garden is a perfect portraiture of himself; here you meet with a row of rare plants almost covered over with weeds; here with a beautiful shrub, even luxuriant amongst the briars, and in another corner an elegant & lofty tree lost in common thicket— on our way from town to his house, he carried me to several rocks & dens, where he showed me some of his rare plants, which he had brought from the mountains etc. In a word, he disdains to have a garden less than Pennsylvania & every den is an arbour; every run of water, a canal; & every small level spot a parterre, where he nurses up some of his idol flowers & cultivates his darling productions. He had many plants whose names he did not know, most or all of which I had seen & knew them— On the other hand, he had several I had not seen & some I never heard of.[103]

As early as 1744, John Bartram's name was proposed as the botanist of the American Philosophical Society, although it was not until 1768 that he was confirmed in that position. His international reputation, however, was assured when, in recognition of his extensive botanical work, Linnaeus elevated Bartram to the status of "The greatest natural botanist of the age."[104] John Bartram must have transmitted at least part of his love for botany to his son, William. The latter, a skillful artist, provided detailed drawings of the birds, insects, and plants that he and his father encountered in their several travels together. Later, William would continue to make such trips on his own, and the fact that he ranged as far afield as his father is indicated by one of his books, *Travels through North and South Carolina, Georgia, East and West Florida* (1791).

At times, unfortunately, rivalry might take precedence over amicability among members of the colonial botanical circle. At one point, Garden took umbrage at Bartram's claim to have found some new plants in the Carolinas. Garden had, it may be recalled, reserved this area as his own "territory," so to speak, when he had offered Linnaeus his services after returning from his trip to New York and Pennsylvania. Bartram made an excursion to South Carolina in 1760, visiting Garden on the way, and it was here that he discovered a new oak. When John Ellis, an English naturalist and a long-time correspondent of Garden, asked the latter why he had not reported on this tree since it was indigenous to Garden's locale, the latter was motivated to write, "Let me assure you that [Bartram] received from me these very specimens . . . he has, it seems, made a different use from what I apprehended."[105]

Shortly thereafter, Garden's ire was again vented when he learned that Bartram had been appointed king's botanist. This led him to tell Ellis, "I find he knows nothing of the generic characters of plants, and can neither class nor describe them. . . . from great natural strength of mind and long patience, he has much acquaintance with the specific characters, though this knowledge is rude, inaccurate, indistinct, and confused, seldom determining well between species and varieties." And, concerning Bartram's new status, he added, "Is it really so? Surely John is a worthy man, but yet to give the title . . . to a man who can scarcely spell, much less make out the characters of any one genus of plants, appears rather hyperbolical."[106] That Garden was sensitive to any real or imagined slight is confirmed by his refusal to submit any further papers for publication to the *Philosophical Transactions* for several years after he had been treated unfairly, as he believed, by some members of the Royal Society.

It was probably the educational disparities between the two men that made Garden envious of Bartram's international reputation as a naturalist. Such issues evidently never intruded in Bartram's relationship with Colden. The two men, as already indicated, got on admirably, even if Colden may have taken a somewhat paternalistic approach to instructing and guiding Bartram in his endeavors. While Colden and Garden shared a common educational background and both employed the Linnaean method, it was Garden who apparently dedicated himself more fully to serving Linnaeus and following his instructions. It would be difficult to imagine Colden being equally obsequious, nor would Colden necessarily have been patient enough to wait several years for a reply from Linnaeus and then abruptly redirect his interests to other fields.

Colden was Garden's senior by forty-two years. He had little of that youthful exuberance or idealism that marked Garden's attitude toward botanical explorations. Again, Colden's work in botany preceded Garden's by nearly fifteen years. Once Colden had been able to grasp and successfully apply the Linnaean scheme of classification and had been given recognition for his botanical achievements, he was apt to turn his attention to other scientific matters. Garden, in contrast, continued his work in botany until a few years before the American Revolution, when he returned to England. Consequently it may be understandable that, whereas Colden could take a more positive if not indulgent, attitude to Bartram, Garden found it difficult to fully acknowledge the inherent significance of Bartram's botanical status.

There is also, in Garden, that pious respect toward nature—especially botany and natural history—that was similar to that expressed by the English botanist, John Ray, in the seventeenth century. Garden remained profusely grateful to Linnaeus for assisting and directing "less powerful minds to examine, study, and adore the evident footsteps of the Supreme Creator, so striking and glorious, even in this world." To John Ellis, he exclaimed, "How many additional arguments has he [Linnaeus] furnished for acquiescence in, and admiration of, the power, the wisdom, the goodness, and providence of the Almighty Author of all."[107] Similar views, perhaps analogous to the Great Chain of Being, were expressed to Colden when he told him "real happiness . . . cannot possibly consist in anything but in a knowledge of the beautiful order, disposition & harmony of the three kingdoms here & the other parts of this system in its higher spheres, which at last leads us gradually to the Great Eternal and first Cause."[108]

For Garden, therefore, reverence toward the handiwork of God as revealed in nature was an outgrowth of scientific investigation. Colden was far more prosaic about such claims, particularly in botany, and was hardly prepared to dwell on the transcendental aspects of Linnaean science. It was perhaps sufficient for Colden that the great botanist had provided a scheme that could be employed with notable success in bringing some order and structure to the study of the various plant forms encountered on his estate. Colden never explicitly imputed or related this to a broader aesthetic or religious dimension, even if he asserted in one of his later philosophical treatises that such order in the cosmos itself could only be maintained by the agency of an Intelligent Being.

One notable foreign visitor who also was to wend his way to Colden's doorstep was the Swedish naturalist, Peter [Pehr] Kalm. As a member of the Swedish Academy, he had been chosen by Linnaeus to travel to North America to investigate native plants and to procure seed material that might be adapted for the improvement of Swedish agriculture. A particular object was to find a mulberry tree that could sustain the rigors of a northern climate and contribute to the development of a silk industry in Sweden. Kalm arrived in Philadelphia in September 1748, and would spend nearly four years on an extensive excursion through Pennsylvania, New Jersey, New York, and Canada. In a published account of his travels, he described his experiences in gathering scientific specimens and information together with various individuals who assisted him in his work, and also included some acute social observations he made as he traveled through the various colonies.[109]

While in Philadelphia, for example, he met both John Bartram and Benjamin Franklin. He was given an opportunity to view Bartram's botanical garden which he particularly admired, adding, "We owe to him the knowledge of many rare plants which he first found and which were never known before."[110] The two men also found time to discuss various scientific topics. Kalm was keen to learn if Bartram, while on his botanical excursions, had formed any opinions on whether the sea might once have covered much of the land. Bartram could tell him that there was certainly sufficient evidence to conclude that much of the eastern seaboard, for a considerable distance inland, must have been under water at one time. Kalm could only speculate that this was due either to major climatic changes or perhaps to a great deluge in past eons. Based largely on fossil remains he had uncovered on his own estate, Colden independently came to similar conclusions.

Due to Colden's botanical achievements, Kalm had apparently been alerted by Linnaeus to write to him prior to setting off on his extensive northern travels. Shortly after his arrival in the colonies, he sent a letter to Colden which was also enclosed with one from Franklin. The latter advised

Colden, "Here is a Swedish Gentleman, a Professor of Botany, lately arriv'd, and I suppose will soon be your Way, as he intends for Canada."[111]

Kalm failed to initiate his trip that fall, however, which meant that this trip had to be postponed until the following spring. In February 1749, Colden informed Linnaeus that he was still awaiting Kalm's arrival and told him, "I hope to see him at my house in his way thither and to have the pleasure if I can be of any use to him in making his voyage more convenient or safe for him."[112] As someone who had himself been on various surveying expeditions throughout the province, Colden was able to assist and guide Kalm as he made his solitary trek through the wilderness. In his later account, Kalm succinctly recalled the discussions the two men had on a number of items that were of particular interest to the Swedish naturalist. These included such arcane topics as the origin of cockroaches in the New World (Colden's opinion was that they had been imported from the West Indies); the medicinal use of skunk cabbage; and the most northerly growth of the white cedar and the *Arbor Vitae* in various geographical areas of North America.[113]

Shortly before he left to return to Sweden, in 1751, Kalm requested a rather detailed catalog from Colden on various species of animals that he might have encountered on his own, including panthers, wolves, bears, porcupines, seals, and fishes. Colden replied that he could give him little satisfaction in providing the kind of specific information required and, except for some general observations, concluded by telling him, "Any country boy you meet can inform you more of fishes than I can." Some of the accounts or reports that Kalm did receive, however, must have certainly tested his credulity. When he inquired whether Colden had ever seen a mouse deer, the latter could only say that he had heard that one had been caught near Albany, but that it reputedly was "as large as an ox." A medically related topic that interested Colden was Kalm's observations regarding the noticeable loss of teeth among the general population. Colden ascribed this to the prevalence of scurvy, due largely to dietary deficiencies, but equally considered it a contagious disease.[114]

In addition to his fastidious collation of material gathered on the flora and fauna of the colonies, which included pressed plants and seeds, Kalm was to add some general observations while making his sojourns. He noted, for example, that he found walking in New York City to be extremely pleasant, as if it were almost like being in a garden, and that the prevalent opinion among the colonists he met was that, due to their continuing growth in population and wealth, they anticipated that, within thirty to fifty years, they would be entirely independent from "Old England." Upon arrival in Montreal, where he was given a lavish reception, he inscribed in his travel journal his comparative impressions of English and French society in North America:

The difference between the manners and customs of the French in Montreal and Canada, and those of the English in the American colonies, is as great as that between the manners of those two nations in Europe. The women in general are handsome here; they are well-bred and virtuous, with an innocent and becoming freedom. They dress up very fine on Sundays; about the same as our Swedish women. . . . Every day but Sunday they wear a neat little jacket, and a short skirt which hardly reaches halfway down the leg, and sometimes not that far. And in this particular they seem to imitate the Indian women. . . . In their domestic duties they greatly surpass the English women in the plantations, who indeed have taken the liberty of throwing all the burden of housekeeping upon their husbands, and sit in their chairs all day with folded arms. The women of Canada on the contrary do not spare themselves, especially among the common people, where they are always in the fields, meadows, stables, etc. and so not dislike any work whatsoever.[115]

Although he would continue to instruct and guide others in their botanical endeavors, Colden himself did little more to add to his stature in botany. For one thing, he soon claimed that he no longer had the same opportunity for wandering afield in search of specimens.[116] To Bartram, he also mentioned his anxieties regarding the Indian danger.[117] Such perceived dangers were not without foundation. As late as October 1757, for example, there was a report that a band of enemy Indians had invaded Ulster County and in August 1758 there was a report that "Indians have killed Samuel Webb on the high road between Goshen and Walkill, burned the house of Isaac Cooley near Goshen, killed a woman and carried off three children. Detachment of Orange and Ulster County militia ordered out."[118] Colden also argued that his eyesight was failing, so that he could no longer make exact and minute descriptions.[119]

Colden soon devised an alternative that would maintain his informal membership in the botanical circle through another member of his family. As he wrote to tell Gronovius,

I have a daughter who has an inclination to reading, and a curiosity for natural philosophy or natural history, and a sufficient capacity for attaining a competent knowledge. I took the pains to explain Linnaeus' System, and to put it in an English form for her use, by freeing it from the technical terms, which was easily done by using two or three words in place of one. She is now grown very fond of the study, and has made such a progress in it as I believe would please you if you saw her performance. . . . If you think, Sir, that she can be any use to you, she will be extremely pleased at being employed by you, either in sending descriptions, or any seeds you shall desire, or dried specimens or any particular plant you should mention to me. She has time to apply herself to gratify your curiosity more than I ever had; and now when I have time, the infirmities of age disable me.[120]

In the same letter, Colden also explained to Gronovius the basis for his original optimism concerning the ability of women to enjoy botanical investigation: "I [often] thought that botany is an amusement which may be made agreeable for the Ladies who are often at a loss to fill up their time, if it could be made agreeable to them[.] Their natural curiosity and the pleasure that they take in the beauty and variety of dress seems to fit them for it."

Obviously, idleness of any kind was repugnant to Colden. By making science sufficiently pleasant and instructive, Colden tried to show his daughter how to make use of her leisure time. His wife again must be given due recognition for her role in the domestic education of her children, ensuring that "her daughters were apt scholars in the accomplishments required of well-bred and trained gentlewomen of the day."[121] Some time later, Colden would reiterate the theme of the use of time when he stated to another correspondent, "Perhaps from her example young ladies in a like situation may find an agreeable way to fill up some part of time which otherwise may be heavy on their hand. May amuse and please themselves and at the same time be useful to others."[122]

Colden demonstrated to his daughter, Jane, how to make ink impressions of leaves on paper as illustrations to accompany her plant descriptions. She eventually produced a folio of 340 drawings, together with information on the medicinal use of certain plants, largely gleaned from local usage or the reports of Indians. Colden may have assisted her in this regard, as he himself had appended such information to some of his own plant descriptions.[123] His daughter would write, for example, "The Country People here make a Tea of the Leaves [of Mountain Mint] and use it for pain or sickness at their stomach. . . . I came to the knowledge of [Gold Thread] by their using a Decoction of the Root, for the Sore Throat that Children often get in the Mouth, they also use it for the Canker sore Throat, as they call it; this has been frequent in this Country, the Leaves and Root are very bitter."[124]

As part of Jane's continuing botanical education, Colden ordered such texts as Tournefort's *Institutiones Herbariae* and Morison's *Historia Plantarum* from England, telling Peter Collinson that "if you know any better books for this purpose, as you are a better judge than I am, will be obliged to you in making this choice."[125] As well, he introduced her to Garden and Bartram while they were visiting Coldengham, and she subsequently exchanged seeds with both men. In 1756, Samuel Bard was sent by his father, a friend of Colden's, to Coldengham for the summer, primarily to recover his health in a rural retreat. Bard would later become a medical doctor and correspond with Colden on various medical topics, but that particular summer would remain especially notable for, as his biographer notes, it was "under [Jane Colden's] instruction [that] he became skilful in botanizing . . . and which owed, perhaps, a part of its attractions to the pleasing associations with which it was originally connected, since to the end of his life, he never mentioned the name of his instructress without admiration and attachment."[126]

After her father introduced her work to the other naturalists, Jane Colden was soon communicating on her own with several of its members. Collinson was sufficiently impressed with her achievements that he wrote to tell Linnaeus that "she is perhaps the first lady that has so perfectly studied your system. She ought to be celebrated."[127] John Ellis, in England, who translated one of her plant descriptions into Latin, forwarded it to Linnaeus with the admonition, "This young lady merits your esteem, and does honour to your System. She has drawn and described 400 plants in your method only; she uses English terms. Her father has a plant called after him *Coldenia*, suppose you should call this *Coldenella*, or any other name that might distinguish her among your Genera."[128] The plant Ellis had suggested was the *Fibraurea* or Yellowroot.

Apparently, Linnaeus was not equally impressed; at least, he did not prove responsive to the several suggestions made by either Collinson or Ellis. In any case, Linnaeus had already named the plant Ellis had proposed as *Helleborus Trifolins*.[129] If Linnaeus did not fully acknowledge Jane's contributions, other colonists continued to do so. Bartram remained one of her more ardent supporters, on one occasion telling her that he read her letter "several times with agreeable satisfactions; indeed, I am very careful of it, and it keeps company with the choicest correspondence—European letters—I shall be extremely glad to see thee once at my house, and to show thee my garden. . . . I showed [William] thy letter, and he was so well pleased with it, that he presently made a packet of very fine drawings for thee, far beyond Catesby's, took them to town, and told me he would send them very soon."[130]

Dr. Garden of South Carolina wrote to tell Colden that he was glad to learn of Miss Colden's "improvements," but he may have somewhat overstated her accomplishments when he wrote to inform Ellis that "[Colden's] lovely daughter is greatly master of the Linnaean method."[131] Jane Colden was more realistic about the importance of her botanical achievements. She was content to regard herself foremost as an ardent novice whose best work was done at the behest and under the supervision of her father or, again, under that of Dr. Charles Alston, who was king's botanist, keeper of the garden at Holyrood, and professor of botany and medicine at the University of Edinburgh.[132] As noted, he had taught botany to both Alexander Garden and John Mitchell. She wrote to Alston with the disclaimer that "[I] blush to think how much you will be disappointed in the expectation Dr. Garden has raised in you, if ever you should have a further knowledge of me."[133] That she did not hesitate to place herself under Alston's tutelage is indicated by her promise that "If I can in any way serve you, either by sending seeds, or the Characters (such as I am able to form) of our Native Plants, I shall always be proud of obeying your Commands."

While she never sufficiently mastered Latin to be able to undertake any extensive classification of plant forms on her own, she obviously deserves some credit, as Collinson told Bartram, for being "the first lady that has attempted anything of this nature."[134] Her efforts not only stand comparison with other botanists of her age but, as one writer concludes, "eighty years before . . . science [was brought] into the education of women, she was recognized in both Europe and America as a botanist."[135]

For this, of course, Colden must be commended. The first to introduce the Linnaean method of botanical classification in the American colonies, he was also the first in the colonies to acquaint a woman with this scientific field. The fact that he had such an apt pupil in his daughter was primarily due to his competence as a teacher. He made Linnaean terminology less forbidding by translating it into English and simplifying its expression. Thereafter, he encouraged Jane to combine the aesthetic and scientific by making artistic ink impressions. This was a shrewd tactic to motivate her to continue on her own and thereafter achieve an easy and rewarding acceptance into the exclusive natural history circle of the eighteenth century.

Colden attained his own status in that circle through his notable botanical contributions, which were fully recognized by Linnaeus himself, and by encouraging and guiding the scientific endeavors of others in botanical exploration. With a membership that included, at times, Dr. William Douglass in Boston, Dr. Colden and his daughter in New York, John Bartram in Pennsylvania, Dr. Mitchell in Virginia, and Dr. Garden in South Carolina, together with Collinson and Drs. Fothergill, Linnaeus, and Gronovius in the Old World, a nascent scientific community was established. Mutual visits, travels, and correspondence sustained their individual and collective endeavors and created that sense of fellowship which promoted the more benevolent aspirations of that age.

NOTES

1. Saul Jarcho, "Biographical and Bibliographical Notes on Cadwallader Colden," *Bulletin of the History of Medicine*, 32 (1958), 323.

2. Cadwallader Colden to Peter Kalm, n.d., *Colden Papers*, IV, 259.

3. John Gilmour, *British Botanists* (London, 1944), 18.

4. *Linnaeus and Jussieu; or, The Rise and Progress of Systematic Botany* (London, 1844), 23.

5. William Martin Smallwood, *Natural History and the American Mind* (New York, 1941), 73 n.

6. Alexander Grant, *The Story of the University of Edinburgh* (London, 1884), 2 Vols., I, 220.

7. John D. Comrie, *History of Scottish Medicine* (London, 1932), 2 Vols., I, 264.

8. Cadwallader Colden to Peter Kalm, n.d., *Colden Papers*, IV, 158.

9. Brooke Hindle, *The Pursuit of Science in Revolutionary America, 1735–1789* (Chapel Hill, N.C., 1956), 56.

10. Louis B. Wright, *The Cultural Life of the American Colonies, 1607–1763* (New York, 1962), 216.

11. Daniel J. Boorstin, *The Americans: The Colonial Experience* (New York, 1958), 211.

12. Russell F. Weigley, ed., *Philadelphia: A 300-Year History* (New York, 1982), 31.

13. Ibid., 39.

14. Cadwallader Colden to Samuel Lowman, November 1711, *Colden Papers*, I, 4; Cadwallader Colden to Benjamin Le Berquier, December 24, 1711, *Colden Papers*, I, 5–6, 23, 25.

15. Cadwallader Colden, "Waterspout," *Colden Papers*, IV, 417.

16. Peter Collinson to Cadwallader Colden, March 10, 1754, *Colden Papers*, IV, 377; Cadwallader Colden to Peter Collinson, May 28, 1754, *Colden Papers*, IV, 445–446.

17. Benjamin Franklin to Cadwallader Colden, 1746, *Colden Papers*, III, 184.

18. Colden's answer to Franklin's letter, *Colden Papers*, III, 186–188.

19. James Chrystie to Cadwallader Colden, April 22, 1715, *Colden Papers*, I, 81–82.

20. Cadwallader Colden, "A Narrative of Some Facts Relating to Mr. Colden," *Colden Papers*, II, 63–64.

21. Cadwallader Colden to Hugh Graham, May 25, 1716. "Copy Book of Letters on Subjects of Philosophy, Medicine, Friendship," in Cadwallader Colden, "Unprinted Scientific and Political Papers," New-York Historical Society. Hereafter referred to as "Colden MSS."

22. Colden Papers, I, 87.

23. David Chrystie to Cadwallader Colden, November 27, 1721, *Colden Papers*, I, 125.

24. Richard B. Sher and Jeffrey R. Smitten, *Scotland and America in the Age of Enlightenment* (Princeton, N.J., 1990), 240.

25. *Philadelphia: A 300-Year History*, 40.

26. See Mary Lou Lustig, *Robert Hunter, 1666–1734: New York's Augustan Statesman* (Syracuse, N.Y., 1983), 146.

27. *Dictionary of National Biography* (London, 1949–1950), XII, 81–83; Frederick B. Tolles, *James Logan and the Culture of Provincial America* (Boston, 1957).

28. *Philadelphia: A 300-Year History*, 41.

29. Frederick E. Brasch, "James Logan, a Colonial Mathematical Scholar and the First Copy of Newton's *Principia* to Arrive in the Colonies," *Proceedings of the American Philosophical Society*, 86 (1942), 3–12.

30. Frederick B. Tolles, *Meeting House and Counting House: The Quaker Merchants of Colonial Philadelphia, 1682–1763* (New York, 1963), 78, 175, 182, passim.

31. Lustig, 146.

32. Ibid., 11.

33. Ibid., 147.

34. *New York: A Chronological and Documentary History, 1524–1970* (Dobbs Ferry, N.Y., 1974), 12.

35. "The Lyne-Bradford Plan" (1730), in Robert T. Augustyn and Paul E. Cohen, *Manhattan in Maps, 1527–1995* (New York, 1997), 54–56.

36. I. N. Phelps Stokes, *The Iconography of Manhattan Island, 1498–1909*, 6 Vols. (New York, 1915–1928), I, 188–189.

37. Cadwallader Colden to John Kearsley, n.d., *Colden Papers*, I, 149–150; Cadwallader Colden to Thomas Graeme, n.d., *Colden Papers*, I, 152–154.

38. Smallwood, 146. Some contemporary opinions relative to this topic are cited in Thomas Bender, *New York Intellect* (New York, 1987), 13.

39. Michael Kammen, *Colonial New York* (White Plains, N.Y., 1987), 243.

40. Frederick E. Brasch, "The Royal Society of London and Its Influence upon Scientific Thought in the American Colonies," *The Scientific Monthly*, 33 (1931), 339.

41. Lustig, 158. Hunter at one point described New York as that "unsettled and ungovernable Province." Ibid., 26.

42. Ibid., 158.

43. Ibid., 144.

44. *Calendar of New York Colonial Commissions, 1680–1770* (New York, 1929).

45. Jessica Kross, " 'Patronage Most Ardently Sought': The New York Council, 1665–1775," in B.C. Daniels, ed., *Power and Status: Officeholding in Colonial America* (Middleton, Conn., 1986), 210.

46. Cadwallader Colden to William Douglass, n.d., *Colden Papers*, I, 271.

47. Ibid.

48. Cadwallader Colden to Benjamin Franklin, November, 1749; *Colden Papers*, IV, 157.

49. *Gentleman's Progress: The Itinerarium of Dr. Alexander Hamilton (1744)*, ed. Carl Bridenbaugh (Chapel Hill, N.C., 1948), 46.

50. Elizabeth Hall, "The Gentlewoman, Jane Colden, and Her Manuscript on New York Native Plants," in J.W. Rickett, ed., *Botanic Manuscript of Jane Colden, 1724–1766* (New York, 1963). Colden's "Farm Journal" is in the possession of the Rosenbach Museum and Library (Philadelphia). See Jacquetta M. Haley, "Farming on the Hudson Valley Frontier: Cadwallader Colden's Farm Journal 1727–1736," *The Hudson Valley Regional Review*, 6, 1 (March, 1989): 1–34.

51. Cadwallader Colden to William Douglass, n.d., *Colden Papers*, I, 272.

52. Cadwallader Colden. "Observations on the Situation, Soil, Climate, Water, Communications, Boundaries, etc., of the Province of New York, (1738)," in E.B. O'Callaghan, *The Documentary History of the State of New York* (Albany, N.Y., 1849–1851), 4 Vols., I, 172–173.

53. Margaret V.S. Wallace, " 'BIG' Little Britain; Cadwallader Colden and His Canal," *Orange County Post*, February 20, 1967.

54. Roxanne M. Gentilcore, "The Classical Tradition and American Attitudes towards Nature in the 17th and 18th Centuries" (Ph.D. Dissertation, Boston University, 1992), 84–85.

55. Cadwallader Colden to Peter Collinson, May 1742, *Colden Papers*, II, 263.

56. William Douglass to Cadwallader Colden, March 11, 1727/8, *Colden Papers*, I, 248; William Douglass to Cadwallader Colden, September 1728, *Colden Papers*, I, 270; William Douglass to Cadwallader Colden, April 22, 1728, *Colden Papers*, I, 257.

57. Edgar J. McManus, *A History of Negro Slavery in New York* (Syracuse, N.Y., 1970), 47–48.

58. Cadwallader Colden to Mr. Jordan, March 26, 1717, *Colden Papers*, I, 39.

59. Cadwallader Colden to Dr. Home, December 7, 1721, *Colden Papers*, I, 51.

60. Kammen, 249.

61. Cadwallader Colden to Mrs. C. Colden, November 10, 1737, *Colden Papers*, VIII, 255.

62. Alice Colden Wadsworth, "Sketch of the Colden and Murray Families" (1819), Transcript, MS Division, New York Public Library, 5, 19.

63. William Douglass to Cadwallader Colden, February 20, 1720/1, *Colden Papers*, I, 115.

64. William Douglass to Cadwallader Colden, July 14, 1729, *Colden Papers*, I, 308.

65. William Douglass to Cadwallader Colden, September 14, 1724, *Colden Papers*, I, 165.

66. William Douglass to Cadwallader Colden, February 20, 1720/21, *Colden Papers*, I, 115.

67. Cadwallader Colden to Capt. James Cunningham, December 6, 1756, *Colden Papers*, V, 101–102.

68. Cadwallader Colden to William Douglass, n.d., *Colden Papers*, I, 272.

69. Cadwallader Colden to Peter Collinson, November 13, 1742, *Colden Papers*, II, 281.

70. Ibid.

71. Cadwallader Colden to Peter Collinson, May 1742, *Colden Papers*, II, 263. The first botanical text to be written and published in America was Humphrey Marshall's *Arbustum Americanum* (1785). See Michael Kraus, "Scientific Relations between Europe and American in the Eighteenth Century," *The Scientific Monthly*, 55 (1942), 265.

72. Cadwallader Colden to ——— [Dr. Whytt?], February 15, 1758, *Colden Papers*, V, 216.

73. Cadwallader Colden to John Frederick Gronovius, December 1744, *Colden Papers*, III, 83.

74. Norman G. Brett-James, *The Life of Peter Collinson, F.R.S., F.S.A.* (London, 1928), 120.

75. E.G. Swem, ed., *Brothers of the Spade: Correspondence of Peter Collinson of London, and of John Curtis, of Williamsburg, Virginia, 1734–1746* (Barre, Vt., 1957), 2.

76. James Edward Smith, *Selections of the Correspondence of Linnaeus and other Naturalists* (London, 1821), 2 Vols., I, 3.

77. Peter Collinson to Cadwallader Colden, March 9, 1743/4, *Colden Papers*, III, 50.

78. Ibid.

79. The full descriptive title is "Plantae Coldenghamiae in provincia Novaboracnesi Americes sponte crescentes, quas ad Methodem Cl. Linnaei sexulem, anno 1742 etc. Observavit et descripsit Cadwallader Colden," *Acta Societatis Regiae Scientiarum Upsaliensis* for 1743, published in 1749; and a supplement in the *Acta* for 1744–1750, published in 1751. See Howard A. Kelly, *A Cyclopedia of American Medical Biography: From 1610–1910* (Philadelphia, 1912), 2 Vols., I, 195.

80. Cadwallader Colden to Linnaeus, February 9, 1748/9, *Colden Papers*, IV, 99.

81. Benjamin Franklin to Cadwallader Colden, October 16, 1746, *Colden Papers*, III, 275.

82. Cadwallader Colden to Joh. Fred. Gronovius, October 29, 1745, Colden MSS, New-York Historical Society.

83. Cadwallader Colden to Joh. Fred. Gronovius, December 1744, *Colden Papers*, III, 86.

84. Ibid.

85. Herbert Thatcher, "Dr. John Mitchell, M.D., F.R.S., of Virginia," *The Virginia Magazine of History and Biography*, 40 (1932), 104.

86. Alexander Garden to Linnaeus, March 15, 1755, in Smith, *Selections*, I, 288.

87. Regarding the French critic, Buffon, for example, Garden stated: "I am vexed at him for snarling so at Linnaeus. Plague on it, why cannot they agree?" Alexander Garden to John Ellis, December 16, 1765, in ibid., 546.

88. Alexander Garden to Linnaeus, March 15, 1755, in Smith, *Selections*, I, 286.

89. Ibid.

90. Peter Collinson to Linnaeus, March 27, 1747/8, in ibid., I, 18.

91. Margaret Denny, "Linnaeus and his Disciple in Carolina: Alexander Garden," *Isis*, 38 (1948), 172.

92. William S. Middleton, "John Bartram, Botanist," *The Scientific Monthly*, 21 (1925), 172.

93. Smallwood, 33.

94. Some of the plants that Bartram introduced into England were the bush honeysuckle, mountain laurel, dog-tooth violet, wild aster, gentian, ginseng, sweet fern, magnolia, locust tree, witch-hazel, spruce, hemlock, red and white cedar, and sugar maple. Middleton, 199.

95. Smallwood, 33.

96 Michael Kraus, *Atlantic Civilizations: Eighteenth Century Origins* (Ithaca, N.Y., 1949), 170.

97. Smallwood, 88.

98. Peter Collinson to John Bartram, February 25, 1740/1, in William Darlington, *Memorials of John Bartram and Humphrey Marshall* (New York, 1967), 142.

99. John Bartram to Peter Collinson, September 5, 1742, in ibid., 161.

100. John Bartram to Cadwallader Colden, n.d., *Colden Papers*, III, 179–180; John Bartram to Cadwallader Colden, October 6, 1746, in ibid., 270.

101. John Bartram to Cadwallader Colden, October 23, 1742, *Colden Papers*, II, 275; John Bartram to Cadwallader Colden, July 15, 1745, in ibid., III, 130–131; John Bartram to Cadwallader Colden, March 6, 1746/7, in ibid., 362–364; Cadwallader Colden to John Bartram, January 27, 1746/7, Colden Letter, *Gratz Collection*, Historical Society of Pennsylvania.

102. Cadwallader Colden to John Bartram, January 27, 1746/7, Colden Letter, *Gratz Collection*, Historical Society of Pennsylvania; John Bartram to Gronovius, December 6, 1745, in Darlington, 353.

103. Alexander Garden to Cadwallader Colden, November 4, 1754, *Colden Papers*, IV, 472.

104. Middleton, 212.

105. Alexander Garden to John Ellis, May 18, 1765, in Smith, *Selections*, I, 532.

106. Alexander Garden to John Ellis, July 15, 1765, in Ibid., I, 538.

107. Alexander Garden to John Ellis, December 24, 1770, in Ibid., 580.

108. Alexander Garden to Cadwallader Colden, November 22, 1759, *Colden Papers*, V, 41.

109. *The America of 1750: Peter Kalm's Travels in North America*, 2 Vols. (New York, 1964).

110. Ibid., I, 61.

111. Benjamin Franklin to Cadwallader Colden, September 29, 1748, *Colden Papers*, IV, 80; Peter Kalm to Cadwallader Colden, September 29, 1748, in ibid., 77–78.

112. Cadwallader Colden to Linnaeus, February 9, 1749, *Colden Papers*, IV, 99.

113. *The America of 1750*, I, 217, 257, 299, 469.

114. Cadwallader Colden to Peter Kalm, January 4, 1751, *Colden Papers*, IV, 261.

115. *The America of 1750*, II, 402–403.

116. Cadwallader Colden to ——— [Dr. Whytt?], February 15, 1758, *Colden Papers*, V, 217.

117. Cadwallader Colden to John Bartram, January 27, 1746/7, Colden Letter, *Gratz Collection*, Historical Society of Pennsylvania.

118. *Calendar of New York Colonial Commissions, 1680–1770* (New York, 1929).

119. Cadwallader Colden to Dr. John Gronovius, October 1, 1755, *Colden Papers*, V, 29.

120. Cadwallader Colden to Gronovius, October 1, 1755, *Colden Papers*, V, 2; James Britten, "Jane Colden and the Flora of New York," *The Journal of Botany, British and Foreign*, 33 (1895), 13.

121. Rickett, 18.

122. Cadwallader Colden to Dr. John Fothergill, October 18, 1757, *Colden Papers*, V, 203. Dr. Fothergill was an eminently successful London physician. Like Collinson and Bartram, he was a Quaker who took a great interest in plants and natural history. He developed an extensive garden in 1762 to cultivate the innumerable plants sent to him from the New World. R. Hingston Fox, *Dr. John Fothergill and His Friends: Chapters in Eighteenth Century Life* (London, 1919).

123. Linnaeus included Colden's observations on the medicinal use of plants, many of which Colden had obtained from the Indians, as a separate entry in his own work, *Nova Plantarum* (1747).

124. Rickett, 20.

125. Ibid.

126. John McVicar, *A Domestic Narrative of the Life of Samuel Bard, M.D., L.L.D.* (New York, 1822), 19.

127. Peter Collinson to Linnaeus, May 12, 1756, in Britten, 15.

128. Ibid. 14–15.

129. *Dictionary of American Biography*, 10 Vols. (New York, 1928), II, 289.

130. John Bartram to Miss Jane Colden, January 24, 1757, in Anna Murray Vail, "Jane Colden, An Early New York Botanist," *Torreya*, 7 (1907), 29.

131. Dr. Garden to John Ellis, March 25, 1755, in Smith, *Selections*, I, 343.

132. Edmund Berkeley and Dorothy Smith Berkeley, *Dr. Alexander Garden of Charles Town* (Chapel Hill, N.C., 1969), 24.

133. Jane Colden to Dr. Charles Alston, May 1, 1756, quoted in Smallwood, 92.

134. Peter Collinson to John Bartram, January 20, 1756, in Darlington, 202.

135. Smallwood, 92–93.

Chapter 2

MATERIA MEDICA

No man who has any share of humanity or regard for the welfare of the
society wherein he lives . . . but will be desirous to give what [medical]
assistance to his neighbours he can by any information which has come
to his knowledge, or by any means in his power.

While Cadwallader Colden's move from Philadelphia to New York in 1718,
at the age of thirty, would eventually require him to relinquish his medical
practice for a career in government, he continued to engage in both medical
and mercantile activities for the first few years. Even thereafter, however, his
continuing contributions to various medical issues reveal that he never gave
up his interest in this field. This is amply confirmed by his extensive correspondence with his fellow physicians both in the colonies and in England
or Europe, by his several treatises on diseases and their cures, by his more
speculative theories on the activities of the body, by the use of his political
office to improve medical services and facilities, and finally by his efforts to
organize societies and lectures for the further training of physicians. All of
these were intended to enhance the status of medicine as a scientific discipline and to benefit society.

Colden continued to improve his own knowledge by ordering medical
and scientific publications from booksellers in Great Britain. Since he was
at some considerable distance from such sources and not always knowledgeable about the latest publications, he would simply ask for "Anything
New in Medicine which is much Valued."[1] Alternately, he would put in

specific requests for such standard texts as Salmon's *London Dispensatory*, Le Clerc's *Histoire de la Medicine*, Boerhaave's *Artis Medice Principes*, Hovius's *De Circulari Humorum*, Ramassini's *Opera*, and others.[2] In addition, Colden occasionally obtained copies of the *Edinburgh Medical Essays* and the *London Medical Essays*.

Relying on booksellers in London or elsewhere, particularly when it came to asking them to select appropriate titles, could have its disadvantages. At one point, following the arrival of a shipment, Colden noted, "I am not so well pleased with some of them." Being parsimonious, he particularly reminded the booksellers "that you would mind what books you have sent that you do not send two copies for there is nobody to take them off my hand."[3] Included in some of his letters to England, while Colden was still a practicing physician, were lists of drugs that he requested to be sent to him. These included such standards of the time as borax, cochinel, cream tartar, calomel, gentian, agaric, oil of vitriol, and so forth. From England, too, came such indispensable items as phials, ivory glyster pipes, glass mortars, crucibles, and flint bottles.[4]

One of Colden's earliest contributions to medicine was his attempt to improve the state of this art in the American colonies. He certainly felt he had apt justification for doing so. Trained physicians were exceedingly rare in the colonies; even at the time of the American Revolution, only 5 percent of medical practitioners held a recognized medical degree.[5] As with Colden, it may explain why few physicians, with notable exceptions, were able to achieve either the social or the economic status they may have anticipated. As such, they would often have to turn to other means to supplement their income. Colden's situation was not unique. A physician in Virginia could state, in 1730, that there was "no way of making money in this country so easy as by merchandizing, this being the occupation that all [that is, all the doctors] come at, for after they have purchas'd a little Stock by their Practice, they presently commence Merchants, and so make their Fortunes."[6]

In rural areas, of course, the opportunity for "merchandizing" on any scale would be almost unknown. This explains why trained physicians generally gravitated to urban centers, in addition to the presumed cultural benefits of working in cosmopolitan areas. Those who lived at any distance from a city had to find—and sometimes practiced—a kind of popular or folk medicine. John Bartram, as noted, found ready acceptance as a farmer-physician among his neighbors on the outskirts of Philadelphia. Works such as Nicholas Culpeper's *English Physician*, John Wesley's *Primitive Physic*, and John Tennent's *Every Man His Own Doctor; or, the Poor Planter's Physician*, were readily available as handbooks to anyone who had the ambition to become a part-time doctor.[7] The lack of any medical licensing standards in the colonies and the emphasis on self-help promoted and sustained this practice.

The absence of professional standards, the dearth of trained physicians, and the prevalence of ignorance could also combine to create a situation that was readily exploited by quacks and imposters. A visitor to New York, a member of the medical profession, recounted the tale of a shoemaker on Long Island who had cured a woman of some affliction and, thereafter, "finding the practice of physick a more profitable business than cobbling, [had] laid aside his awls and leather, got himself some gallipots and, instead of cobbling of soles, fell to cobbling of human bodies."[8] As late as 1775, a complaint to the Assembly at Philadelphia could lament that many parts of the country were "infected with a set of men, who taking upon them the offices of physicians and surgeons (though in reality no better than empirics or quacks) administer drugs so unskillfully and ignorantly, that some persons have, in all probability, thereby lost their lives, and others been rendered cripples."[9] In 1757, William Smith, Jr., historian of the province of New York, could lament: "Few physicians amongst us are eminent for their skill, Quacks abound like Locusts in Egypt, and too many have recommended themselves to a full practice and profitable subsistence. This is the less to be wondered at, as the profession is under no kind of regulation. Loud as the call is, to our shame be it remembered, we have no law to protect the King's subjects, from the malpractice of pretenders. Any man at his pleasure sets up for physician, apothecary or surgeon. No candidates are either examined or licensed, or even sworn to fair practice."[10]

Colden's correspondent in Boston, William Douglass, would also write in his *Summary, historical and political, of the . . . present State of the British Settlements in America* (1775) that "A young man without any liberal education, by living a year or two in any quality with a practitioner of any sort, apothecary, cancer doctor, cutter for the stone, bonesetters, tooth-drawer, etc. with the essential fundamental of ignorance and impudence, is esteemed to qualify himself for all the branches of the medical art."[11] Writing to Colden, Douglass could agree with his assessment regarding the low state of medicine in the colonies but could also admit, at least in his own case, that he lived "handsomely by the incomes of my practice, and save some small matter."[12]

One of Colden's early proposals for the improvement of medicine was the funding of an allowance as a physician to the poor of Philadelphia. Subsequently, he suggested a series of lectures on medical topics to be subsidized by an annual fee imposed on every unmarried male above twenty-one years of age.[13] Both of these were presented to James Logan, but the latter regarded them as overly ambitious and confessed: "These things I owned very commendable, but doubted our Assembly would ever go into them, that of the lectures especially."[14] Logan's pessimism was confirmed when the assembly took no action on either measure. Still, Colden can be credited for making the first attempt to improve medicine through public lectures in the colonies.[15] Thereafter, Colden did nothing further along these lines while he was in Philadelphia.

Not long after his move to New York, however, Colden wrote a letter to Governor Hunter in which he expressed his belief that as astronomy had been brought to perfection so, too, could the art of medicine. The hindrances that impeded its progress, however, could only be removed with the assistance of government.[16] Colden then explained that the low repute of medicine was due to two specific factors: the kind of men who practiced medicine and the lack of a proper method in medicine itself.

Concerning the former, he suggested that, whereas astronomy was pursued by gentlemen of leisure and wealth, in medicine, on the other hand, "sordid gain" attracted men of ignorance or with little education. In his view, those that became wealthy in medicine did not desire to undertake any scientific investigations, whereas those that remained poor had to apply themselves to other occupations. Moreover, those that continued in medicine, Colden added, "die martyrs of that religion which pushes on Violently Good Souls in persuing the general Good of Mankind [and] to Avenge whose Death we may say God suffers Quacklike Plague and Pestilence to Destroy his People."[17] In these words, an impulse toward philosophical benevolence to mankind was given a quasi-religious dimension that was probably an expression of Colden's exasperation with the state of medicine in the colonies. What he was hinting at might well have been some form of medical licensing standards.

In his submission, Colden went on to argue that medicine would arrive at perfection if the "proportions" of geometry and the laws of motion were applied to the human body. Here, Colden's implicit belief in progress is evident, even though he was forced to admit that curing all the ills of nature might be unattainable. By making frequent and exact observations of the human body—as the astronomer does of the heavenly bodies—the physician could calculate the motion of fluids and secretions and thereby "discover the true causes of the Effects with as great Certainty in Physic as is done in Astronomy."

Similar considerations prompted Colden's proposal to William Douglass for the formation of a society that would aid in the diffusion of scientific knowledge and initially, at least, might be made up of the medical community.[18] Such an organization was not exclusively designed for the improvement of medicine, but in inviting the participation of physicians, Colden recognized that their common educational and professional background could serve as the basis for developing a scientific community. For Colden, of course, it was one means of compensating for that isolation and infrequent communication that he probably assumed were felt by all those who, like himself, had at one time lived or studied in the great urban centers of England and Europe.

Douglass, however, had the singular advantage of living in an urban environment and this may have been one reason why he did not take immediate steps to implement Colden's progressive proposals. Admittedly, it was still somewhat premature to form an inter-colonial society for, as Douglass pointed out, "Your project of a Society . . . is very desirable but not practicable . . . I know but few . . . who are qualified for such a correspondence, and even these few can not with the Poet say *nobis* . . . [torn] but must mind their particular business or Profession."[19]

It may be worth noting, then, that at the height of an epidemic in 1735, the town council of Boston invited the leading physicians to meet with it in order to discuss proper methods to protect the public from contagion. On the basis of this initial meeting, a medical society was eventually formed in Boston and it, under Douglass's leadership, would become the first such society in colonial America.[20] It failed, however, to attain either that broader scientific or inter-colonial emphasis that was an integral part of Colden's conception. A medical society was also formed in New York during the first half of the eighteenth century, but it remains doubtful whether Colden had any direct role in this later development.[21]

Greater awareness of the need for some kind of inter-colonial scientific association arose in the 1740s, when a rudimentary natural history circle was in the process of formation. Increased contacts between the various members of this group created the desire for a scientific society through which correspondence and an exchange of information would be established on a regular basis. In 1739, Bartram recognized this need and proposed the development of a scientific society in Philadelphia.[22] Gradually becoming aware of the work of botanists and naturalists in the colonies, Benjamin Franklin published his *Proposal for Promoting Useful Knowledge among the British Plantations in America* in 1743. That it was meant to attract and, in part, grow out of the members of the botanical circle is evident in Franklin's recommendation that one of the subjects to be considered was "All new-discovered plants, herbs, trees, roots, their virtues, uses, etc." This was not all, of course, but the relation of such a society to the Enlightenment was expressed in the proposal that a study should be made of "all philosophical experiments that let light into the nature of things, tend to increase the power of man over nature, and multiply the convenience or pleasures of life."[23]

Colden was glad to lend his support to this venture, giving the somewhat terse and crabbed comment that, after having made "great progress in Aping the Luxury of [the] Mother Country," the colonists were finally making a noticeable "endeavor to imitate some of its Excellencies."[24] Colden surely expected to be elected to membership in the society. This occurred promptly in 1744. Peter Collinson, to whom Bartram first addressed his ideas on a scientific academy, having heard of the formation of the American Philosophical Society, wrote expansively to Colden that it would be "a Means of Uniting Ingenious Men of all Societies together and a Mutual Harmony be got which will be Dayly producing Acts of Love & Friendship" and that it would "Influence them to Benevolence and Good will to Each Other in every Capacity."[25]

Collinson's statement reflects that philosophy of benevolence that was so evidently associated with the advance of science and that of a scientific fellowship in the eighteenth century. Franklin's proposals were meant to serve immediate and practical aims, for his desire was to bring together persons who "are widely separated and seldom can see and converse or be acquainted with each other," but this, too, was for the benefit of mankind. Thus, Colden's original proposal for a "Voluntary Society for the advancing of Knowledge" saw its first fruition in Franklin's achievements. While Bartram's role must also be acknowledged, it took Franklin's personal resourcefulness to bring such schemes to reality.

Alas, that society confirmed neither Franklin's nor Collinson's original expectations. Franklin soon had to admit to Colden that "The Members of our Society here are very idle Gentlemen; they will take no Pains."[26] At one time, Colden also proposed to Franklin, as an alternative, the publication of a collection of scientific papers at periodic intervals.[27] This might possibly serve as an interim measure until a more permanent form of organization had been found. Franklin proved receptive to this suggestion and went on to tell Colden that he was prepared to do all the work and take the responsibility for its publication.[28] Franklin proposed to call it an "American Philosophical Miscellany" and to publish it on either a monthly or a quarterly basis. Nevertheless this, too, failed to materialize and it was not until the 1760s that the American Philosophical Society was put on a firm foundation.

After 1760, when Colden once more became more fully engaged in political and administrative matters in the province of New York, he lent his assistance to improve medical facilities in the city of New York. In 1770, he received a petition from several physicians, including Samuel Bard, for a charter of incorporation for the New York Hospital. Bard, who had gained his medical degree from the University of Edinburgh, returned to New York intent on improving the level of the medical profession and medical services in the city. Colden evidently recognized the need for such an institution and was sympathetic to the request. In July 1771, a charter of incorporation was granted to several prominent citizens of New York. These were to be known as "the Society of the Hospital in the City of New York in America." Upon the appointment of a board of governors, the first meetings took place in the same month.[29]

In addition to making such practical suggestions for the improvement of medicine as establishing a series of lectures, proposing the formation of a society, and using his political offices for the scheme mentioned, Colden was also to become involved in writing numerous medical treatises on the topics that attracted the attention of the physicians of that age. Through these treatises, some of which took the form of private correspondence while others were published in newspapers and periodicals, Colden was able to exert a personal influence on medical ideas and practices in the colonies. In this way, too, Colden maintained a continuing membership in the medical community of the eighteenth century.

One of Colden's early treatises on medicine was written at the request of Governor Hunter. Originally entitled *An Account of the Climate of New York*, it was subsequently revised as *An Account of the Climate and Diseases of New York*.[30] The latter, in particular, can be regarded as an important introduction to Colden's mature considerations on the prognosis of fevers since, in this work, he draws certain parallels between the variation in seasons and climates and the prevalence of specific fevers.

For Colden, the etiology of most diseases was primarily due to environmental factors. In New York City, for example, Colden observed that the summers were sometimes almost as "torrid" as the tropics, whereas the winters were at least as cold as those in northern Europe. It was not only these temperature extremes but equally the sudden change of the seasons which accounted, in his view, for the onset of "pleurisies" and "inflammatory fevers" in the spring. People living in rural areas were particularly predisposed to the "distemper" since they were most liable to be exposed to cold temperatures during the winter months. That New York had several extreme winters during the eighteenth century is confirmed by contemporary accounts noting that the lower Hudson River had become completely frozen or that it had been possible to drive a carriage from Manhattan across the East River to Long Island during the winter months.

Colden went on to describe the summers in New York—lasting from May to September—as hot, rainy, and sultry, since the air was always humid, and he associated the oppressiveness of the heat with the "quantity of vapor in the air."[31] July to September, in particular, were regarded as the most sickly months of the year, since

more people being sick and more children dying than in all the rest of the year. The epidemical diseases are intermitting fevers, cholera morbus, and fluxes. The intermitting fevers are not near too frequent in this province as in those to the southward, but I think fluxes are more frequent in this time than in Philadelphia. Two reasons may be assigned for this: first, the poor people at this time eat an abundance of water melons and other such kinds of fruits more than they do in Philadelphia: the other is, that the water in the town is not near so good as there, being brackish and so hard (as it is commonly termed) that it will not dissolve soap.[32]

Although fall was agreeable, the coming of winter brought with it the danger of "rheumatic pains," while in February people were in danger of "bastard pleurisies."

This rather depressing account of the climate and diseases of New York would hardly seem to make it a suitable place for human habitation. Yet Colden concluded that "As it is at present I prefer it to the climates of

England, and I believed most people that have lived any considerable time there, and are returned to England, will confirm this." One reason for this was that the air was generally clear and, consequently, there were few consumptives. He concluded by remarking that "People inclined to be consumptive in England, are often perfectly cured by our fine air, but if there be ulcers formed they die in a little time."[33]

Since this treatise was meant to be a brief summary, Colden did not elaborate on the nature or cause of these several diseases and his nosology of fevers remains necessarily vague. By recognizing, however, that there was a correspondence between such factors as climate, geography, latitude, diet, and certain diseases, Colden made a useful contribution to what might be termed "environmental medicine." Even if broadly sketched and somewhat conjectural at points, the treatise was an attempt to provide—in the context of the time—some theoretical explanation for the cycle of fevers that affected New York City throughout the year. In the same treatise, Colden suggested that the growth of cities had a distinct moderating effect on climate, thus implying that growing urbanization might alter local meteorological conditions to some degree.

During the 1720s, Colden was also introduced to the ongoing controversy surrounding the value of smallpox inoculation. Smallpox was a disease that had assumed epidemic proportions several times in the seventeenth and eighteenth centuries. Massachusetts, in particular, seems to have suffered repeated visitations and this apparently motivated the first medical publication in the colonies, Thomas Thatcher's *Brief Rule to Guide the Common People of New England, How to Order Themselves and Theirs in the Small Pocks or Measles* (Boston, 1677–1678).[34]

In 1721, Boston experienced smallpox with more severity than at any other time in its history. During this episode, William Douglass became one of the most outspoken opponents of inoculation. In 1722, and again in 1730, Douglass published essays condemning the practice in no uncertain terms. He wrote to tell Colden that "I reckon it a sin against society to propagate infection by this means and bring on my neighbor a distemper which might prove fatal and which perhaps he might escape (as many have done) in the ordinary way."[35] Douglass's attitude was one that was probably taken by most of the medical profession in all countries, including the colonies.[36] In New York, Colden also intended to remain one of the unconverted. He may well have confirmed Douglass in his opinion, for the latter wrote to Colden that "Your reasons against inoculation of the small-pox are strong."[37]

In 1731, ten years after its appearance at Boston, New York City also experienced a severe epidemic of the disease. The *New York Gazette* reported, in August of that year, that "the smallpox now spreads in this city pretty much."[38] In September, the same paper printed an extract from the *Philosophical Transactions* on the use of smallpox inoculation. It is not certain what impact the article had within the environs of the city but on Long Island, at least, inoculation was quickly adopted.[39] While Colden may have abstained from taking any active part in the matter, it may be significant to note that as late as 1747, Governor Clinton issued a proclamation prohibiting such inoculation within the confines of New York City.[40]

Whatever role Colden might have had in the debate regarding inoculation, it was his theories on the effect of inoculation and the proper treatment to be employed when infected with smallpox that are of some interest. Colden expressed his views on this topic not to Douglass, but to an early correspondent in England, Dr. Hugh Graham. In 1716, Colden wrote to Graham to tell him that Philadelphia was experiencing a smallpox epidemic, something that had been absent for fourteen years.[41] As a practicing physician, Colden had first recommended bloodletting, but he found that this was not fashionable. Concerned that some untoward consequences might result if he persisted in giving this aggressive treatment, he turned to a less drastic form of therapy. This was his noted "cool regimen," to which he ascribed the fact that not one of his patients had died.

Deriving at least some of his ideas from works by the English physician Thomas Sydenham, Colden argued that as long as the fever continued unabated the motion of the blood would be too violent for the "pox" to separate from the blood. The "cool regimen," by regulating the heat, would provide that proper motion which permitted the "gross parts" to be released. In addition, it offered the advantage of preventing the excessive evaporation of the body's fluids that would contribute to a thickening of the blood. Were the "gross parts" to stagnate, they would once more mix with the blood and revive the fever. Although Colden admitted to Graham that "I have observed my rules about fevers answers like Oracles, you may think I am full of them & I think I have reason," he also argued that they "pointed me to these methods of cure by which I have been very lucky in my practice."[42]

Even so, Colden did not believe that the "cool regimen" was equally valid as a treatment in all smallpox cases. While part of Colden's theory on the treatment of smallpox was derived from observing the physical changes of the body after being affected with the disease, a good portion is based on primarily theoretical considerations; it is quite evident that Colden was, at times, more certain of his theory than of its application. He reminded Graham that cures are "corollaries" from a general theory of fevers and that the former are, in effect, to be deduced from the latter.[43]

The reason why Colden adamantly opposed smallpox inoculation may now be more understandable. His rational conception of disease led him to the supposition that inoculation introduced that gross matter which, by causing fevers resulting from stagnation, prevented its release. Lacking knowledge of immunology, he could not be expected to appreciate how some matter (as he might term it) would have to remain in the body to ward off more serious consequences in the future. In urging depletion or evacuation, Colden was being entirely consistent with rational criteria and traditional norms. Colden never really accepted inoculation, although he did later agree to allow it to be performed on a member of his family. It must be added, however, that Douglass subsequently proved himself flexible enough to adopt the practice in 1751, and could then write that inoculation "is a very considerable and most beneficial Improvement in that Article of Medical Practice."[44]

In addition to his private correspondence with physicians in the colonies, Colden was also interested in what would be termed public health issues. He wrote a series of articles on the fevers that had prevailed in New York City for two years, which were subsequently published in 1743 and 1744 in the *New-York Weekly Post Boy*. As in his earlier treatises, Colden began by stressing the seasonal appearance of these fevers. He was quick to point out, however, that there must be additional factors since, while New Yorkers suffered repeatedly from such diseases, rural areas remained virtually untouched.[45] What was unique to New York City, he decided, was the effect of stagnant waters in that locale; this became, in effect, the major thesis in the articles and justified his recommendations for improved sanitary conditions. The publication of these articles in a newspaper were evidently meant to inform and activate public opinion on such issues. Ultimately, it proved to be a successful appeal.[46] The articles are now regarded as the first to deal with the problems of public health in the city of New York.[47]

Much of the material in Colden's articles, including his description of fevers and his emphasis on stagnant waters as a cause of these fevers, was drawn from Giovanni Maria Lancisi's classic, *De noxiis paludum effluviis* (On Harmful Emanation from Swamps, 1717) and perhaps to a lesser extent from another writer, Bernardino Ramazzini. Colden had ordered their texts from England and, indeed, would claim that he probably was the only person in the colonies to have a copy of Lancisi.[48] In resorting to such texts, Colden evidently sought to take his theories on fevers from important authorities in the field.

Lancisi based much of his material on the history of the city of Rome, which itself was built on swampy ground. The city had suffered several epidemics, Lancisi noted, whenever its magistrates failed to take proper steps to drain or divert its stagnant waters. The noxious vapors that resulted were due to "fermentations" that were dependent on atmospheric and seasonal variations. In a similar vein, Colden observed that New York, like Rome, was also built upon a "swamp or moist slimy ground" and had poor drainage. He remained especially critical of the docks which often contained garbage and animal offal and the many cellars filled with stagnant waters. Since little had been done in the past to correct these problems, Colden now urged that responsibility for drainage and the removal of filth be taken out of the hands of private persons—primarily supported by voluntary contributions—and be delegated to a tax-supported corporation.[49] If necessary, he argued, the magistrates of the city should appeal to the assembly for legal authority to enforce compliance with new sanitary regulations.

In 1744, a committee was appointed to investigate such conditions and laws were passed to prevent skinners and leather dressers from operating south of the Fresh Water Pond, a large body of water in lower Manhattan. Both hatters and starch makers were prohibited from pouring their solutions into street gutters. Finally, more stringent regulations were adopted for the disposal of garbage.[50] In view of his public services and as an expression of their gratitude, the Common Council of New York tendered Colden a vote of thanks.[51]

Other than the periodic episodes of smallpox that affected the colonies, there was probably no disease that contributed to more of an ongoing discussion among physicians in the colonies than the dreaded appearance of the yellow fever. While this seems to have been a term that was applied to several epidemical fevers, Colden's first clinical account of the disease was provided by John Mitchell of Virginia. Mitchell actually wrote two accounts of yellow fever in Virginia. One, prepared in 1744, was sent to Cadwallader Colden in New York. The second, an abbreviated version, was submitted to Benjamin Franklin in Philadelphia in the expectation that it might be read before the members of the American Philosophical Association.[52] Franklin also mailed the account sent to him, or perhaps a copy of it, to Colden so that the latter would have the benefit of any additional information that Mitchell had to offer.[53] Franklin had earlier sent Colden's "Observations on the Fevers" to Mitchell in Virginia and thus served, for a time at least, as an intermediary between these two men.

Yellow fever aroused more fear among the population than any other comparable disease. Its dreadful symptoms and rapid, often fatal, progression baffled and dismayed colonial physicians throughout the eighteenth century. This may explain Mitchell's careful clinical description and his reluctance to provide any speculative theories. It was only on this basis that there could be "a foundation to build a theory upon, and on which to deduce a rational cure for the disease."[54]

At one point, Mitchell described yellow fever as "malignant" on the assumption that it had some similarity with the malignant fevers that had prevailed in New York in 1741 and 1742. Since yellow fever reappeared in Virginia in both those years, there was some justification for this supposition. Should the fevers prove to be identical, then Colden's opinions on a proper method of treatment would prove useful.

Yet, whereas Colden's views on yellow fever were apt to be—as Mitchell had tried to avoid—deductions from an established theory, those of Mitchell were not only based on some clinical experience with this disease but, more importantly, on several postmortem examinations. It was particularly the "yellowness in the eyes or all over the body" that marked the external pathological symptoms of this fever. To Colden, Mitchell felt justified in reporting that his anatomical dissections confirmed that the same yellowish appearance could be detected on the internal surface of the body. Mitchell had carried out his first two autopsies in 1737, one of them on a female slave, and by 1742, having completed three more, was certain that his diagnosis was confirmed. It was only then that he proceeded to send his reports to Colden and Franklin.

These postmortem examinations were perhaps Mitchell's most positive contribution to the literature on yellow fever. While such examinations had become fairly common in Europe—performed traditionally by the various surgeons guilds—there were neither these precedents nor any guilds to introduce the practice in the colonies. Consequently, it remained the responsibility of individual physicians to make such examinations, and it is almost certain that Mitchell was the first to do so.[55] As a European-educated physician, rather than a mere "empiric" (as untrained colonial doctors were often termed), he realized the importance of making a clinical observation of the condition of the viscera. To that extent, at least, he exemplified the doctrines associated with such notables as Herman Boerhaave and Morgagni, both of whom emphasized the relation between symptomatic lesions on various organs and specific diseases.[56]

Mitchell also devoted a portion of his letter to methods of treatment for yellow fever and recommended that such factors as its state of development and the season of the year be taken into account. Noting that it was primarily the abdominal viscera that were affected by the inflammatory effects of this disease, he argued that the best procedure would be to remove that morbid matter which was responsible for "mortifications, putrefaction and dissolution." Consequently, in seeking a rational cure, he recommended one or more depletives, including lenitives, concoctions, emetics, purgatives, sudorifics, and so forth. Mitchell believed that yellow fever was similar to the epidemical diseases mentioned by Hippocrates in his *Prognostics* and, consequently, that it was not peculiar to the New World.[57] The only novel method of treatment that Mitchell was interested in trying was the use of a bark that was alleged to possess antiseptic properties. This is almost certain to have been the cinchona bark that was introduced into Europe by Spain in the 1630s. It soon proved effective in the treatment of malaria. Thereafter, it was used in the amelioration of several other fevers; hence, its particular interest to Mitchell.

When Colden replied to Mitchell's letter the following year, he must have also seen a copy of the letter that Mitchell had sent to Franklin. At the outset, Colden made the concession that "I have never seen any ill of the Yellow fever, and hope I never shall, and therefore I can only speak speculatively of the distemper."[58] The only claim Colden might have to discuss his views on this topic was the general, and rather inclusive, use of the term "fevers" by most eighteenth-century physicians. In any case, Colden's letter provides some useful insights into his theory regarding fevers and their effects on different states of the body. He defended his recourse to speculation by also telling Mitchell: "I have for many years declined the practice of physic, and any thoughts I now entertain on that subject, are only by the way of amusement, to fill up a vacant hour in a solitary part of the country; and for this reason you can expect little else from me than mere speculations, and which must always give place to that knowledge which arises from accurate and judicious observation."[59]

Even though Colden, at this time, had not actually seen any cases of yellow fever and his clearest conceptions of the disease were derived from Mitchell's letter, he disagreed with Mitchell's contention that it was "an inflammatory in the proper sense of the work, arising originally from a stagnation." Instead, Colden suggested that it was due to "corrosive humours" that required a different approach from that used in the case of inflammations. While he did not entirely reject the depletive method of treatment that Mitchell favored, he felt this could only be introduced when the blood had a certain velocity. The role of the physician under these circumstances was to regulate the velocity by all means at his disposal.

Their different medical theories soon proved to be a worthy topic for further discussion. Shortly after he received Colden's letter, Mitchell wrote to tell him that "I should indeed have done myself the pleasure of writing to you before . . . had I thought that my philosophic notions would either have proved acceptable to you, which they are in so few in this part of the world, who are commonly busied about other pursuits," and offered to treat Colden's views with the same philosophic freedom with which he hoped his own would be received.[60]

Mitchell could admit that, from the point of theory at least, Colden was correct, except that he himself had found that the circulation was too rapid rather than languid. Mitchell defended his mode of treatment, particularly the use of sudorifics, by telling Colden that yellow fever was due to some form of "morbid matter" which quickly became turgid at the onset of fever. Consequently, it had to be removed as soon as possible.

This cautious approach, together with its emphasis on empirical verification, is evident throughout Mitchell's letter to Colden. Although he was dependent on such terminology as "morbid matter," he complained, "What is meant by a turgescence of the morbid matter is too little explained, & hardly touched upon by our modern writers of Physick." In the same letter to Colden, he mentioned that he believed that he had found a root (known to the colonists as rattlesnake root), which might have some value in the treatment of yellow fever, and advised Colden that it was beneficial when given in small quantities.

Finally, in response to Colden's suggestion that he should publish his account of yellow fever, Mitchell replied that he felt that he had to know more about the disease and its mode of propagation before taking this step.

He had been, he told Colden, "very careful to trace its origin, no less than four times . . . and find that it was always imported in British vessels," and that it was even more important to know its affinity for the southern climes. At the time, yellow fever was generally regarded as having originated in the West Indies and was carried to the colonies largely through commercial transactions.

In his next and final letter to Mitchell—for the latter left shortly afterward to go to England for health reasons—Colden would offer the view that the two differed little in their medical views on yellow fever. Since Mitchell had actually observed its symptoms, Colden added, "I would have entirely acquiesced in your judgment and have given up my own opinion."[61] The only thing Colden could do now was to rephrase portions of his own articles dealing with malignant fevers in order to explain why these fevers had appeared in New York. Mitchell most likely had seen the articles, so Colden was not able to offer anything really novel on that score. It was primarily the wharfs and filthy docks that he blamed for these fevers, and he concluded that while the sickness might not necessarily be due to the putrid vapors, it assuredly owed its propagation to them.

The somewhat surprising aspect of Colden's last letter to Mitchell is Colden's claim that the fevers of 1743 and 1745 were due to yellow fever, in spite of his prior admission that he had not seen any cases of yellow fever in New York. He asked Mitchell to be particular in providing information for making a diagnosis, since local practitioners usually lagged in making accurate diagnoses until the disease had reached either fatal or epidemical proportions. Perhaps the real reason why he wanted a more detailed report from Mitchell is suggested when Colden wrote, "Tho' by my situation in the country we may here keep free from the Infection, yet I have children and grandchildren in the City who are every year exposed to it."[62]

Mitchell's vivid description of the progress of yellow fever in Virginia may have alarmed Colden sufficiently that he wondered if it had not already arrived in New York. He now asserted that yellow fever had become epidemical in New York in 1743, did not appear in 1744 due to the various sanitary measures that had been adopted, but had again infected portions of the city during the summer of 1745. It is not certain what altered Colden's mind over a period of some six months. It is possible, even probable, that included in the malaria-typhoid sequence of 1743 and 1745 were some cases of yellow fever.[63] If Colden altered his opinion, it was not due to any direct clinical evidence but on the basis of a revised theory that all fevers of a certain type could be reduced to variations of yellow fever. He now pronounced to Mitchell that all the "nervous fevers" that have "passed under different denominations at different times and in different places" were originally due to the yellow fever imported from the West Indies.[64] Only in this way might Colden have been able to defend his speculative ideas on its treatment and cure.

In his letter, Mitchell also raised the controversial issue regarding those diseases that could be considered native to the New World and those that were derived from Europe. It was a topic that fascinated many physicians of the eighteenth century. Mitchell, for example, wanted Colden to tell him if he had ever seen the distemper called "yaws" which a French writer, La Hontan, identified with the "pox" among Indians.[65] If so, Mitchell added, he would appreciate a particular history or other account of the disease. In his reply, Colden rejected the contention that these two diseases were similar, and told Mitchell that he believed that yaws had been imported from Africa, whereas he believed the "French Pox or Lues Venera [syphilis] to have been originally from America."[66] He promised to send Mitchell an account of the cure of yaws by tar water as written by Dr. Johnson of Stratford, Connecticut, probably in lieu of the particular history that Mitchell had requested.

Another epidemical fever that attracted Colden's attention was the noted "throat distemper" that ravaged principally the New England colonies between 1735 and 1740. Within that five-year period, it sometimes assumed such dangerous proportions that it was actually feared that, left unchecked, it would destroy the colonies. Whether it also could have had some psychological repercussions leading to that noted religious revival, the "Great Awakening," remains a distinct possibility.[67]

The throat distemper first appeared in New Hampshire in the summer of 1735. Thereafter, it spread through numerous New England communities until, by late summer, it had reached Boston, Massachusetts. That same year it made an appearance in New Jersey; by 1736, it had reached both New York and Connecticut.[68] It was quickly noted that the disease afflicted mainly the young, often causing multiple deaths in a single family. For some reason, it was not generally believed to be contagious. William Douglass in Boston, for example, could attest:

I can not acct [account] for the general invasion of this Distemper; it was not imported; it affected only some particular Towns here and there & neighbourhoods, but not progressively or by Spreading. In the same town it seized families as it was at random without infecting the neighbourhood or visitors who without any reserve did frequently see their sick neighbours; where it enters a family constitution, scarce any of the family escape being seized: in some family constitutions it is generally mortal, in others very favorable—Some fear I observed in the common way of judging Received it by personal infection. . . . The Subjects of this Illness are generally those under the age of Puberty, some adults even old people have been seized and died of it.[69]

The extent and persistence of this disease throughout the northern colonies prompted several medical treatises. William Douglass in Boston, Cadwallader Colden in New York, and the Reverend Jonathan Dickinson, a minister-physician in New Jersey, all contributed to the literature on this epidemic. In his *Observations on that terrible Disease vulgarly called the Throat Distemper*, written in 1738–1739 and published in Boston in 1740, Dickinson observed that "The long Continuance and universal spread of [this Distemper] among us, has given me abundant opportunity to be acquainted with it in all its Forms. The first Assault was in a family about ten miles from me, which proved fatal to eight of the Children in a fortnight."[70]

Douglass' own treatise was entitled *The Practical History of a New Epidemical Eruptive Miliary Fever, with an Angina Ulcusculosa, which prevailed in Boston, New England, in the years 1735 and 1736* (1736). Douglass described his approach to this work as founded on "observations or phenomena, that is, upon the Symptoms that appeared in the course of the Epidemical disease; it must therefore be of permanent truth."[71] Among other signs, his clinical observations included "soreness in the throat, tonsils swelled and spekt, uvula relaxed, slight fever, flush in the face, and an Erysipelas like efflorence in the neck, chest and extremities." This is now regarded as the first scientific description of scarlet fever in English, or perhaps any language.[72] By the time that Douglass wrote to Colden, in 1739, when the throat distemper made its reappearance, it also included cases of diptheria.[73] This explains its more fatal consequences, at least in Boston at that time. The throat distempter was apparently a mélange of these two diseases: some communities had the milder scarlet fever, whereas others experienced the more severe repercussions of diptheria. In a letter to Colden, Douglass's description of the throat distemper suggests this difference:

A putrid heat different from the parched skin of common fevers, pulse not high but inconstant, a languid countenance, great prostration of strength, no considerable thirst, tongue much fever'd Tonsils and other parts of the Fauces infiltrated and Speck'd. . . . The slough casting off from time to time, if the ulcer appears of a mellow red the patient do well; but if of a fiery raw excoriated like colour the patient generally dies; blackish crusts or Seals, or hemorrhage upon the last scratch are fatal omens. . . . The last complaint is of an oppression and stricture in the upper part of the Chest (from the failure of Vis Vitae to carry on the circulation) asthmatick breathings, a deep pulmonary hollow hoarse cough, ending in a loud strangled contenances and death.[74]

The letter that Douglass sent to Colden was published the following year by Peter Zenger as *An Account of the Throat Distemper, in a letter from Wm Douglass to ——— of New York* (1740).[75] Douglass had actually encouraged Colden to publish his letter, "If you think these informations may be of any benefit to your neighbours." It was primarily Douglass's letter on the throat distemper and Mitchell's on yellow fever that prompted and guided Colden in forming his own theories on both diseases.

In this case, however, Colden expressed his views on the throat distemper not to William Douglass but to Dr. Fothergill, a London physician. He did so largely at the request of Peter Collinson.[76] In his letter, Colden affirmed his indebtedness to Douglass, but then went on to make several additional observations and suggestions of his own. In the first place, he traced the importation of the throat distemper into New York by noting that, "it appeared first in those places, to which the people of New England chiefly resorted for trade, and in places through which they traveled."[77] Second, he emphasized that it proved more contagious to the "poorer sort of people" than "those who live well" and to those "in the country than in great towns." Third, he remained completely baffled by its sporadic appearance without any previous cases, and could only conjecture that, after the disease abated, "It seems as if some seeds, or leaven, or secret cause remains, wherever it goes; for I hear of the like observations in other parts of the country." This certainly has some relevance to recognizing the latent stages of communicable diseases. Regarding therapy, Colden was of the opinion that the only successful cure had been found by William Douglass in Boston, and that it was best to adhere to his regimen.

Many of the Boston physicians, like Douglass, argued that the distemper was caused by some "morbific matter" in the blood, a view that seems to have been generally employed in the etiology of fevers. The most efficacious treatment was one that would force the poisons to erupt through the skin surface, thus liberating the body from this febrific substance.[78] For Colden—in contrast to the recommended treatment for smallpox—it justified the use of the "warm regimen," in which the patient was to be kept in bed, given gentle diaphoretics, and in this way forced to perspire freely. The most common diaphoretic that Colden preferred was sage tea—which, he averred, he had used successfully both within his family and with local neighbors. However, this could only be employed at the onset of the disease, for then it went through its course mildly.

Colden concluded his letter to Dr. Fothergill by giving a summary statement of his views on the distinguishing aspects of various fevers, their causes and proper treatment:

I distinguish the humours of the body into three different stages or classes. First, that which circulates only within the larger ramifications of the veins and arteries, and which is properly called *blood*. Secondly, that which moves slowly in smaller ramifications than those in which the red globular parts can pass, and from which the sensible secretions are made. Thirdly, and lastly, that humour which moves and is contained in still finer ramifications, and which is sometimes distinguished by the name of *lymph*. This last I take to be the principal instrument in the vital and vegetable functions of an animal. I suppose that the animal food or nourishment undergoes three different concoctions or digestions, after it has entered the course of the circulation, in these different ramifications; in all of which, the humours move slowly; That by a fault in any one or more of these digestions, diseases of different kinds are produced, which may be properly distinguished and ranked, according to the different stages in which these humours circulate, and where the digestion is faulty.

From this distinction it follows, that the morbid matter in the first class may be most effectually carried off by venesection; in the second, by one or more of the sensible secretions; and in the last, by insensible perspiration only.[79]

While Colden would have regarded all fevers as equally serious, only his treatment for the first, the so-called "inflammatory fevers," involved some operative procedure, since the fever resulted from the disturbance of the humors associated with the blood. The remaining two fevers could be treated more gently. In any case, they would prove unresponsive to more aggressive approaches. Consequently, some method of perspiration was generally preferable—either "sensible" or "insensible." Whereas with the throat distemper Colden had recommended sage tea, those in the third category, or "nervous fevers," were best treated with Madeira wine. It was a therapy Colden submitted for Fothergill's consideration, adding that it had been used successfully in an epidemic of the "nervous fevers" at Albany in 1746. In a letter to Bartram that year, Colden was equally insistent in giving this advice, telling him, "Madeira wine proved the most effective Specific which most people were surprised at when I advised it, but I had so old an authority as Hippocrates for the use of wine in some kind of fevers. This was attended with so much success that the use of it became common."[80] The use of wine was also cited in Jean Baptist van Helmont's *De Febribus*. Obviously, Colden's patients must have quickly discovered that this cure, unlike venesection or the reliance on diaphoretics, was decidedly more agreeable than conventional therapy.

After Colden had sent his treatise on the throat distemper to Dr. Fothergill, the latter read it to a medical society that was just in the process of formation. As one who had attempted something similar in the colonies, this led Colden to remark that through such societies "the healing art will advance farther in the age of one man than it has hitherto done in several ages."[81] It was an evident expression of the Enlightenment of that age and its belief in progress and the advance of knowledge.

In 1763, Colden's treatise was published in the (London) *Medical Observations and Inquiries*, thus conforming to Colden's general injunction that "I wish that Authors in all medical publications would submit their works to the judgment of others of established reputation for their skill before the publication, which ought to be determined solely by the use & public benefits."[82] The recognition given to his medical theories must have vindicated, for Colden, his various efforts to retain membership in the medical community of the Old World as well as the New. Indirectly, it also contributed to the international reputation of Douglass, who had died in 1752.

Much the same views on fevers that Colden expressed in his treatise on the throat distemper can be found in another essay that he wrote, entitled,

An Abstract from Dr. Berkeley's Treatise on Tar Water, with some Reflexions Thereon. Colden first expressed his opinions on the medicinal virtues of tar water in a series of anonymous newspaper articles that were printed in the *New York Weekly Post Boy* (1744–1745). These were subsequently collated and republished by J. Parker in New York in 1745.[83]

Much of the treatise is an extended commentary on a preexisting work on the same subject. It was primarily because Bishop Berkeley's book might prove tedious to the average reader that Colden felt justified in condensing its contents by separating the "historical" from the "argumentative" parts, and then concluding "with some Reasoning more adapted to common Understandings than the Bishops' are, to show what Grounds one may have to trust to the Virtues attributed to TAR WATER, in the several cases mentioned by the Bishop."[84]

It is almost certain that it was Bishop George Berkeley's visit to the American colonies between 1729 and 1731 that acquainted him with the use of tar water by the colonists.[85] Tar water may have been one of those popular curatives which the colonists could have learned from the Indians and adopted for their own use. The last year that Berkeley was in the colonies also witnessed the peak of one of the smallpox epidemics, and he subsequently observed that a cold infusion of tar water was generally employed by some colonists as a preventive against smallpox.

When he returned to Ireland, therefore, Berkeley was determined to try the same therapy among those of his parishioners who had been similarly affected by smallpox.[86] Believing that he had no small measure of success in these treatments, he continued to experiment with tar water for a variety of ailments. It was not until 1744 that, with all the zealousness of a recent convert, he extolled its benefits in no uncertain terms. The two publications that helped to proclaim its virtues, both printed in 1744, were *Philosophical Reflections and Inquiries Concerning the Virtue of Tar Water*, and *Siris; A Chain of Philosophical Reflections and Inquiries Concerning the Virtues of Tar-Water, and Divers other Subjects connected together and Arising One from Another.*

Berkeley's optimistic account of the efficacy of tar water made it appear a virtual panacea for nearly all the ills that afflicted mankind. He suggested, for example, that it had value for any or all of the following: cutaneous eruptions, ulcers, consumptive coughs, dropsy, indigestion, asthma, scurvy, and several other ills. Evidently realizing that many readers would remain dubious about these purported cures, Berkeley concluded: "From my representing Tar-Water good for so many things, some perhaps, may conclude it is good for Nothing; But Charity obligeth me to say what I know, and what I think, howsoever it may be taken: Men may censure and object as they please, but I appeal to Time and Experience."[87]

Colden, however, did not suspend his belief in order to await the further trial of "Time and Experience." He may have been only slightly less credulous than Berkeley, but at least he had a theory at hand to explain the curative properties of tar water. His own treatise on this subject, it should be noted, was primarily intended to illustrate its uses by some further observation and "reasonings" with more emphasis, perhaps, on the latter than the former.

Thus, largely on the basis of Berkeley's experiments, Colden was led to propose that tar water possessed special therapeutic value for the treatment of contagious fevers that are contracted from "some noxious vapor or atmosphere." These vapors tended to act on all the parts of the body that were exposed to air and more particularly on those "animal juices" that resided within the capillary vessels. At first, the noxious vapors only rendered them "unfit for the animal function," but eventually their toxic influence was communicated throughout the body like a "leven" (leaven) and could cause, in its most extreme state, a "violent fermentation of all the humours in the body."[88]

Since it was not within the powers of a physician to regulate the disease once it reached this state and death became imminent, his primary role was to intercept or arrest the distribution of the "morbific matter" within the body. In this task, the physician was directly aided by a fever that was caused whenever these noxious vapors invaded the body. The resulting fever accelerated the velocity of the blood to the point where it effectively prevented the "depraved juices" from entering the larger vessels of the body. Consequently, the physician had to maintain the proper velocity in order to aid the recovery of the patient.

The significance of tar water in this regimen was that it was extracted from a resin that, as Colden argued, contained "volatile acid spirits." When tar water was made sufficiently dilute, on the order of one gallon of cold water to one quart of tar (as Bishop Berkeley had recommended), a solution resulted that could be easily and gently absorbed by the body. In this process, the "volatile spirits" were gradually introduced into the finest ramifications of the various ducts of the body's system. Thereafter, the "morbific matter" was removed and the proper motion of the lymphatic juices restored. If more conventional treatments were used, such as the usual evacuations, the "stagnating poisons" would not be allowed to escape through the skin surface; instead, they would be drawn into the recesses of the body through the blood stream and cause serious, if not fatal, consequences.[89]

Much the same thesis, of course, was also presented in Colden's treatise on the malignant fevers. In the treatise on tar water, however, he included in this category not only the summer or warm weather fevers, for example, malaria and typhoid, but also smallpox, measles, the throat distemper, yellow fever, and scurvy. Colden's primary purpose in writing the treatise was to inform and educate the general public in a manner that was more readable than Berkeley's book and to warn them of the dangers of living in regions that, at times, were subject to fevers caused by noxious vapors.

Another convert to the benefits of tar water was James Alexander of New York. He gave it to his daughter when little hope was left for her survival, and only after a local physician had been unable to restore her to health. Her condition apparently improved after she was given some tar water and as Alexander stated, "whether Tar Water has preserved her I cannot say, but every one of the family drinks it plentifully every night before going to bed."[90]

Colden must have evidently been looking for other converts, for he wrote to John Mitchell in Virginia, giving him accounts of tar water's curative properties and urging him to add it to his pharmacopoeia. Mitchell remained somewhat dubious, if not an outright skeptic, about the alleged benefits of tar water. He had no hesitation in letting his esteemed colleague know that "as for the surprising treatise that has been wrote of it, I think that if it had been wrote by Dean Swift instead of Berkeley, it might have been reckoned a very proper performance for his wit, & a good banter upon the many extravagant publishers of new medicines."[91]

Another popular folk remedy that came to Colden's attention and which he hoped to popularize was the use of pokeweed (*Phytolacca Americana*) to cure cancerous growths. He had first learned of its uses from Dr. Samuel Johnson of Stratford, Connecticut. The latter supplied Colden with several accounts that confirmed its alleged therapeutic benefits.[92] This prompted Colden to publish articles on the "Cure of Cancers" in the British periodical, *Gentleman's Magazine*, in 1751 and 1758.[93] Since physicians had had little success in treating this problem, once he had learned of this folk remedy he felt compelled to bring it to public attention.

In his articles, Colden gave a detailed botanical description of *Phytolacca*, remarking that it was the corrosive juices of this plant that were to be externally applied to the lesion or ulcer. He further justified the use of pokeweed in a letter to Franklin, telling him that he could confirm that it had cured a cancer that had been found in a woman's breast and was much preferred over the conventional "cruel method of extirpation." He added: "Though this juice gives much pain in the application, it is not a caustic but rather such kind of pain as Arum gives without destroying the substance of the flesh. I have never heard of any ill consequences from the use of it, where the sick had the patience to endure the pain."[94]

In his articles, Colden declined to provide any explanation that would account for the success of pokeweed in treating cancer. His preference was that others interested in the plant should pursue this investigation. In any case, he claimed that there was no rational basis for its properties; only further observation and trials could determine whether it was beneficial or prejudicial in specific cases. In short, its value was based on the "empiric" standard of proof, rather than on any theoretical construct.

While Colden also admitted that he could not tell "wherein the nature of a cancer consists," he contended that it was similar to the tumors caused by insect eggs deposited in the bark or leaves of trees: "The embryo seems like a point, from whence some peculiar force and action proceed, so that upon examining of them, while these tumors are tender, there seem to be numerous tubes and fibres all tending to or from the embryo. The eggs of some insects lie several years without any apparent increase or alteration, but after they have passed a certain time, their life or force of vegetation begins, and they encrease greatly in a short time." Colden inferred that cancer had a similar embryonic and radiating activity, remaining dormant beneath the skin until, "at the end of that term [it] encreases very fast, and spreads its parts like roots, through all the adjoining parts of the body, and thereby occasions the obstruction and swelling of the vessels."[95] From this, he concluded, we can form some notion of the nature of cancer. As a botanist and gardener, Colden must have observed such growths and evidently perceived their analogy, in several respects, to cancerous tumors in man.

The letters, articles, and treatises that Colden wrote were his contributions to the medical literature of his age. The theories that he expressed in many of them are generally a blend of both ancient and modern authors. He made use, for example, of Hippocratic and Galenic doctrines of humors but modified the latter to suit the scientific developments and attitudes that exerted an influence on medicine in the eighteenth century.

Colden's mechanistic conceptions of the body were in keeping with that period and largely derived from the iatro-mathematical or iatro-physical tradition, which was primarily dominated by Italian scientists, mathematicians, and physicians. To make the body analogous to a machine emphasized its structural components and that dynamic balance of forces that promoted its efficient and orderly operation. Subsequent advances in chemistry and an understanding of chemical processes furnished the basis for the iatro-chemical school, which took issue with the iatro-mechanical tradition by pointing out some of its inherent limitations.

While the iatro-mechanical school was represented in the works of several Italian notables, such as Giovanni Borelli's *De vi percussionis* (1667) or Lorenzo Bellini's *De urines et pulsibus* (1685), the iatro-chemical approach was most indebted to Jean Baptist van Helmont, a pioneer in the chemistry of gases. He suggested that processes such as nutrition, movement, and digestion were not mechanistic in nature—comparable to the actions of bellows and pumps—but based on various chemical fermentations that took place within the body.

Both schools would continue to attract adherents but there were also those such as Thomas Sydenham (1624–1689) who refused to identify themselves with either school and instead emphasized the necessity for observation and interpretation of the phenomena of disease. In the American colonies, Sydenham's influence on Mitchell, who pursued the practice of clinical observations and careful description, is evident. The effect of Syndenham's authority is also manifest in the writings of William Douglass.[96]

Cadwallader Colden had evidently also read some of the works of this noted English physician.[97] It is quite probable, for example, that Colden derived at least some of his ideas on the interrelationship between climate and disease from Sydenham's *Constitution Epidemica*, as well as from Lancisi's classic treatise on the same subject.

While observational skills were important, a university-trained physician was expected to have some overall philosophical conception regarding the operations of the body; in this context, at least, the role of the iatromechanists continued largely unabated throughout the early eighteenth century. Teachers from universities in northern Europe gradually supplanted the Italian authors who had largely dominated a tradition that was itself an outgrowth of Cartesian philosophy. In England, too, the Royal Society was instrumental in fostering the mechanical philosophy for a time.[98] Again, the influence of Isaac Newton's natural philosophy also lent some credence to this development.

Foremost among his adherents was Herman Boerhaave, who taught his students that the body exemplified Newtonian mechanics and that the particles and fluids that flowed through its tubes were governed by definite laws of motion. In his *Method of Studying Physic* (1719), Boerhaave recommended Newton as the "Prince of Philosophers" and proposed that the mathematical knowledge of fluids, or hydrostatics, was "absolutely necessary for a Physician (for all things that happen in a Fluid are found in our Bodies) that he may thence know what is Life, Increase, Decrease."[99] In addition, such knowledge would help the physician understand all the philosophical books relating to medicine, as well as medical theory, reasoning, and argument. A student of Boerhaave, Archibald Pitcairne, the founder of the medical faculty at the University of Edinburgh, also published a similar work entitled *The Philosophical and Mathematical Elements of Physik* (1718).

Colden's educational background, his scientific interests, and his importation of books primarily authored by physicians of the iatro-physical school initially predisposed him to a mechanistic conception of the body. This is evident in many of Colden's letters and treatises on medical subjects, especially on the topic of fevers. As noted, these included such items as his letters to Governor Hunter on the perfectibility of medicine, to Hugh Graham on the issue of infectious fever, and to William Douglass on the nature of smallpox. It can only be surmised that his lost treatise on "Animal Secretions" would also reflect some of the main tenets of that tradition. Again, Colden's letters to John Mitchell on yellow fever and to Fothergill on the "Throat Distemper," as well as his *Abstract on Tar Water* expanded on his earlier views on fevers and now included an analysis of the role of secondary fluids, such as secretions and lymph, within the human body.

In these several letters and articles, Colden gave a predominantly mechanical interpretation to the doctrine of the circulation of the blood by arguing that the rate of its circulation—as would be the case with other fluids—was directly determined by the degree of heat in the body. Later, he added that the blood and its secondary fluids were also affected by the diameter of the various ducts through which they had to pass. It was on the basis of such theories that Colden was able to deduce several specific recommendations regarding the treatment of fevers.

Colden's disenchantment with the claims of the iatro-mechanical philosophy probably began to develop in the 1740s, for it was during this time that he expressed his qualms to Mitchell:

That at my first entrance in the Study of Physic I imbibed the Mechanic System with great greediness[.] It giving the only Satisfactory account of the Animal Oeconomy which I had seen and the other Systems containing only confused notions of things without communicating distinct ideas of what they intended[.] But after more serious consideration, I found the Mechanic system was very defective and at last am convinced that the alterations in the Animal juices very little depend on Mechanical principles and that even the first and principle mover in the Circulation is in no way Mechanical.[100]

Colden was further confirmed in his skepticism concerning the merits of the iatro-mechanical philosophy when he tried to account for such biological phenomena as fertilization, birth, and growth. He reexamined this problem in more depth in his *An Inquiry Into the Principles of Vital Motion*, and in a shorter work, *Notes on Physiology*. In his *Animal Oeconomy*, for example, Colden put it quite simply when he stated that animal motion was produced by fire, which is an "active principle" in the blood. Certain medications, therefore, such as caustic salts that contain fire, ought to be used by the physician to revive circulation and promote recovery.[101]

A much more practical and compelling instance of the limits of the mechanical philosophy pertaining to medicine confronted Colden when he was forced to decide whether to have his youngest son, David, be given the smallpox vaccination.[102] Colden probably had little hope that his son, a sickly, deformed child, would survive smallpox contagion. In time, he agreed to the procedure, believing that there was less risk with this method than through a common infection.[103] The technique of immunization, together with the results of inoculation, disabused Colden of his early commitment to the iatro-mechanical school.

I was educated in the Mechanical Philosophy, & considering the evidence on which its principles are founded, & the Mathematical method which the Professors used in explaining the Animal Oeconomy, & accounting for the disorders which arise in it from these principles, it is not to be wonder'd at, that I intertained a notion of the perfection of the Science, & that I began to practice with that assurance which Young Men commonly obtain at the Universities.

The Professors generally are solicitous to establish an opinion of their great knowledge, but are not sufficiently careful to show to their pupils how far that knowledge is deficient; that the Mechanical principles do not reach to every part of the Animal Oeconomy. The mutual effects of the Intelligent on the material constituent parts of the Animal, or of the material on the Intelligent do not depend on mechanical principles: and yet these mutual effects are constantly observed in the Animal Oeconomy, which in no manner depend on mechanic principles but are produced by physical causes of which perhaps we are entirely ignorant.[104]

Colden then went on to give a detailed description of the method of inoculation, noting its various stages, progress, and appearance, and adding that none of it could be explained according to iatro-mechanical theory. Moreover, he doubted that any other physician could so explain it, "however knowing & skilful in other respects they may have been." It is here, he admitted, that "Theory absolutely fails the Physician."[105]

Colden's growing disenchantment with the iatro-mechanical or iatro-physical philosophy did not lead him to reject theoretical considerations altogether. It was still necessary, in his view, that the physician be acquainted with general principles, both of the animal oeconomy, that is, physiology, and of physics or natural philosophy. The physician who operated outside the scope of a theoretical framework had no guide to interpret his observations and thus "must perpetually wander in the dark."

After confessing his inability to explain the process of inoculation in strictly mechanical terms, Colden proposed that the only way of accounting for its activity was "from an analogy with what is observed in fermenting liquors, *viz* that the variolous pus is a kind of leven or ferment, which being mixed with the blood of a living man produces a fermentation or fever, that by this fermentation a considerable quantity of the animal juices is assimilated into the nature of the variolous pus or leven: that the crisis or cure of this disease is by separation of the assimilated matter from the other circulating fluids, & by its expulsion in pustles on the surface of the body."[106] When Colden went on to argue that "the whole art of cure of the disease, simply taken, consists in regulating the fermentation," he concurred with a key doctrine of the iatro-chemists. He subsequently developed and applied his theory of fermentation to such biological processes as circulation, generation, and digestion, in a work entitled *The Principles of Vital Motion*.

Although a portion of this treatise is necessarily speculative, Colden insisted that in regard to such topics at least "where we have not *Data* Sufficient for Demonstration, hypothetical and conjectural reasoning may be allowed: for they often give hints for future discoveries."[107] In Colden's opinion, the problem of generation, for example, deserved more attention for it was only recently that the sexuality of plants and the existence of the spermatozoon (*animalcula seminis*) had been revealed. The reference to plant sexuality was an obvious reference to Colden's reading of Linnaeus, although Linnaeus was admittedly not the first to recognize this feature.

While Colden mentioned that he had performed some experiments of his own on the fertilization of corn, he believed that the results of male-female fertilization in animals would be best studied in eggs while they were hatching. In the process of fertilization, the male sperm contributed "something essentially necessary for producing that kind of intestine motion or fermentation in the humours of the egg, which is proper for the nutrition and growth of the foetus."[108] This intestine motion was sustained by heat that, in turn, created a "yeast" as "no kind of machine can do." Again, the nourishment that passed between the placenta and uterus resulted from the "pulsion" of the fermenting fluid.

The digestion and absorption of food would also confirm this general theory, Colden averred. It was such juices as saliva, bile, and pancreatic secretions that entered into this process and produced a fermentation which forced the food to be absorbed and its nutrients transported throughout the body. Somewhat more detailed and important was Colden's theoretical explanation of the circulation of the blood and other animal fluids in the body. He argued that the decreasing velocity of the blood at a distance from the heart and its increasing velocity as it returned to this organ made it possible to propose that the motion of the blood "begins in the veins and that the principle of Vital Motion resides in them." No mechanical apparatus or force could sufficiently explain this velocity.

Colden went on to declare that it was very probable that the nerves provided that ferment or leaven in exciting the intestine motion of the blood in the veins. The nerves did not themselves contain any fluids, but were like lines or filaments surrounded by "an extremely subtle elastick fluid, whose parts mutually repel each other, and which adheres to these filaments like an extremely thin atmosphere."[109] The nerves also caused glandular secretions for, when they were obstructed, a "morbid state" of the secretions resulted. Colden also speculated that "one reason why animals grow to a certain bulk [is] because the nerves do not admit of a farther division."[110]

Although Colden would conclude by stating that "a peculiar kind of fermentation is the principle of all vital motion," it was in response to issues relating to the design of the body and the activity of fermentation that compelled Colden to introduce the role of intelligence or that of an Intelligent Being. Colden concluded that the complicated and interrelated structure of the body could not have occurred by accident. "The Direction of an Intelligent Being," he wrote, "is necessary in regulating the vital fermentations, and in forming the secretions: for otherwise they could not always remain regularly the same."[111] The role of the Intelligent Being was to direct activity without itself acting in place of the vital motions, for "Intelligence gives no motion or force, but only of direction." Its primary purpose, in this scheme, was to achieve a balance between either excessive or deficient fermentations—in the body, as well as between opposing passions and appetites. Thus, the singular role of the physician was "the art of preserving health . . . in keeping all the vital fermentations in their regular and natural order."[112]

In these later treatises, Colden enunciated a more balanced, one might almost say "conservative" approach to the issue of a proper medical therapy. What was recommended was a mean between an active and passive method of treatment and between theory and observation. Such conclusions may well represent a summing up, as it were, of a lifetime spent in reading, reflection, and correspondence on various medical topics, and the influence these had in altering some of his earlier views. He could now regard these with some indulgence and even as based on a certain naiveté. His initial enthusiasm for the iatro-mechanical school, which he had absorbed from his teachers, was no longer a viable proposition. His experience with small-pox together with his views on the several biological processes in the body gradually forced him into making a fairly thoroughgoing reexamination of that tradition.

Although Colden could only speak of fermentation in an analogous manner, and his discussion of its activity is often vague and obscure, he remained certain that something of this nature, rather than a variation of the laws of matter in motion, could best describe the intricate processes that combined to sustain and perpetuate life from one generation to the next. And this led Colden to posit the existence of some agency (mind or intelligence) which directed and guided this active metaphysical principle, fermentation, to certain ends and purposes.

It was approximately at this stage that Colden was introduced to two eminent physicians at the University of Edinburgh who had themselves abandoned the iatro-mechanical tradition that had dominated medical education at that institution for much of the eighteenth century. Both physicians became adherents of the teachings of George Stahl, who suggested that the body was sustained by a supreme life force, or *anima*, comparable to that immaterial principle regulating fermentation among the iatro-chemists.[113]

Robert Whytt, an eminent neurologist at the University of Edinburgh, wrote several works on human and animal physiology.[114] The vitalistic thesis is evident in one of the early treatises that Whytt published, entitled *An Essay on the Vital and other Involuntary Motions of Animals* (1751). Here, Whytt proposed to analyze such processes as respiration, muscular contraction, and circulation. Since both respiration and circulation were, in Whytt's view, dependent on muscles, much of the discussion was devoted to a study of their operation within the body.

Whytt proposed that the heart, like all other muscles in the body, was animated by an "active sentient principle" that caused contractions. In so doing, he rejected the myogenic theory of the iatro-mechanics in which muscle irritability was a sufficient explanation for its alternate contraction and dilation. Neither the circulation of the blood nor the continuation of life, Whytt claimed, could be ascribed to any mechanical device, but only to "the agency of a living principle capable of generating motion." It was, then, the power and agency of mind which was that very "sentient principle." Whytt justified his contention that there is no need to know *how* the soul acts on the body, as long as "we know from experience, that it feels, is endowed with sensation, and has a power of moving the body."[115]

Whytt furnished Colden with a copy of his *Physiological Essays*, which included *An Enquiry into the Causes which promote the Circulation of the Fluids in the very small Vessels of Animals,* and *Observations on the Sensibility and Irritability of the Parts of Men and other Animals.* At that time, Colden had already written a work on natural philosophy, entitled *The Principles of Action in Matter,* and while he confessed that the way the body acted on the mind, or *vice versa,* was a difficult problem, he could not readily conceive how Whytt's answer was entirely consistent with the latter's notion of the inactivity of matter.

In his letter to Alexander Garden—to whom he addressed his response to Whytt's treatise—Colden disclosed that the stimuli on the mind must be "the actions of some material parts on the body exciting uneasy or some kind of sensation on the mind."[116] It was due to these stimuli that the mind motivated the muscles to act. He concluded: "I am strongly inclined to think with Dr. Whytt that muscular motion is allwise excited by some action of the mind, though I despair of ever being able to conceive in what manner this is done."

Another defender of the vitalistic hypothesis was William Porterfield. In his *Treatise on the Eye, The Manner and Phaenomenon of Vision* (1759), he advanced the theory, for example, that the pupillary activity of the eye could be explained on the basis of the soul's reaction to strong light. He, too, rejected mechanism because it was not an adequate description of the activity of the body nor could it account for the complete pre-formation of animals before birth. Since mechanism could not account for the generation of animals, he wondered why, after birth, "so great concern should be shown to reduce all to mere Mechanism, and to exclude an intelligent and active Principle from having any share in the government of those motions on which Life depends."[117] Porterfield maintained that not only the voluntary, that is, conscious, but also "the vital and natural motions of the body are under the influence and interposition of this active principle." He equated this "vital principle" with the mind or intelligence.

Colden's general position was that the soul had an important, though limited, role in the body. Its major function was to direct the activities of the body, rather than promote such activities. Neither Whytt nor Porterfield would find this distinction convincing, since it would detract from and circumscribe the power of that vital principle that was a central feature of their philosophy. When Colden, for example, suggested at one point that the soul might alter or change "the direction of the force or moving power in the Blood, but that it did not communicate any new force to them," Whytt contended that, as the "Deity has communicated motion to the whole matter of the universe . . . why may not a finite Spirit Communicate motion to a smaller portion of matter?"[118]

For Colden, it was not intelligence, but light alone—conceived as a propulsive force or perhaps as a form of energy also exemplified in heat—that was able to initiate motion, for reasons which are made more evident in his scientific, rather than medical, treatises. Colden regarded a knowledge of scientific philosophy as an indispensable introduction, even a prerequisite, for some of his medical theories. Whytt was sufficiently acquainted with Colden's views to realize that neither individual was fully able to explain how the soul, as Whytt proposed, or light, as Colden would claim, moved matter. As Whytt noted: "I shall only add on this head, that if light gives motion to bodies not by impulse, but in a manner quite unknown, why may not mind or Spirit give also motion to matter, although it cannot act on it in the way of common impulse; & if this be so, why should we restrain the power of the Soul to the changing the direction of the force or moving power of the body?"[119]

Colden remained adamant in his original position for he did nothing to apply this analogy to his scientific philosophy. At this stage, he had already formulated his theory and, for reasons that are suggested elsewhere, retained his basic presuppositions.[120] Colden may have transformed his medical views to incorporate some iatro-chemical conceptions, but this, in effect, was his final position on such medical speculations.

Sometime after Colden had received Porterfield's treatise, he felt motivated to compose a rather lengthy treatise of his own.[121] It was ostensibly meant to be a commentary on Porterfield's treatise, but it has only a superficial relation to that work. It is more accurately a collation of views which Colden had formed on a number of topics that evolved out of his ongoing reflections and conceptions relating to medicine. In his treatise, Colden covers such diverse subjects as the role of ideas, the function of memory and dreams, and the contribution of fermentation in the activity of the body. Scattered through the treatise are statements which largely refer to his *Principles of Action in Matter*—a work that he was in the process of revising for further publication.

While the treatise itself may have been written as one of those "private amusements," as Colden would have termed it and thus have never been intended for publication, this does not detract from its importance as one of Colden's last works on various topics related to medicine. It is largely made up of a series of somewhat rambling and obscure, sometimes redundant, collation of speculations. Here, as sometimes elsewhere, Colden sketches his thoughts in a broad manner, often abruptly terminating or reintroducing a particular subject.

One of the issues that Colden introduces at the outset is the role of sensation to knowledge. He asserts that all our ideas of the external world must be derived from sensation, and that it is a mode of knowledge that both men and animals share. Such ideas, though admittedly subjective, do not "deceive us," but are meant to serve "the common uses of life," an evident reference to Cartesian metaphysics. Thus, even if men could have knowledge of things as they are in themselves, independent of experience, "We should not be able from our infancy to take the necessary care for food, choose the good & avoid the evil without the Appetites & Sensations we now have. We could have none of the Social pleasures nor the appetites necessary for continuing the Species."[122] These sensations are transmitted to the mind by an "impulse" which is conveyed by "some elastic fluid" contained in the nerves. The strength of this impulse is directly proportional to the elasticity of the transmitting fluid. Older persons have less of such elasticity, while that in hysteric cases is "praeternatural."

Once sensation is communicated to the mind, it impinges on the "common sensorium" and, in turn, is acted upon by the Intelligent Being. Strictly speaking, the Intelligent Being does not act solely due to this stimulus, but in response to the ideas or perceptions of things which already exist in the mind. In this way, the function of memory is to guide and direct the Intelligent Being to serve the purposes of animal life. It is, in effect, a principle of continuity.

The Intelligent Being directs a chain of operations, or perhaps a chain of experience, past and present, that establishes the habits or disposition of the mind. In the body, the Intelligent Being directs the intestine motion to certain ends, but Colden adds that the Intelligent Being is equally dependent on the intestine motion, for when the latter ceases, so do the physical and mental processes of the body. Herein, Colden finds one solution to the problem of the interaction between the intellectual and material activities of the body or between the soul and matter by proposing: "May it not then be concluded that the Union of the Intellectual powers with the Material system is preserved by the vital intestine motion of the Animal fluids?[123]

A related topic that Colden discusses at some length is the several operations of the mind. He divides these into three processes or powers: (1) the power to form ideas, (2) memory, and (3) judgment. The first is that by which the actions of material powers are communicated to the common sensory through the nerves. It is, in other words, the transmission of those impressions and experiences by which an external object produces an idea. The second is the sum of recollections or the process by which the present is integrated with the past, as already noted. The final power, that of judgment, may be subordinate in status to the first, the formation of ideas, but is the faculty of knowledge for comparing these ideas, for all knowledge is concerned with discovering and establishing such relationships.

Judgment is again subdivided into intuitive judgment or instinct and will. These are essentially concerned with the mind's reaction to pleasure or pain, which leads it either to desire or to avoid the object presented to it.[124] Its highest attainments are to create maxims or principles while, in the case of animals, it accounts for such activities as protection of the young, finding food, and so on. Colden did not consider these three basic functions of the mind to be an interdependent unity. They are, he asserts, the "powers of separate beings [for] the operations of the second & third may be destroyed or greatly impaired without any diminution of the first."

Thus, the physiology of the body is a complex structural system, with its several distinct activities and processes all tending to the preservation of life, the collection of information, and the extension of knowledge. It is primarily sustained by the vital fermentation that is directed by the mind. Individualization is attained through (1) a set of particular experiences and (2) the process of fermentation, which varies from one individual to the next. The unity of the self is due to the nerves that connect the body with the brain, or the physical with the mental, and which permit it to function as a living entity.[125]

The intellectual and scientific influences that shaped these views are basically the same as those which appeared in Colden's earlier productions. The later iatro-chemical tenets are much in evidence; so, too, are some Lockean contributions on the topic of the nature of ideas. In other respects, the treatise can be treated as a continuation of Colden's interest in physiology, both human and animal, the effects of disease and drugs, the process of generation, and those other philosophical and scientific subjects that he would examine in greater detail in other works.

When this treatise is added to the numerous letters and articles that Colden contributed to the medical literature of that age, it becomes apparent that he was an individual of impressive intellectual appetite and vigor. In medicine, he may have had only a limited clinical background, but he always recognized that observation and experience must be the physician's first guide in seeking a proper therapy. Yet the quest for a theoretical context and understanding was in the forefront of his mind, and prompted his extensive speculation on a range of *materia medica*. In most respects, his theories were based on the common intellectual and scientific influences that were prevalent amongst physicians at that time. This does much to explain the ease with which Colden was able to attain an informal membership in the medical community of the eighteenth century, in the American colonies as well as in Britain and Europe. As a counterbalance to his speculative work, Colden's contributions to the practical improvement of medicine—lectures, societies, legislation, and the publication of medical treatises—should also be recalled at this point. In many of these endeavors, he can be credited with taking a leading role not only in enhancing the status of medicine, but also in providing for the needs of his fellow man. Both of these were essential Enlightenment concerns. Indeed, his belief in progress and philosophical benevolence or humanitarianism, as well as his ongoing interest and involvement in contemporary medical issues, confirm his status as a colonial physician of his age.

NOTES

1. Cadwallader Colden to Mr. Richard Hill, November 23, 1716, *Colden Papers*, I, 33.

2. Cadwallader Colden to Mr. Innis, August 6, 1718, *Colden Papers*, I, 41–42. Cadwallader Colden to Messrs. W & J Innys Booksellers, n.d., *Colden Papers*, I, 42–43.

3. Cadwallader Colden to Mr. William & John Innys Booksellers, June 14, 1720, *Colden Papers*, I, 46.

4. Cadwallader Colden to Mr. John Fair Apothecary, January 22, 1716/17, *Colden Papers*, I, 37–9.

5. Richard H. Shryock, *Medicine and Society in America, 1660–1780* (New York, 1960), 9.

6. Whitfield J. Bell, Jr., "Medical Practice in Colonial America," *Bulletin of the History of Medicine*, 31 (1957), 446.

7. Ibid, 447.

8. Carl Bridenbaugh, ed., *Gentleman's Progress: The Itinerarium of Dr. Alexander Hamilton (1744)*, (Chapel Hill, N.C., 1948), 91.

9. Bell, 442.

10. Ibid. 443.

11. John B. Blake, "Diseases and Medical Practice in Colonial Virginia," *International Record of Medicine*, 171 (1958), 359.

12. William Douglass to Cadwallader Colden, February 20, 1720/1, *Colden Papers*, I, 114.

13. Francis R. Packard, *History of Medicine in the United States*, 2 Vols. (New York, 1931), 286.

14. Ibid.

15. Ibid.

16. Cadwallader Colden, "To His Excellency Brigadier Hunter, Governor of New York, January 16, 1719/20, "Copy Book of Letters on Subjects of Philosophy, Medicine, Friendship," 1716–1721, *Colden MSS*, New-York Historical Society, unpaginated.

17. Ibid.

18. Cadwallader Colden to William Douglass, n.d., *Colden Papers*, I, 272.

19. William Douglass to Cadwallader Colden, March 31, 1729, *Colden Papers*, VIII, 191.

20. William Douglass to Cadwallader Colden, February 17, 1735/6, *Colden Papers*, II, 146. Ernst Caulfield, "A History of the Terrible Epidemic Vulgarly Called the Throat Distemper, as it Occurred in his Majesty's New England Colonies Between 1735 and 1740," *Yale Journal of Biology and Medicine*, 11 (1938–1939), 246.

21. Maurice Bear Gordon, *Aesculapius Comes to The Colonies* (Ventor, N.J., 1949), 176.

22. Brooke Hindle, *The Pursuit of Science in Revolutionary America*, 1735–1789 (Chapel Hill, N.C., 1956), 64.

23. David Hawke, *U.S. Colonial History—Readings and Documents* (New York 1966), 344.

24. Cadwallader Colden to Peter Collinson, June 1744, *Colden Papers*, III, 61.

25. Peter Collinson to Cadwallader Colden, August 23, 1744, *Colden Papers*, III, 69.

26. Benjamin Franklin to Cadwallader Colden, August 15, 1745, *Colden Papers*, III, 143.

27. Cadwallader Colden to Benjamin Franklin, December 1744, *Colden Papers*, III, 93.

28. Benjamin Franklin to Cadwallader Colden, November 28, 1745, *Colden Papers*, III, 182.

29. Gordon, 170.

30. The latter was written sometime in the early 1720s. A copy of this treatise can be found in the *American Medical and Philosophical Register*, I (1811), 304–310.

31. Ibid., 307.

32. Ibid., 308.

33. Ibid., 310.

34. Blake, 355.

35. William Douglass to Cadwallader Colden, May 1, 1722, *Collections*, Massachusetts Historical Society, II (1854), 170.

36. George H. Weaver, "Life and Writings of William Douglass, M.D. (1691–1752)," *Bulletin of the Society of Medical History of Chicago*, 2 (1917–1922), 235.

37. William Douglass to Cadwallader Colden, May 1, 1722, Massachusetts Historical Society. *Collections* (4th series), 2 (1854), 167.

38. Claude E. Heaton, "Medicine in New York during the English Colonial Period," *Bulletin of the History of Medicine*, 17 (1945), 23.

39. James Alexander to Cadwallader Colden, December 23, 1731, *Colden Papers*, II, 42.

40. Heaton, 25.

41. Cadwallader Colden to Hugh Graham, October, 1716, in Saul Jarcho, "The Correspondence of Cadwallader Colden and Hugh Graham on Infectious Diseases (1716–1719)," *Bulletin of the History of Medicine*, 30 (1956), 205.

42. Cadwallader Colden to Hugh Graham, Ibid., June 1717, 208.

43. Cadwallader Colden to Hugh Graham, Ibid., [1719?], 210.

44. Weaver, 236.

45. Cadwallader Colden, "Observations on the Fever which prevailed in the City of New-York in 1741 and 2, written in 1743," *American Medical and Philosophical Register*, 1 (1811), 311.

46. James Alexander to Cadwallader Colden, January 22, 1743/4, *Colden Papers*, III, 46; Cadwallader Colden to Alderman Johnson, December 1744, *Colden Papers*, III, 95–96.

47. Gordon, 13.

48. Colden, "Observations on the Fever," 311.

49. Ibid., 325.

50. I.N. Phelps Stokes, *The Iconography of Manhattan Island, 1498–1909*, 6 Vols. (New York, 1915–1928), I, 197.

51. Martha J. Lamb, *History of the City of New York: Its Origin, Rise and Progress* (New York, 1877), 2 Vols., I, 589.

52. John Mitchell, "Account of the YELLOW FEVER which prevailed in VIRGINIA in the years 1737, 1741, and 1742, in a Letter to the late CADWALLADER COLDEN, Esq. In New York," *American Medical and Philosophical Registrar*, IV (1814), 181–215; John Mitchell, "Additional Observations on the YELLOW FEVER of Virginia, addressed to Benjamin Franklin," in ibid. 383–387.

53. Benjamin Franklin to Cadwallader Colden, October 25, 1744, *Colden Papers*, III, 77–78; John Mitchell to Benjamin Franklin, September 12, 1745, *Colden Papers*, III, 151–154.

54. John Mitchell, "Additional Observations," 383.

55. Thomas Cadwalader of Philadelphia is credited with carrying out, in 1742, the first scientific autopsy in the American colonies. William Postell, "Medical Education and Medical Schools in Colonial America," *International Record of Medicine*, 171 (1958), 367. However, Mitchell claims to have performed his first autopsy in 1737, thus preceding Cadwallader by several years.

56. Herbert Thatcher, "Dr. Mitchell, M.D., F.R.S., of Virginia," *The Virginia Magazine of History and Biography*, 40 (1932), 49.

57. Mitchell, "Account of the YELLOW FEVER," 197.

58. Cadwallader Colden, "Observations on the YELLOW FEVER of Virginia, with some remarks on Dr. John Mitchell's Account of the Diseases," June 8, 1745, *American Medical and Philosophical Register*, IV (1814), 378.

59. Ibid.

60. Dr. John Mitchell to Cadwallader Colden, September 10, 1745, *Colden Papers*, VIII, 314.

61. Cadwallader Colden to Dr. John Mitchell, November 7, 1745, *Colden Papers*, VIII, 328.

62. Ibid., 328.

63. Saul Jarcho, "Cadwallader Colden as a Student of Infectious Diseases," *Bulletin of the History of Medicine*, 29 (1955), 105.

64. Cadwallader Colden to Dr. John Mitchell, November 7, 1745, *Colden Papers*, VIII, 333.

65. Dr. John Mitchell to Cadwallader Colden, September 10, 1745, *Colden Papers*, VIII, 322.

66. Cadwallader Colden to Dr. John Mitchell, November 7, [1745], *Colden Papers*, VIII, 334–335.

67. Caulfield, 220.

68. Ibid., 314.

69. William Douglass to Cadwallader Colden, November 12, 1739, *Colden Papers*, II, 196–197.

70. Caulfield, 315.

71. Weaver, 238.

72. Ibid.

73. Caulfield, 261.

74. William Douglass to Cadwallader Colden, November 12, 1739, *Colden Papers*, II, 198.

75. Caulfield, 298.

76. Peter Collinson to Cadwallader Colden, June 2, 1755, *Colden Papers*, IV, 392.

77. "Extract of a Letter from Cadwallader Colden, Esq: to Dr. Fothergill, concerning the Throat Distemper," *Medical Observations and Inquiries*, 1 (1763), 212.

78. Caulfield, 272.

79. "Extract of a Letter," 222.

80. Cadwallader Colden to John Bartram, January 27, 1746/7, *Gratz Collection*, Historical Society of Pennsylvania; John Bartram to Cadwallader Colden, March 6, 1746/7, *Colden Papers*, III, 362–363.

81. Cadwallader Colden to ———— , January 8, 1756, *Colden Papers*, V, 64.

82. Ibid. Fothergill told Colden: "I was so much pleased with thy instructive account, that I could not forbear producing it, in the medical society lately formed here for revising & publishing such essays as may seem conducive for the improvement of medicine. It was received with unanimous approbation." John Fothergill to Cadwallader Colden, October 23, 1755, *Gratz Collection*, Historical Society of Pennsylvania.

83. [Cadwallader Colden], *An Abstract from DR. BERKELEY'S Treatise on TAR WATER, with some Reflexions Thereon, Adapted to Diseases Frequent in America* (New York, 1745).

84. Ibid., Preface.

85. Arthur A. Luce and Thomas E. Jessop, eds., *The Works of George Berkeley, Bishop of Cloyne*, 5 Vols. (London, 1949–1953), V, v.

86. Saul Jarcho, "The Therapeutic Use of Resin and of Tar Water by Bishop George Berkeley and Cadwallader Colden," *History of Medicine in New York State*, 55 (1955), 834.

87. Colden, *An Abstract*, 6.

88. Ibid., 14.

89. Ibid., 17.

90. James Alexander to Cadwallader Colden, September 22, 1745, *Colden Papers*, III, 155.

91. Dr. John Mitchell to Cadwallader Colden, September 10, 1745, *Colden Papers*, VIII, 325.

92. John Hubbard to Dr. Samuel Johnson, n.d., *Colden Papers*, III, 123–125; "An Account by John Patterson," July 12, 1745, *Colden Papers*, III 128–129.

93. Cadwallader Colden, "The Cure of Cancers," *Gentleman's Magazine*, 21 (1751), 305–308; 22 (1752), 302.

94. Cadwallader Colden to Benjamin Franklin, March 16, 1753, *Colden Papers*, IV, 317.

95. Colden, "The Cure of Cancers," 308.

96. Weaver, 230.

97. Cadwallader Colden to Dr. John Fred Gronovius, 1745, *Colden Papers*, III, 98.

98. Theodore M. Brown, "The Mechanical Philosophy and the 'Animal Oeconomy'—A Study in the Development of English Physiology in the Seventeenth and Early Eighteenth Century" (Ph.D. Dissertation, Princeton University, 1968).

99. Herman Boerhaave, *A Method of Studying Physic* (London, 1719), Preface.

100. Cadwallader Colden to Dr. John Mitchell, November 7, 1745, *Colden Papers*, VIII, 354.

101. Cadwallader Colden, *A Treatise on the Animal Oeconomy*, Colden MSS, New-York Historical Society, 2.

102. Cadwallader Colden to Dr. Bard on Small Pox, July 5, 1758, *Colden Papers*, V, 236.

103. Colden also eventually agreed to permit his daughter to receive the smallpox inoculation. Peter Collinson to Cadwallader Colden, March 6, 1759, *Colden Papers*, V, 297–298.

104. Cadwallader Colden to Dr. Bard on Small Pox, July 5, 1758, *Colden Papers*, V, 240–241.

105. Ibid.

106. Ibid., 243.

107. Cadwallader Colden, "An Inquiry into the Principles of Vital Motion," Colden MSS, New-York Historical Society, section 2, section 6, 3.

108. Ibid., section 2, 1.

109. Cadwallader Colden, "Notes on Physiology," Colden MSS, New-York Historical Society, section 23, 9.

110. Ibid., section 24, 27.

111. Colden, "Notes on Physiology," section 28, 29.

112. Colden, "Vital Motion," section 38, 22.

113. Paul Diepgen, *Geschichte der Medizin* (Berlin, 1949–1951), 3 Vols., I, 299.

114. Robert Whytt, *The Works of Robert Whytt*, M.D. (Edinburgh, 1768).

115. Ibid, 145.

116. Cadwallader Colden to Alexander Garden, June 23, 1757, *Colden Papers*, V, 162.

117. William Porterfield, *A Treatise on the Eye, the Manner and Phaenomenon of Vision* (Edinburgh, 1759), 2 Vols., I, 29.

118. Dr. Robert Whytt to Cadwallader Colden, October 20, 1760, *Colden Papers*, V, 352.

119. Ibid., 354.

120. See Alfred R. Hoermann, "Cadwallader Colden and the Mind-Body Problem," *Bulletin of the History of Medicine*, 50 (1976), 392–404.

121. Cadwallader Colden, "The Reading of an elaborate Treatise on the Eye by the learned & ingenious Dr. Porterfield was the occasion of the following Reflections." Colden MSS, New-York Historical Society.

122. Ibid., section 6, 3.

123. Ibid., section 13, 9–10; section 33, 26.

124. Ibid.

125. Ibid., section 37, 29.

Chapter 3

A MAN IN THE WOODS OF AMERICA

It is not improbable that . . . any attempt of a man in the woods of America to correct or improve Sir Isaac Newton would have appeared so ridiculous that it could not have drawn their attention so far as to consider it.

In these words, Cadwallader Colden expressed his growing sense of despair regarding the fate of his treatise, *The Principles of Action in Matter*. The predicament of a colonial philosopher, physically isolated from the cultural and intellectual community of Europe and thus dependent on others to present his scientific labors to public scrutiny is poignantly revealed. At the time that Colden uttered these sentiments, he had spent at least twelve years making substantial revisions and additions to the treatise. The amount of time and energy that Colden was willing to devote to this work and the tenacity of his belief that it was a major scientific contribution to the age makes it evident that he considered this particular treatise to be his *magnum opus*. Next to this treatise, Colden's work in botany and medicine—the two other fields that he tried to dominate with more success—pale by any measure of comparison.

Although Colden provided some penetrating insights and underwent some intellectual transformations in his medical theories, his treatises and articles on medicine were usually written on an ad hoc basis, often prompted by clinical works on the same subject. Again, his contributions to botany were primarily limited to the several years he spent examining and classifying the plants found near his estate. His failure to do much more in botany may have been the result of several factors, such as the distractions caused by his political responsibilities, but it appears likely that it was his attention to this treatise which soon occupied the major portion of his leisure time.[1] It would not only complement the fame he had achieved in botany but, more important, would far exceed in originality anything else he had yet done. He therefore attached a measure of personal reputation on the success of this work that was hardly the case, for example, with his theories in medicine. Regarding the latter, he was quite apt to admit his clinical limitations and welcomed criticism and correction. This was never the case with the *Principles of Action in Matter*, for here he demonstrated a measure of obstinacy in defending its merits which, in itself, may be quite unusual in the annals of such intellectual lucubration.

What Colden intended to accomplish in his treatise was certainly no small task. It was, in effect, nothing less than to complete Isaac Newton's masterwork, *The Principles of Natural Philosophy*, by supplying explanations for those several issues that Newton himself had left intentionally vague or unresolved. Exactly when Colden decided to initiate this rather momentous undertaking is not certain, but it is quite evident that, even while he was an undergraduate at the University of Edinburgh, Newton's natural philosophy exercised an early influence on Colden's own intellectual and scientific interests. In time, Newton's work may have come to dominate these to such an extent that Colden could not resist the blandishment of making his own singular contribution to Newtonian science.

Cadwallader Colden was admitted to the University of Edinburgh in 1702, although he did not matriculate until February 1703 as a "superveniens anno secundo" in the class of Regent William Law. The title of "superveniens" was reserved for those who had shown sufficient proficiency in Latin and Greek to be permitted to enter directly into the second year's work.[2] Under the system introduced by the Town Council of Edinburgh in 1628, the same regent was required to teach all courses leading to the M.A. degree, except for the first year. Knowledge of Latin and Greek formed an important part of the curriculum. It was also stipulated that the regent should introduce his pupils to several Aristotelian texts, while subjects such as geography, Hebrew, and anatomy were reserved for the third and fourth years.[3] A major change in the curriculum came with the introduction of Newtonian science at the University of Edinburgh under the auspices of David Gregory. In 1683, at the age of twenty-two, he became professor of mathematics and remained at Edinburgh until 1691, when he was appointed Savillian Professor of Astronomy at Oxford.[4] His brother, James Gregory, succeeded him at Edinburgh.

In his last year at Edinburgh, Colden took William Law's course in general physics. It was here that he was given an acquaintance with Newtonian science. His notes on the lectures given by Law—while fragmentary and sometimes illegible—reveal the extent to which Newton's stature must have been impressed on the young student. Phrases such as "Celeberrimus Newtonus," "Clarissimi Newtoni," and "illustris auctor" occur frequently in Colden's notes. He made careful translations of such terms as *vis centrifuga, vis centripeta,* and *gravitas,* defining the last as "vis ferens deorsum qua corpora recta ad terram tendunt."[5]

At the time of graduation, students were required to defend a thesis. Here, again, Newton's influence is apparent. His name and those of Flamsteed, Huygens, and other scientists appear in several of the theses.[6] Colden graduated with the degree of M.A. on April 27, 1705. Within another five years, he had completed his medical training in London, presumably with members of the London College of Physicians, and thereafter emigrated to the American colonies.

The early, positive response to Newtonian science by Scottish universities proved to be an important factor in the development and intellectual rigor of the Scottish Enlightenment. In much the same manner, the acceptance of Newtonian science at several American colleges gave an impetus to the development of the Newtonian epoch in the American colonies. As early as 1714, for example, Yale College introduced Newtonian mathematics into its curriculum.[7] In 1727, Harvard followed suit while, in the southern colonies, the New Philosophy was adopted at William and Mary College at approximately the same time.[8] Some of the newer colleges established during the eighteenth century, such as the College of Philadelphia (now the University of Pennsylvania), also intended to devote one-third of the curriculum to mathematics and natural sciences.

It was principally through the endeavors of individual scientists and through academic instruction that the dominance of Newtonian science was eventually assured. Newton had reinforced for many colonists a disposition toward scientific investigation. In the eighteenth century, astronomy was one science that became particularly popular. Its general acceptability in the American colonies was probably due to the fact that the colonists could furnish important data for use by European scientists as part of a cooperative scientific venture. It usually generated the most activity when preparations were made for the observation of comets or eclipses.

For a time, at least, Colden was also actively involved in making astronomical observations. While still in Philadelphia, he participated with James Logan in using a telescope the latter had purchased from England and mounted in his backyard. There, both men made the attempt, in 1717, to determine the effect of the earth's motion on the annual parallax of the stars.[9] After settling in New York, Colden corresponded with William Douglass in Boston about the various observations Colden had made in 1723 and 1724 on the eclipses of the moons of Jupiter.

Closer to home, another man who showed enthusiasm for astronomy was James Alexander. As one means of getting started, he proposed to Colden that the two men should test and, in time, exchange their compasses in order to detect any variations in deflection.[10] After having purchased a quadrant, Alexander invited Colden to assist him in setting it up to make some observations. Alexander's devotion to astronomy increased over time. Early in 1753, for example, he took the initiative in stimulating colonial interest in the transit of Venus across the sun, which would occur in May, 1763, a phenomenon that would not be visible again until the year 2004.[11] He expected that the Jesuits in China and observers in the East Indies would also make a major contribution in viewing this unusual phenomenon. For colonial astronomers, however, it would offer a unique opportunity to demonstrate their commitment to scientific endeavors. Alexander fully expected the various colleges to bear a large part of the responsibility for undertaking such tasks. As he wrote to Franklin, "As there are now sundry nurseries of learning springing up in Pennsylvania, [New] Jersey, New York, Connecticut & Boston; all ways should be thought of to induce each of those to provide a proper apparatus for making such observations, long before the year 1761, [so] that they may be expert in taking observations of that kind before that transit happens."[12]

In the interim, he urged Colden to come to New York to assist him in preparing apparatus for observing the transit of Mercury in May, 1753. Unfortunately, poor weather conditions prevented any sighting of the transit of Mercury that May. The only useful account of this event came from Antigua.[13]

There is no evidence that Colden complied with Alexander's request for assistance. This may not have been altogether unforeseen by Alexander.[14] At this time, Colden was fully involved in making revisions and additions to his treatise, and whatever interest he had in astronomy was secondary to this work. To Dr. Betts, a professor at Oxford University, Colden was candid enough to admit that "Astronomy was never properly my study any further than as an amusement and to obtain some general conceptions of Sr. Isaac Newton's theory till lately I entertain'd the notions of the first principles of Action in Matter."[15]

In addition to astronomy, electricity also had a continuing popular appeal. As a science that was still in its infancy in the eighteenth century, it invited experimental investigation and, in some cases, information derived from such work had demonstrable uses as well. Franklin's invention of the lightning rod, for example, was an important contribution that combined theory and experiment toward useful ends. Electrical phenomena proved an endless source of fascination and stimulated the curiosity of that age concerning the mysterious forces in nature. Collinson remarked, "Now the Virtuosi of Europe are taken up in Electrical Experiments" and added, "Electricity Seems to furnish an inexhaustible fund for enquiry."[16] In the colonies, Alexander Garden and, more particularly, David Colden, the youngest son of Cadwallader, performed various electrical experiments investigating the properties of electricity—David largely at the behest of his father and with the anticipation that the experiments could be related to the latter's treatise on natural philosophy.

At one time, Colden intended to make an improved quadrant that would be helpful not only to astronomers but also to geographers and mapmakers. Consequently, it had to be both portable and accurate. Colden himself had previously shown some interest in making a map of North America but here his proposal was prompted by his participation in a commission that was given the responsibility of settling the boundaries between Massachusetts and Rhode Island.[17] Such disputes generated a good deal of controversy and Colden probably believed that an improved quadrant would serve a useful purpose. Through Collinson's assistance, Colden was able to submit his plans to an English instrument maker who commented that the proposed device was not altogether practical.[18] Instead, he recommended that Colden investigate the products made by a Mr. Sisson, described as a "Mathematical Instrument Maker in the Strand." Colden accepted this judgment and sometime later purchased a "Circumferenter" from Sisson.[19]

Another invention that seemed to have some useful application was Colden's proposal for a new method of printing. In a letter to Franklin on this subject, Colden stressed the interrelationship between the art of printing and the advancement of learning, and concluded that any method that would produce more copies at a lower cost was an important contribution to the "republic of letters."[20] The method itself—which subsequently became known as stereotype printing—required making a matrix that could be used to produce permanent printing plates. If preserved, the plates could be used as often as desired, with additional copies becoming cheaper with each edition. In theory at least, this had certain advantages over the more conventional methods of printing, especially with regard to "books in the sciences and to such only which have an intrinsic value independent of the governing humour or taste, the value of which are known to few and will always be esteem'd & sought after by some."[21]

Colden sent a description of his invention to Collinson, pointing out that he himself had been unable to make any such plates; Collinson subsequently sought out a printer who would be more knowledgeable about such matters. After examining Colden's proposal, the printer reported that, while a laudable scheme, it would not have the advantages Colden might have expected. The sales of the several titles that Colden had mentioned were quite insignificant and, in any case, Colden was informed that printers "would not easily, if at all, be induced to try any other method of printing than what they have been used to."[22] Even if nothing further was done with regard to his printing scheme, Colden remained convinced of its intrinsic merits.

It is not altogether improbable that one reason, at least, why Colden took an avid interest in book publication was that he himself, at this time, was preparing a scientific treatise for publication. It, too, would be one of those books that could not meet the "governing humour or taste," as he termed it, for there was comparatively little demand for works of a strictly philosophical nature in the colonies at that time. Colden surely realized this when he wrote to Collinson, "I have often wished for to communicate some thoughts in natural philosophy which have remained many years with me undigested, for we scarcely have a man in this country that takes any pleasure in such kind of Speculations."[23]

Colden had some justification for expressing such sentiments, for he had received little encouragement that such speculations would be welcomed. Not long after he arrived in the colonies, Colden suggested to James Logan that the two men initiate a correspondence on philosophical matters.[24] What Colden may have subsequently submitted to Logan is not certain, but in response to one of Colden's "hypotheses," Logan told Colden that "for some time past I have been very dull in such inquiries, being persuaded that they are but guesses and that the Truth in these cases is placed designedly without our reach, that is, that we have no organs fitted for their discovery, and that all that remains for us, is to make the most advantageous uses of what certainty discovers to us."[25]

This may have proven sufficient to deter Colden from pursuing such speculations for some time, yet his philosophical interests must have come to the attention of Governor Hunter, once Colden settled in New York. After returning to England, Hunter wrote to Colden to encourage him in his speculations on "Natural Philosophy or any thing else without reserve for they give pleasure to others as well as my self."[26] One individual who may have proven responsive to sharing Colden's interest in a philosophical dialogue was William Douglass in Boston, to whom Colden later reminisced about "The speculations that gave you & me the greatest pleasure in the pleasantest time of our Life, while we were in the Garden of Eden, before we knew good & evil, before we knew men."[27]

It was, however, only after he retired to Coldengham that Colden more fully committed himself to natural philosophy, for some years later he wrote, "After I had passed a great part of my life in action, age and some incidents made it proper for me to retire to a solitary part of the country. I had at all times a strong inclination to philosophical speculations, and this turn of thinking has enabled me to pass away that part of my life very agreeably to myself, which in most people is accompanied with more pain than pleasure."[28]

It is most probable, therefore, that Colden began the initial work on his scientific treatise sometime in the early 1740s. He sent a rough draft of his speculations, late in 1744, to both Benjamin Franklin and James Logan.[29] Thereafter, Colden expanded this draft and published the first edition in New York City with the title, *An Explication of the First Causes of Action in Matter and of the Cause of Gravitation* (dated 1745). It became the first such scientific treatise to be published in the colonies.

Colden may not have originally intended to publish the treatise; at one point, he even considered abandoning the project altogether. One of the first to know of Colden's early plans on this subject and to encourage him to complete the task was James Alexander.[30] It was probably for this reason that Colden dedicated the first edition to him. Since it was not possible for Colden to be in New York City much of the time, Alexander also took a major share of the responsibility for supervising the publication of the treatise, sometimes sending Colden proof sheets as they came from the press.[31] Eventually, some three hundred copies were printed, nine of which were sent to Peter Collinson by Colden for submission to friends and associates.[32]

It must have pleased Colden when he learned that Collinson had been so impressed with the "greatness of [Colden's] design" that he had distributed the treatise "to our greatest people on these studies both at home and abroad in Holland, Germany, Paris, Sweden, Scotland, Dantzig, etc."[33] Collinson also submitted a copy to the Royal Society where "it is so well esteemed and admired." The general curiosity and interest shown in the treatise even prompted one publisher to print an unauthorized version. All of this makes it understandable why it was only to Franklin that Collinson disclosed that some mean-spirited person could not believe that the treatise was actually Colden's work, but must have been the "Ship wrack papers of some ingenious European" that had fallen into Colden's hands.[34]

In spite of the initial flurry of interest shown in Colden's treatise, Collinson found it difficult to obtain any informed opinion on the merits of its contents. In 1747, he noted ominously that "I find the more it is examined, the more they are at a loss what to offer & so in short say nothing," but promised Colden that "I persuade myself some or other will at last say something for it or against it."[35] The only indication that the treatise might have some scientific value came from Professor Betts at Oxford. In 1749, he wrote to James Alexander expressing his interest in the treatise and his concern that a person of Colden's "philosophic turn" should not desist from "such useful and pleasing speculations for a few inconveniences."[36]

Colden, of course, had not been idle in this respect. His attachment to the treatise was not going to be influenced by the lack of any positive response from its European readers, for he informed Betts that "this did not slacken my pursuit of an amusement so agreeable to my own humour, for after having made repeated & repeated reflections on the principles which I attempt to establish & consider'd all the objections to them which have in any shape occurr'd to me, I am fully persuaded that they will at last prevail & though they may not suit the present taste of learning, they will somehow or other be embraced perhaps when the author is dead & forgot."[37]

After recounting some of the interruptions that had constantly interfered with his attempt to complete the work, Colden explained to Betts the steps he had taken to prepare an enlarged, corrected, and revised edition. This was subsequently published in London in 1751. Abstracts from this edition were printed in such periodicals as the *Monthly Review*, the *Gentlemen's Magazine*, and the *London Magazine*.[38] The treatise was also translated into both French and German. Even if Colden admitted that, as far as the Hamburg and Leipzig editions were concerned, he could not understand one word, he proudly announced to Franklin that "I find my name often in company with those of the very great ones: Newton, Leibnitz, Wolfius."[39]

While aspects of Colden's speculative productions can be found in numerous smaller treatises, such as *An Introduction to the Study of Philosophy*, or, *Of the Transmission and Reflection of Light*, and *An Enquiry into the Principles of Vital Motion*, it is his *Principles of Action in Matter* that contains the most complete expression of Colden's natural philosophy. In this work, Colden reveals a quest for those universal laws or principles that might explain the operation of certain physical forces in terms of the activity of matter.

Thus, the several chapters that were added to the 1751 edition were intended to demonstrate the practical application of Colden's principles to certain heavenly phenomena, such as "The distance and eccentricity of the orbits of the planets and comets" and "the inclination of the axes of the sun and planets to the ecliptic," as well as an attempt to illustrate the principles on the basis of the astronomical observations of Flamsteed, whose tables had been used by both Alexander and Colden. In addition, Colden appended an introduction to the "Doctrine of Fluxions" or what he termed the "Arithmetic of Infinites," which was intended "to assist the imagination in forming conceptions of the principles on which that doctrine is founded."

The use in the 1751 edition of the phrase "to assist the imagination in forming conceptions" is revealing, for it suggests the kind of purpose Colden may have had in mind for the treatise itself. The fact that the first edition contained only 48 pages, whereas the London edition had been expanded altogether to 215, indicates the extent of Colden's arduous efforts to make the *Principles* more comprehensible.

The gist of Colden's natural philosophy can be extracted from the first three chapters of the 1751 edition. These three chapters are entitled: "The Principles of Action in Matter," "The Cause of Gravitation," and "The Motion of the Planets." Perhaps the best explanation for Colden's motivation to write on such abstruse problems is summarized in the preface to the treatise itself:

The doctrine of the mutual attraction of matter had in it something so unphilosophical, something so like the occult qualities, which had been exploded, that nothing could have made it pass with the learned, but the accurate agreement which Sir Isaac Newton showed it had with the phenomena. However justice must be done to this great author, that he nowhere calls it a *real* attraction, only apparent, the cause of which we know not.

In this tract, the author presumes to think, that he has discovered the cause of this apparent attraction, and from which all the phenomena in gravitation evidently follow, as necessary consequences: and that he has likewise discovered an error, which had slipped from the sagacious Sir Isaac, by his not knowing the cause of this apparent attraction.

Sir Isaac Newton no where gives the cause of the motion of the planets, but only supposes a certain degree of velocity to have been impressed upon them: in consequence of which no reason is given for the most general and obvious phenomena of the motion of the planets, as particularly for the different distances at which the planets severally, and the comets revolve, and the different eccentricity of their orbits. The author pretends to have discovered the true cause of the motion of the planets and comets, and from thence to deduce the reason of all the phenomena.[40]

Colden was quite right in arguing that Newton had not given a convincing explanation for his doctrine of gravitational attraction. This criticism was not unique to Colden nor was he the first to recognize the dimensions of this particular issue. Alexander Pope's famous dictum, "And God Said/Let Newton Be/And All Was Light," was not the universal rule. Almost a half-century earlier, following the publication of the first edition of the *Principia Mathematica* (1687), scientists were baffled by the meaning and status of this doctrine. It certainly could not be placed within the context of traditional physics. Of course, Newton's original intention was to give a mathematical description rather than a physical explanation of gravitation—a point he stressed in the second edition of the *Principia* (1713).

The enduring problem associated with gravitational attraction, given an atomistic philosophy and the doctrine of space void of matter, was that of "action at a distance." The scholastic axiom that "matter cannot act where it is not" was sufficiently viable to retain its relevance as a metaphysical principle for eighteenth-century natural philosophy. For Newton, it should be added, the notion of action at a distance proved equally repugnant; so, too, did the view that gravity could be considered an innate property of matter. When pressed for some explanation of the nature of gravity, Newton could only state that "Gravity must be caused by an agent acting constantly according to certain laws; but whether this agent be material or immaterial, I have left to the consideration of my readers."[41]

The closest Newton came to suggesting the cause of apparent mutual attraction was in the "Queries" attached to the second edition of the *OPTICKS* (1717). It is here that he gave an explicit account of the relation of a subtle diffused medium termed "aether" to gravity, and speculated that it was much more dense within the bodies of the sun, stars, planets, and comets than in the celestial spaces between them. He concluded: "if the elastic force of this medium be exceeding great, it may suffice to impel bodies from the denser parts of the medium towards the rarer, with all that power which we call gravity."[42]

These queries were made by Newton "in order to [encourage] a farther search to be made by others." They were conjectures or "hints" that might stimulate and guide subsequent scientific investigation into various areas. By putting them in the form of questions and suppositions, Newton, of course, was relieved of the responsibility for defending or retaining them as absolute or final philosophical propositions. The limited experimental insight available to him on these problems hardly permitted him to do more. To some degree, these speculations may even be regarded as the hypotheses that he had so scrupulously avoided in his *Principia*. Evidently, there was some justification for further investigation along some of these lines. In spite of the unfinished quality of the *OPTICKS* (or, perhaps, because of it), it became, together with the *Principia*, a part of the Newtonian legacy to the eighteenth century.

It is understandable, then, that Cadwallader Colden could appreciate the necessity of, and visualize the opportunity for, completing several aspects of Newtonian science. Although he noted, for example, that Newton had spoken of mutual attraction as an apparent, not real, phenomenon, and offered the hypothesis of an aether as the cause of gravitation, Colden regarded the hypothesis as one that Newton was "forced to leave . . . to excite others to pursue." He criticized Newton for not having "clear conceptions of what I call oether though he perceived from the phenomena that some such medium must necessarily exist between the several bodies in the Universe & within them between their component parts."[43]

Colden then set about the task of discovering the nature of this medium. He proposed that aether was composed of small elastic bodies that occupied space. These were absolutely contiguous in that there "cannot be the least distance between the points of aether." As a "middle thing" or medium, aether received and transmitted any action impressed upon it, by a kind of expansive power proceeding in all directions from each point, as from a center. In order to communicate both resistance and motion—the other two primary powers described in Colden's treatise—aether must act by "fits and turns." In this way, it could propagate resistance in the same direction in which it was transmitted, as well as in the opposite direction.[44]

The second primary power in Colden's natural philosophy was what he termed the "force of resisting." This was his equivalent of what was described as *vis inertiae* by Isaac Newton, who had stated that "The *Vis Inertiae* is a passive principle by which bodies persist in their motion or rest, receive motion in proportion to the force impressing it, and resist as much as they are resisted."[45] For Newton, therefore, the term expressed the tendency of a body to remain either at rest or in motion unless impressed with a force sufficient to alter its state: it was a passive quality of matter. For Colden, however, it could be assigned a "real or positive force or power in matter" since "a meer negative power, or passive power, as some call it, that is, an unactive power, cannot be augmented or lessened; because it is a negation of all power and action, and is truly a non-entity."[46]

Here, Colden revealed his discomfort with what he regarded as a negative power. It became an intellectual paradox for him to comprehend how any "power" could remain passive. The requirements of his natural philosophy were such that a "primary agent" always acted or exerted its force. The logical dilemma inherent in this premise led him to state: "Power, force, and action are so essential to the conception of resisting, that the denying of it necessarily included a contradiction in terms. For the power of resisting either does something or nothing: if it do anything, it acts; if it do nothing, it does not resist in contradiction to what is supposed. Therefore that resisting is acting, may be reckoned among the self-evident maxims, which cannot be denied without falling into an absurdity."[47]

The third and final primary power or principle that Colden analyzed in his treatise was that of the "moving power." Like resistance, it could be daily observed in those things that gained or lost motion with varying rates of velocity. This, Colden insisted, must be the effect of some agent that had "its active principle in itself." As resistance opposed motion in all directions, so the moving power asserted motion in all directions "and its assuming one direction rather than another, or its changing its direction, [was] only from the opposition of some resisting power," for they remained mutually impenetrable. Its absolute force, he added, was composed "of the velocity and the quantity of the moving thing."[48]

In the third chapter of his treatise, Colden examined the nature and activity of the moving power and, at the outset, emphatically rejected the thesis that "motion comes immediately from the Divine Being, or that he is the cause of all motion, as he must be, if no other thing have the power of moving in itself; and therefore, that every new motion, at least, is generated by the immediate power of the Creator." To accept such an argument would violate the very principles that Colden had established as the basis for his natural philosophy. It would have little scientific import because the "laws of actions of such an agent can never be discovered by any mathematical inquiry, because quantity is its sole object."[49]

Here, it might be recalled that in his medical theories and in his correspondence, particularly with Dr. Whytt, Colden had also questioned the necessity for the dependency of the body's motions or activities on the mind. For Colden, the mind guided or regulated motion, but it did not directly cause it; instead, much of the body's physiological activity was assigned to the principle of fermentation. There is some apparent similarity between this proposition and Colden's theories concerning the universe which he saw, in several respects, as a macrocosm consisting of body (matter) and mind ("Divine Being"). In a later chapter, Colden expanded on the role of an "Intelligent Being," to which such terms as "mind," or "God," or "Divine Being" appeared synonymous. The fact that Colden devoted only one of the eight chapters of his treatise to this topic, almost as a kind of appendage, suggests something of its limited importance, both within the operation of the universe and within the context of his particular philosophical concerns.

Since the Intelligent Being cannot be the cause of motion, it must come from something that (1) has that power in itself, (2) must be quantifiable, and, therefore, (3) must be some kind of matter. Colden continued:

When we see all animal and vegetable motion, and the fluidity of liquors, increased or lessened, by the approach or withdrawing of the sun, or by the falling of his rays more perpendicularly or obliquely on the surface of the earth, or in greater or lesser quantity, we are naturally led to the rays of the sun or light as the cause of this motion. In the most violent and rapid motion produced by fire, we likewise discover light in proportion to the greatness of the fire. The same is observed in the motion produced by the firing of gunpowder.[50]

It was such observations, together with the hints supplied by Newton in his *OPTICKS*, that seemed to justify this assertion for Colden. On this basis, he was now prepared to establish his metaphysical principle concerning the cosmic action of light: "We shall be more directly led to light, as the cause of motion in the planets, so as to almost put it out of question, by considering that the motion or degree of velocity in the planets is reciprocally as the squares of their distance from the sun: which proves, that whatever it be which puts them in motion, it must be by an emanation in straight lines from the sun."[51]

A brief synopsis of Colden's natural philosophy might be given as follows: The universe is composed of bodies of resisting matter surrounded by aether. The sun, as befits its status, contains the greatest quantity of such matter; in addition, a thin layer of light encloses it. Normally, this light or moving matter would cause the disintegration of the resisting matter within, except that the atmosphere of the sun is extremely dense. Consequently, the light streams outward in the form of particles that constantly strike the surfaces of other bodies of resisting matter, such as planets. This creates a centrifugal force that is counterbalanced by the reaction of the aether that is strongest on the side opposite to the sun, even as light itself is most concentrated on the side facing the sun. At a certain point they are both equal in force, with the result that "the body impelled will move in a line equally inclined to both directions, and therefore must move at right angles to the direction of the impelling actions."[52]

Although this is a seemingly complete rational construct, certain imponderables, ambiguities, and even inconsistencies remained in Colden's presentation. One of these, for example, was why the planets should move at all, rather than remain perfectly suspended or fixed between equally opposing forces. That Colden himself may have had some residual qualms about this issue is revealed in a subsequent chapter, where he introduced the role of the Intelligent Being, as a kind of *deus ex machina*, to resolve this problem. Even more confusing, perhaps, is Colden's discussion on other aspects of his natural philosophy.

His analysis of the nature and activity of aether is a case in point. He began his inquiry with the caveat that aether was a primary or simple power and, therefore, "nothing of shape or parts" must enter our conception of it. Yet he went on to describe it as being both "particulate" and "elastic." At another time, he claimed that aether was "neither a fluid or elastic." Again, his statements on the nature of gravitational attraction remain vague. They do more perhaps to perplex than inform. The usual explanation for gravitational attraction was that it was due to differences in the elasticity of the aether. Subsequently, Colden proposed that gravitation "is in proportion to the quantity of matter," but he appeared to subvert this statement when he argued that gravitation "is not caused by the quantity of matter . . . but by the . . . degree of resistance."[53]

Finally, Colden's vacillating descriptions concerning the essence of light remain to be noted. In his *Principles*, he made light, the moving power, a material entity comparable to aether and resistance. It was, in other words, one of the three species of matter that governed the operation of the physical universe. Nevertheless, in one of his smaller treatises, Colden professed the belief that light was not a material power. He wrote: "Is not light a being essentially different from Matter? Is there any absurdity in supposing that some beings exist which are neither Matter, nor Spirit, or Intelligence[?]"[54] Shortly after the publication of the 1751 edition of his *Principles*, he again expressed the view that "Light is a substance as Being essentially distinct from what we commonly call Matter or Body, that they have nothing in common between them, except that we consider or conceive both as consisting of Quantity, that is, that in the same space there may be a greater or less quantity of either, and that a certain quantity of either may be confined within certain bounds and consequently have some shape or form."[55]

Colden also recognized that there was a basic difficulty in trying to explain how rays of light could mutually interpenetrate without "stopping" or hindering each other, if they were material bodies. This evidently occurred, as he observed, when rays of light were reflected from all points within a room. It led him to suggest that light was not a material entity and even that "rays of light cannot be composed of particles or atoms of any size or shape."[56]

These examples suggest the inconsistent manner in which Colden developed and presented his philosophical conceptions. For this reason, he often found himself invited to revise, if not abandon, some of his earlier scientific tenets. Readers of the treatise might find themselves somewhat confused and baffled by its contents, with the result that Colden was often called upon to explain and elaborate its contents.

James Alexander, for example, found it difficult to conceive how the aether, a material power, could be described as perfect inactivity. This became a paradox for him.[57] Again, he did not understand the necessity for an agency, that is, light, to sustain the motion of the planets. To this doctrine, he responded, "I have not the least knowledge or notion of any second cause used by the Almighty to give the progressive motion of projectile force to bodies of resisting matter; that's a thing that being once done wants not to be done again."[58] Finally, Colden's contention that the planet's forward motion was due to the reaction of aether and light proved especially problematical. Here, Alexander merely confessed that "This I cannot conceive tho' before and now I have as well as I could considered what you say on it." With the publication of the second edition of the *Principles*, and its various additions, Colden evidently hoped to win Alexander over to his views, but all the latter did—except for repeating some of his former reservations—was to tell Colden that, due to age, he was no longer able to form a "Sufficient Judgment of it."[59]

Benjamin Franklin expressed an early interest in viewing Colden's treatise. At one time, he had even offered to print the first edition of the *Principles*, proposing to do so at his own expense and risk. In the expectation that the treatise would "excite the Curiosity of the Learned," he assumed that he would not lose his investment in the venture.[60] Although Colden did not take up Franklin's offer, he later sent Franklin several copies of his treatise in the expectation that the latter would distribute these to his friends and associates in Philadelphia. In this way, Franklin functioned in the same capacity in the colonies as Collinson did in England, for Colden was largely dependent on both men to obtain comments on his treatise.

Within a month after he had sent Franklin copies of the treatise, Colden became impatient for a response. Two of the individuals to whom Franklin had given the treatise were Bartram and Logan. The former could only reply that he "apprehended he should find it out of his reach," while Logan and others had yet to give their comments.[61] In the interim, all Franklin could convey to Colden was that "There are so many things quite new in your Piece, and so different from our former Conceptions and Apprehensions, that I believe the closest and strongest thinker we have amongst us, will require much longer time than you are willing to allow."[62]

Some months later, Franklin was prepared to inform Colden that several of his friends had read some parts of the treatise, but all uniformly found it beyond their comprehension. Even Logan, whom Franklin would have expected to offer an opinion, was baffled and added only that he believed Colden's theory concerning the action of aether in gravity had been originally proposed by Bernouilli.[63] Franklin doubted, however, that Colden knew this author and, for his part, had to confess, "I am almost ready to join with the rest, and give it up as beyond my reach."[64]

Neither Franklin nor his friends were prepared to abandon their attempts, however. Franklin assured Colden that he, for one, would continue to examine the treatise and make notes and queries to "show you that I have been endeavoring to read and understand your Piece." As might be expected, little that was positive came from these professed intentions. By 1748, Franklin had turned his share of responsibilities in his printing business over to his partner, and this now gave him the leisure to pursue more fully his investigations into assorted natural phenomena. The year before, Collinson had sent the Library Company in Philadelphia an "electrical tube" with directions for its use, and this soon proved so fascinating that, as Franklin expressed it, "I never was before engaged in any study that so totally engrossed my attention and my time as this has lately done."[65]

For some time, therefore, it was this subject, rather than the contents of Colden's treatise, that dominated their mutual correspondence. It is doubtful that Colden had given much serious attention to electricity before Franklin stimulated his interest in its phenomena. If he now became attentive to Franklin's electrical experiments, it was not only for what they might reveal about electricity but also, more importantly perhaps, for the value they might have in demonstrating the relevance of his own theories. Colden apparently anticipated that the data Franklin was collecting would serve to illustrate his *Principles*, just as he expected the astronomical observations and calculations of others to serve as a useful demonstration of his theorems. Consequently, it would not have been unwelcome to Colden when Franklin sent him a glass tube for Colden's amusement; the first part of his "Electrical Journal," and a promise to mail the second part when it was completed. [66]

Franklin continued to send Colden his observations on electricity, sometimes including copies of letters he had written to Collinson on the same topic. By 1750, he had prepared his "Essay towards a new Hypothesis of the Cause and Effects of Lightning, etc." and submitted copies to Colden and to Mitchell, who now lived in England.[67] Thereafter, Franklin continued to pursue further experiments with lightning, and was able to confirm that it was an electrical phenomenon.

Impressed with Franklin's experimental successes, Colden was prompted to make at least one such experiment on his own. He also attempted to form some views on the cause of electricity but confessed to Franklin, "I find it difficult to form any conceptions." He could not resist supposing, however, that it had to be related to a "most subtile elastic fluid," similar to air but even "more subtile and more elastic." The extent to which this fluid was retained by particular substances would largely determine whether they were to be considered as electric or non-electric.[68] Colden admitted the necessity for further experiments into electricity in order to test some of these suppositions, but declined to perform these himself.

Franklin rejected Colden's distinction between electric and non-electric as no longer useful; instead, he stated that the words "conductors" and "non conductors" would be more suitable.[69] More positive was his response to Colden's notion of an "elastic fluid," which he regarded as "undoubtedly just," but aside from giving the opinion that this elastic fluid would have to be more "subtile" than air—since the latter seemed to impede the electric atmosphere—he could only conclude, "There is no end to Conjectures. As yet we are but Novices in this branch of natural knowledge."[70]

Colden remained optimistic that electrical phenomena could be accounted for on the basis of his *Principles*. In this task, he invited Franklin's assistance since, as he told the latter, "you have such sagacity in contriving proper experiments for any purposes you have in view."[71] It was not Franklin, however, but Colden's youngest son, David, who made an attempt to provide such assistance. Colden proudly regarded David as the "most intellectual" of his children and thus the one best suited to carry out electrical experiments.

From the first, David endeavored to explain various electrical phenomena in terms of his father's treatise.[72] In 1757, he wrote to his cousin in England that his father had given him "the first principles on which to go to work, & was always the Square and Plummet, to keep me within the bounds of just reasoning and philosophy."[73] Aside from any theoretical considerations, David's interest in electricity was sustained by a fascination with natural phenomena. He conducted several electrical experiments on his own to confirm some of the scientific data that Franklin had sent him. These experiments included attempts to electrify a bottle filled with water; to electrify a soapy bubble on wax and to electrify a "naked Phial" and some observations on the repulsive force between the ends of silk threads. The results of several such experiments led him somewhat caustically to inform the Abbé Nollet, Franklin's critic in France, that "I am in many places of the Abbé's book surprised to find that Experiments have succeeded so differently at Paris from what they did with Mr. Franklin & as I have allwise observed them to do."[74] Colden sent his son's experiments and observations to Franklin who regarded them as "judiciously made" and suggested they be sent to England for publication.[75]

Whereas Franklin continued to be absorbed by electricity, Colden's attention was more apt to be drawn to matters of abstract speculation. It was almost inevitable, therefore, that the subject of his treatise would reassert itself in their mutual correspondence. At first, Franklin declined to comment on Colden's work, probably because he felt he was hardly qualified to do so. His preference, generally speaking, was to allow others to exercise that option. This, however, did not prevent him from making certain spirited observations concerning Colden's theories.

Regarding Colden's doctrine of light as "very curious," Franklin had to admit that he remained "much in the *Dark* about *Light*."[76] Franklin could not conceive how the sun could continually emit particles of matter and not diminish in size. He presumed that the motion or speed of light—at least according to Colden's theory—must be so "prodigious" that its force must exceed "That of a 24 pounder discharg'd from a Cannon." This, he inferred, could very well drive the planets away from, rather than around, the sun.

In an attempt to come to terms with Colden's suppositions, Franklin proposed that the matter emitted by the sun must be returned as part of a continual cycle. Only in this way might it be possible for the sun not to be wasted by the discharge of its matter. He also offered an alternative hypothesis: "May not all the Phenomena of Light be more conveniently solved, by supposing Universal Space filled with a subtle elastic Fluid, which when at rest is not visible, but whose Vibrations affect that fine sense the Eye, as those of Air do the grosser Organs of the Ear?"[77]

Colden rejected Franklin's concept of light as a fluid because it was obviously at variance with his corpuscular doctrine of light and added, by way of instructing Franklin, "The Vibrations of a Fluid will in no manner explain the Phenomena of Light as is very expressly pointed out in Sr. Isaac Newton's Optics." He then added, somewhat superciliously, "On this occasion I think it proper to observe to you that in the Treatise before mentioned, what Sr. Isaac has proved is generally taken for granted & supposed to be known."[78] In response to Franklin's helpful suggestion regarding the recovery of matter by the sun, Colden dismissively remarked: "It may take a hundred or a thousand years to diminish the sun's diameter by one Inch."[79]

Still, Franklin could not resist the temptation to inject some banter into their discussion on such weighty philosophical matters. Doubting that Colden's description of aether as "perfect inactivity" was meant to be taken literally, Franklin remarked: "it may be some kind of Dutch wit, and intended to joke that QUIETISM which in Germany is supposed to be very prevalent in Pennsylvania, many of their Quietists having removed thither."[80] Colden was hardly one to appreciate such a witty comparison. In any case, Franklin apparently never intended to give a serious or sustained analysis of Colden's natural philosophy.

After he had read a sizable portion of the treatise, the most that Franklin would say was that there were some things in it that were pleasing, some that were wrong, and some that required further clarification.[81] Although Franklin promised to amplify these remarks in further letters, his preference had always been to await the comments of European readers; as he once told Colden, "I long to see from Europe some of the deliberate and mature Thoughts of their Philosophers upon it."[82] Franklin himself refrained from making any further comments on the treatise.

Initially, at least, Colden remained optimistic regarding the fate of his treatise in European circles, believing that it was only a question of time until it would receive its due recognition. Following the publication of the second edition, he informed Franklin that distinguished gentlemen in London, Oxford, Leipzig, and Paris "have given so favourable an opinion of the little treatise you have seen," and felt encouraged in continuing with further additions and revisions to the work. Yet, Colden must have had some intimation of the difficulties the treatise might encounter, for he concluded his letter with the observation: "I cannot expect that my sentiments so contrary to the commonly received notions should suddenly prevail. A French gent writes: *il a bien donné la torture a nos Metaphysiciens*, but I am confident they will at last."[83]

Not long afterward, Colden found less cause for optimism when he learned the reaction of one of his readers in Europe. This was from the eminent mathematician, Professor Euler of Berlin, who transmitted his remarks on the treatise through Collinson. He began with the rather slighting observation that Colden's philosophy contained many "Ingenious Reflections . . . for a Man that has not entirely devoted himself to the study of physic." Euler was quick, however, to point out that Colden had not actually resolved the problems he had proposed to examine. He reprimanded Colden for attacking "the best established propositions of the late Sr. Isaac Newton," while some of Colden's own theories were based on "reasons destitute of all foundations."[84] Again, Colden's description of planetary motion about the sun was rejected for showing little knowledge of Newton's principles of motion, and disqualified Colden "from establishing the true forces requisite to the motion of the planets, from whatever cause he may attempt to derive them." Finally, Euler described Colden's theory of the elasticity of the aether as so ill imagined that it was "absolutely contrary to the first principles of hydrostatics."[85]

Such devastating criticisms only prompted Colden to tell Franklin: "He [Euler] writes much like a Pedant highly conceited of himself."[86] To Collinson he wrote that opposition to the *Principles* came mainly from those who erroneously thought that the work contradicted Newton's philosophy.[87] It was only on this basis that Colden could explain the sentiments of Euler and the general lack of interest in his own *magnum opus*.

In Colden's mind, at least, this continued to be the primary reason for the poor reception of the treatise. Being put on the defensive, he reiterated to several of his correspondents that his treatise was never designed to criticize but to complement or complete the Newtonian natural philosophy. To Collinson, he professed that "surely it may be hoped that some improvement may be made in knowledge besides what he [Newton] has done."[88] It was precisely because of the status of Newtonian physics that the need existed to "perfect" his scheme. To another correspondent in England, Colden affirmed: "One strong prejudice I observe against me is that it is thought what I advance is contrary to what Sr. Isaac Newton has demonstrated. Now, I mistake exceedingly if this be true in any one instance. I only presume to think that I have advanced in some cases farther than he has done, in cases which he has left indetermined, or where he is silent, or where he speaks doubtfully."[89]

It may have been Collinson who was partly responsible for giving Colden this perspective on the reception of his treatise when he informed Colden that, "everyone is so satisfied with Sr. Isaac's that they have no curiosity to examine yours."[90] In his defense, Colden reminded Collinson that "all men do sometimes err and very great men have sometimes fallen into paralogisms," without mentioning Newton by name.[91]

Thus, Colden was placed in the unenviable position of trying to convince others that he merely desired to improve on Newton without necessarily casting aspersions on Newton's deserved stature. In intellectual and scientific matters, Colden readily condemned reliance upon authority, especially if it hindered further investigation. Such reliance, Colden suggested, was induced through education or social pressure, and could become strong enough to deter men from the "conviction[s] of sense" or "arguments that reason can add."[92]

For Colden, there was sufficient historical evidence to conclude that progress had been often attained only when popular idols were removed; almost invariably, they were replaced with new authorities that could become just as repressive as those they had replaced. In this context, Colden noted that Aristotle's preeminence lasted until the time of René Descartes, and Descartes himself remained dominant until the advent of Newtonian science. Implicit in these remarks is Colden's apparent belief that Newton had become the "idol" of the age, with all that implied for those who, like himself, were committed to enhancing scientific progress.

As one of the few means left for vindicating himself, Colden proposed to Collinson that his response to Euler, together with Euler's remarks on his treatise, be printed either as a pamphlet or in a periodical. In the meantime, he still planned to continue his work on the *Principles*, in order "to give some other instances of their use in some other parts of natural philosophy."[93] He ruefully discovered that the printer would print neither the remarks nor, later, a further revised edition.[94] Thereupon, Colden suggested to Collinson that the latter should organize a subscription, since "persons of knowledge" would readily understand why his treatise might deserve such support.[95] As if to emphasize the futility of such designs, Collinson reluctantly informed Colden that "as to your Principles, I do not find they are espoused by anyone."[96] Even then Colden obstinately remained, as he said, "strongly possessed with the opinions of the truth of them & they make the same impressions on my mind, which the truth of the clearest conceptions do, & while I do not perceive the mistake, I cannot avoid continuing of the same opinion."[97]

A final comment from Europe on Colden's treatise came from a Professor Kastner, who had translated it into German. A patently condescending attitude toward a colonial philosopher is evident in his initial remarks: "It would be something remarkable, if we should obtain from America, the solution of difficulties in physics, which have seemed insurmountable to the greatest geniuses in Europe, & if that, what was incomprehensible to a Newton should now be cleared up, by a countryman from the New World."[98]

Like Euler, Kastner charged Colden with having failed to give a meaningful explanation concerning the operations of the physical universe. Colden had not, for example, given the cause of his principles and, until that were done, Kastner remarked, "he has at least not told us Europeans anything new." He criticized Colden's description of the moving and resisting powers as "too light to be right." More specifically, like James Alexander, he saw no need for an active material power, for "A motion . . . which in the beginning of the creation has been communicated to bodies, will, therefore, because of this inertia, have continual actions as long as there are bodies."[99]

Again, while the phenomenon of resistance was undeniable, there was no justification for making resistance itself a conceptualized power or agency. While Kastner admitted that the notion of *vis inertiae* might be difficult to comprehend, he declared that Colden's concept only made it all the more confusing. This could only lead to the kind of operations that were "like to the contrivers of the Primum Mobile which carries the other crystalline globes of Heaven along with it," an evident reference to discredited Aristotelian physics.

Finally, Colden's concept of elastic matter was dismissed by Kastner, who found himself unable to develop any such concept. Using an analogous reference similar to Franklin's, Kastner informed Colden that this doctrine appeared as if it were "not framed in N.Y., but in Pennsylvania." If he declined to add anything further to his remarks, it was because "I unwillingly enter into such things as I take to be fictions." A final rebuke informed Colden that "we have natural philosophers enough in the Old World who have endeavour'd to explain gravitation from Matter the effect[s] whereof are in some measure easier to be comprehended."[100]

None of these criticisms deterred Colden from further work on his *Principles*. For the time being, at least, he abandoned the idea of publishing a revised edition, but once more he turned to Collinson to obtain readers for the additional chapters he had completed. After making an attempt to find suitable "connoisseurs," Collinson eventually obtained the agreement of Dr. Bevis to examine the treatise, adding, "I could get nobody else to peruse it."[101] For Bevis, in turn, Colden's scientific notions presented such difficulties that his only alternative was to forward the treatise to another mathematician. The latter stated flatly that Colden's principles were in opposition to the "unalterable laws of mechanics."[102] Bevis, who tried to be more conciliatory, assessed Colden's view on the nature of the resisting power as "unexceptionally just," but took him to task for not fully comprehending Newton's doctrine of *vis inertiae*, which largely obviated the need for any moving power in matter. More to the point, however, was Bevis's contention that self-motion could not be separated from direction, as Colden had argued. It led Bevis to exclaim: "into what unfathomable depths, both in philosophy and divinity, must such a notion lead?" In spite of Colden's attempts to explain his position, Bevis could not resolve his qualms so easily and remained apprehensive of "the use which the materialists would make of an hypothesis which supplied the grand desideratum in their system."[103] This comment—perhaps more than anything that was nominally "scientific" in Colden's treatise—would remain a formidable issue among several of its readers.

Such news could only have been discouraging for Colden, for it concluded nearly a decade of repeated attempts to have his treatise accepted by informed commentators in England and Europe. Bevis was the last individual who had deigned to show some interest in Colden's philosophy and his judgment became, in effect, the final word on that subject.

During the period when Colden's *Principles* went the rounds among the international community, several colonial scientists remained keenly interested to learn how an American philosopher would fare among the *cognoscenti* of the Old World. In general, colonial scientists had succeeded well enough in such matters as scientific observation, experimentation, and botanical collection and classification, but it was in intellectual topics, particularly abstract speculation, that they had yet to make a significant contribution. Franklin's remark at one time to Colden that his treatise would do "honour to America" reflects an incipient nationalism regarding the kind of impression a colonial philosopher might make in Europe. Indeed, if Colden attained some recognition it might give additional evidence of American cultural and scientific progress by the middle of the eighteenth century.

Hearing, then, of Colden's frustrating appeals to obtain readers for his treatise could not but make Franklin sympathetic toward Colden's predicament. Franklin, too, had had his critics among European scientists and, after having seen a copy of Kastner's remarks, was prompted to console his fellow scientist by telling him, "I see it is not without reluctance that the Europeans will allow that they can possibly receive any instruction from us Americans."[104] Alexander Garden could express the same sentiments. Realizing the difficulties that Colden encountered in having his treatise accepted in England, Garden declared: "you have not been the first whose works had been denied the countenance of the English Society: They appear to me to be either too lazy and indolent to examine or too conceited to receive any new thought from any one but from an F.R.S. [Fellow of the Royal Society]." After recounting the slow acceptance of both Newtonian and Linnaean science in England, he concluded by remarking: "Your works, I think, are another testimony against them, for it's a thousand to one but they will implicitly receive your notions if only countenanced by foreigners, though they would stumble at them promulgated by one in America."[105]

The only individual in England who had actually read and become enthusiastic about the contents of Colden's treatise was the self-proclaimed philosopher Samuel Pike. He introduced himself to Colden by way of a letter in 1753, in which he indicated how fortunate he felt to have seen a copy of the *Principles* some years previously. It had, he explained, "laid the first foundation for those enquiries into nature & scripture which I have now ventured into." One of these was to account for that elasticity that Colden had taken for granted. Pike found an explanation by searching the Bible and presuming that "the scripture word *Firmament* or *expansion* might mean the same with this elasticity."[106]

After he had formulated his "Scripture Philosophy," Pike had received the revised and enlarged edition of Colden's treatise and now—more convinced than ever of the connection between Colden's philosophy and revelation—wrote to inform him of this revealing discovery. In this way, as Pike expressed it, he was "in great hope that you may see how your principles are confirmed, cleared, & explained in Revelation." Although Pike had read some of the works of John Hutchinson, it was still Colden's treatise that "approached nearer the truth of Revelation."[107]

Pike was a Hutchinsonian, and his attempt to relate scriptural revelation to natural philosophy was a task that was equally the concern of other members of this school, such as George Horne, William Jones, Robert Spearman, and Duncan Forbes. Hutchinson's own symbolic exegesis of the Mosaic account of creation is expressed in one of his more important treatises, *Moses' Principia*. The manner in which he was able to extrapolate an esoteric philosophical meaning from Genesis is aptly revealed in the following example:

AND GOD CALLED THE FIRMAMENT HEAVEN. The Meaning of the sixth Verse must be:—Let the Motion which is in the Airs, and has produced Light, go a Step further, make the Parts of the Fluid of the Air *Liquidum.* A thin Fluid expanding and diffusing; and let it act in the Pores, or press in, or act among or between the parts of the Mixture called Waters, and compress itself and other things, and thereby make a Separation, and of the Parts separated a Division between the one and the other Waters.[108]

Hutchinson's antipathy to Newtonian science is revealed not only by the allusive title of this work, but in such disparaging phrases as "the Heathens may take back their Idols of Projection, attraction, Gravity, Elasticity, etc.," "as long as Gravity stands, *Moses* cannot be explained," and "gravity has got the better of revelation." In his *Treatise of Power*, Hutchinson criticized Newton for not having studied Hebrew and, in an allusion to Newton's investigations into the phenomena of light, commented, "even women and children can become philosophers by . . . staring at soapy Vesicles." The allegation that Newton had professed the doctrine of "action at a distance" was, in Hutchinson's words, "more senseless, if possible, than transubstantiation." Its corollary, the "void" or space without matter, was regarded as a "puzzle."[109]

Such notions, Hutchinson declared, were not warranted by the Bible; indeed, they were in direct opposition to the philosophy contained in Scripture. He contended that not only was scientific knowledge to be found in the Bible, but anyone who attempted to investigate nature outside the scope

of revelation could only further the cause of atheism. The concepts of gravitational attraction and the "void," found in Newtonian science, had negated
for Hutchinson "the revealed power in fluids, and the visible evidence of
the power of God." Instead of empty space, the Scriptures spoke of an
"absolutely full" universe or a *plenum*. Hutchinson's theory was that "The
whole universe, to the utmost circumference, is replete with this fluid; so
that it must be infinitely more in quantity than all other sorts of matter
within our knowledge; and so is really omnipresent, and in sober seriousness
abhors a vacuum."[110]

These general tenets are also evident in the writings of the Reverend
William Jones, who characterized Newtonian philosophy as based on "nostrums" that defied comprehension.[111] The Reverend George Horne, a friend
of Jones, also complained that one reason Hutchinson's "discoveries" had
not been more readily accepted was that Newton's philosophy was commonly regarded as certain and infallible. Horne's own book was designed
to reconcile some of the differences between Hutchinson and Newton by
showing that Newton had only intended to give a mathematical description
of the operations of the universe, whereas Hutchinson had devoted himself
to writing a philosophy of physics.[112] For Horne, the Hutchinsonian philosophy was derived not from mathematical analysis but from Genesis, where
the notion of a fluid that took the forms of fire, light, and air or spirit could
be found.

The publication of Colden's *Principles* in England in 1751 came at a time
when the Hutchinsonian movement was already fairly well established.
Hutchinson died in 1737, but an "Abstract" of his works appeared in 1753.
Duncan Forbes' *Reflections on the Sources of Incredulity* and George Horne's
A Fair, Candid and Impartial State were printed in 1750 and 1755, re-
spectively. It was approximately at this time that both Horne and Jones
propagated Hutchinsonian doctrines at Oxford and the movement found
supporters at Cambridge.[113] Then, too, Samuel Pike, as he informed Colden, had initiated his own attempt to create a scriptural philosophy sometime in the 1740s. The appearance of Colden's book sometime thereafter
may have been a coincidental factor in convincing Pike that the *Principles*
were a contribution to the Hutchinsonian literature.

Colden's doctrine of a diffused aether as a cause of universal gravitation
had an approximate relationship to Hutchinsonian theories. In his *Enquiry
after Philosophy and Theology* (1755), another Hutchinsonian, Robert Spearman, credited Colden with having perceived the inconsistencies in Newtonian philosophy and went on to give a brief synopsis of Colden's treatise.
However, he regarded Colden's proposal on the activity of matter as both
unphilosophical and unacceptable.[114] In contrast to Pike, Spearman concluded that Colden's theories (like Newton's) were incompatible with scriptural philosophy and simply demonstrated the limits of human reason. Of
course, Pike shared the general apprehension of the Hutchinsonians toward

anyone who would assign matter an active status. He proposed to Colden that, if the latter could align his philosophy with revelation, "You will not be under any temptation to believe the eternity of matter; nor under any obligation to suppose that any matter is penetrable, or resisting or elastic or moving in its own nature: but that all matter is of the same nature, only different in shape & size, & that it is in itself a dead motionless thing."[115]

The contents of Pike's first letter must certainly have taken Colden by surprise. At first, he was pleased enough to thank Pike for "promoting knowledge and love of truth benevolence," even if he had some qualms regarding the uses to which his *Principles* might now be put.[116] To Franklin, Colden was candid enough to admit, "If his [Pike's] book had not come with his letter, I should have suspected him to be a wag."[117] Perhaps it was an ambivalent attitude toward Pike's treatise that led Colden to tell Franklin that his own *Principles* appeared to be authenticated by revelation. Yet he added that Pike's book "has not increased my vanity much."

Having now found an interested correspondent and one who, for a change, could be quite flattering, Colden certainly could not miss the opportunity to instruct, correct, and if possible convert his reader to the only authorized interpretation of the *Principles*. To begin with, he told Pike that he never consulted the Bible in order to establish philosophical principles, since its value was primarily for moral instruction. While Colden admitted that the Mosaic account of creation might have some relevance in solving the problem of how the Intelligent Being had separated the sun and planets from the primeval chaos, he declared himself not fully convinced of its scientific value. More emphatic was his rejection of Pike's opinion of matter as nothing more than a dead, motionless thing, for he informed Pike, "you have not in several instances comprehended clearly my Principles." Concerning this crucial point, he wrote to Pike: "In this opinion you have almost all the world with you and against me, and yet I am clearly persuaded that this universal opinion is an universal error."[118]

Colden also queried Pike's attempt to relate aether to other powers, presumably meaning the "firmament" or "expansion" that Pike had derived from Scripture. Colden observed: "I find that the using the word elastic has led you & several others into mistakes of my conceptions."[119] In spite of such evident differences, Colden proceeded to study Pike's *Philosophia Sacra* and at one point forwarded it to Franklin. The latter, however, refused to be drawn any further into abstruse philosophical discussions and returned Pike's treatise with the brief comment, "His manner of Philosophizing is much out of my Way."[120]

It was not until Colden had finished reading Pike's book that he was prompted to make some additional remarks. One of these concerned Pike's use of the word "Darkness" to connote a being or substance distinct from light; for Colden, this distinction was meaningless, since darkness did not connote anything positive or real. Instead, he proposed that it might be interpreted to mean the same as his concept of resistance. Apparently, Pike remained indifferent to this suggestion, for Colden subsequently admonished Pike for being "in the wrong to continue to use the word *Darkness* to express a distinct substance from *Light.*"[121] This may have been largely a matter of terminology, but there were other, more important issues that remained to be resolved.

One of these concerned Pike's supposition that matter itself was undifferentiated, and might produce various effects. Colden, however, was prepared to assign only one causal activity to each material principle. If it were otherwise, he wrote, one would remain in a state of uncertainty regarding the nature of physical causation. He also mentioned to Pike that while he did not believe Pike's treatise contradicted Scripture, he himself was not prepared to study Hebrew to determine the extent to which his philosophy was confirmed by revelation. He concluded with the statement that if his treatise did not meet the approval of "proper Judges," he thought it wrong "to trouble the world by publishing the meer conceits of perhaps a heated Imagination."[122]

As might have been anticipated, Pike made it evident in his last letter that he had become somewhat disenchanted with Colden's explanations, if not with the latter's philosophical principles as well. He pointed out, for example, that Colden's doctrine of matter as extension was incomplete without assigning solidity to matter. Without this property, neither the moving nor the resisting power would be able to make any contact with, or impression upon, other material objects.[123] Equally, he denied that motion or resistance could arise from matter itself; it could only be received initially from the Deity or resolved into an "Immediate Divine Power." Colden's attempt to retain his own notion of elasticity proved altogether unconvincing to Pike, who admonished Colden: "good Sir, I desire you would be cautious of running into unmechanical, unmeaning, principles & occult qualities one upon another," and invited him to "come to that which is demonstrable upon the principle of true mechanism & divine revelation & then you will feel a real substratum to your philosophical opinions."[124]

Colden, of course, was hardly prepared to accept such a paradigm. In any case, he never thought of Pike as one of the "proper judges" of his *Principles,* and those he did consider proper authorities had made it quite apparent that his natural philosophy was either too complicated or too incomprehensible to provide sufficient intellectual assurance or scientific elucidation as an "improvement" on Newtonian science. Still, in spite of all such setbacks, he continued to revise his treatise until by 1759, by which time he had expanded it to twelve chapters, he made a final effort to have another edition published, confident that the additional material would salvage the original scheme.[125] When no publisher could be found in England to print it, Colden acquiesced to the suggestion made by Robert Whytt, a professor at the University of Edinburgh, to have the manuscript deposited at the university library.[126] This arrangement not only protected Colden's vanity but would also keep the massive tome intact for study by the "Gentlemen of that university" in the expectation that it might still prove useful.[127] A measure of that conviction is the fact that, even at the age of eighty-four, Colden still busied himself by making some minor additions to the treatise, in spite of his complaints of poor eyesight and failing health.

Colden's inability or unwillingness to accept the criticisms directed against his treatise can perhaps best be ascribed to his personal obstinacy regarding the scientific convictions that he held. He never fully understood the several reasons for the rejection of his treatise. He often berated his readers for having either misinterpreted or misunderstood his philosophy, and assumed that his task was to instruct and enlighten his critics rather than permit himself to be corrected. He also blamed the poor reception of his *Principles* on its novelty and originality and on his own situation as "an obscure person living in an obscure corner of the earth."[128] A more general factor that he cited was the cultural climate of the times. It was, in his view, one of "general luxury" and "dissipation"; what was required was a reformation in public taste, so that "books which require some attention may obtain reputation and be generally read."[129]

The difficulties that the treatise encountered were, as his readers noted, more likely to have been found within the work itself. The scope of its contents reflects a penchant for speculation that led Colden far astray from the tempered, measured, and tentative approach that had become the norm for scientific investigation in the Newtonian age. He had, in effect, reversed the Newtonian methodology of proceeding from "analysis" to "composition" or synthesis, by "assuming the causes discovered, and established as principles, and by them explaining the phenomena proceeding from them, and proving the explanation."[130]

For Colden, it was the most general causes that became the "Grand Object of Physics." Their discovery, he once wrote, involves a kind of "philosophic genius" that manifests itself "in readily making the only hypothesis which can solve all the phenomena."[131] All first inquiries, he asserted, were hypothetical. It was only when these were established that "the truth of their discovery may be afterward demonstrated." Consequently, he apparently saw his own role as one of creating hypotheses suitable for use by subsequent investigators. His emphasis throughout the treatise was on perfecting the rational evidence for his theories. Phenomena were used more for procedural illustration than as demonstrable and incontrovertible proof.[132]

If any comparison needs to be made, it might even be argued that Colden's philosophical tenets were closer to some aspects of Cartesian metaphysics than to Newtonian science. While Colden himself dismissed Cartesian philosophy as "hypothetical" and a "romance," his own treatise may well be considered as a variant of one of those classical cosmologies, rather than as a scientific construct of the eighteenth century, as it was meant to be. An apparent area of agreement between Colden and Descartes was in regard to their definition of matter. The Newtonian concept of mass proved incomprehensible to Colden, as it would also have been to Descartes. This may be one reason why Colden felt it necessary to introduce an active material principle to sustain the planets in their orbital motion. For Newton, the concept of *vis inertiae* made this unnecessary. James Alexander, Kastner, and others recognized the implications of this doctrine; Colden, for his part, did not.[133]

A similarity between Descartes' and Colden's views may also be more than coincidental with regard to the following theory: Descartes had proposed that three forms of matter had evolved out of primeval chaos.[134] One form was the sun, with its luminosity; the second was interplanetary space; and the third was the dense opaque matter of the earth. In the order given, they could approximate Colden's moving power (light), the ethereal substance, and resistance (planets and other material bodies). Again, Colden may reveal some similarity to Descartes' identification of matter and space, or the *plenum*, in his own concept of aether. In one of his smaller treatises, Colden wrote that aether was a "Universal Medium" and also that it was "a being universally diffused through all space."[135]

In the *Principles*, at least, Colden was emphatic in rejecting the Newtonian concept of the void. He asserted that the term itself was meaningless, a kind of non-concept or word without signification. As he stated, "If one have no conception of an absolute void, we cannot affirm that it is, or is not: and what conceptions can a man have of a place void of everything, and of which nothing can be affirmed?"[136] As one writer notes, "the void, according to Descartes, is not only *physically impossible*, it is essentially impossible. Void space—if there were anything of that kind—would be a *contradictio in adjecto*, an existing nothing . . . nothing can have no properties and therefore no dimensions."[137]

Colden's rejection of negative (empty) concepts is related to his opposition to anything that remained unintelligible or even mysterious in nature. His ideal of science—as he reiterated several times—was to clarify conceptions and to establish indubitable ideas. Colden's emphasis on such logical structure, and on science itself as a kind of pictorial representation, is reminiscent of the Cartesian rather than the Newtonian mode of scientific explanation.

Colden's attempt to "improve" Newtonian philosophy failed largely because he subverted some of its most essential aspects. Moreover, by rejecting the advice and criticism offered by his various readers, he forfeited whatever instruction he might have obtained from their comments. The inevitable result was that the fate of his treatise remained—as he himself once profoundly recognized—the singular work of a man "in the woods of America."

NOTES

1. To Collinson, Colden once wrote: "It is probable that my application to Botany may be interrupted not only by business, but by my thoughts being turn'd to another Subject." Cadwallader Colden to Peter Collinson, June 1744, *Colden Papers*, III, 60.

2. Alexander Grant, *The Story of the University of Edinburgh* (London, 1884), 2 Vols., I, 264.

3. "The Forme and Ordour of Teaching and Proceiding of the Students in Thair Foure Yeires Course in the Colledge of Edinburgh," in Alexander Morgan, ed., *Charters, Statutes, and Acts of the Town Council and the Senatus, 1583–1858* (Edinburgh, 1937), 110.

4. Andrew Dalzel, *History of the University of Edinburgh* (Edinburgh, 1862), 2 Vols, II, 245; W.G. Hiscock, *David Gregory, Isaac Newton and Their Circle: Extracts from David Gregory's Memoranda* (Oxford, 1937), Preface, v.

5. Cadwallader Colden, "Annotationes in Physicam Generalem," University of Edinburgh Library, 95, 97, passim.

6. *Edinburgh University Theses [Theses Philosophicae], 1705.*

7. Frederick E. Brasch, "The Newtonian Epoch in the American Colonies (1680–1783)," *Proceedings of the American Antiquarian Society*, 48–49 (1939), 319–320.

8. Theodore Hornberger, *Scientific Thought in the American Colleges*, 1683–1800 (Austin, Tex., 1945), 45; Brasch, 319.

9. Frederick B. Tolles, "Philadelphia's First Scientist, James Logan," *Isis*, 47 (1956), 25.

10. James Alexander to Cadwallader Colden, January 22, 1743/4, *Colden Papers*, III, 47.

11. James Alexander to Benjamin Franklin, January 26, 1753, *Colden Papers*, IV, 363.

12. Ibid., 364.

13. Peter Collinson to James Alexander, March 6, 1754, *Colden Papers*, IV, 433.

14. James Alexander to Cadwallader Colden, February 15, 1743/4, *Colden Papers*, III, 48.

15. Cadwallader Colden to Dr. Betts, April 25, 1750, *Colden Papers*, IV, 294.

16. Peter Collinson to Cadwallader Colden, March 30, 1745, *Colden Papers*, III, 110.

17. Cadwallader Colden to Peter Collinson, n.d., *Colden Papers*, II, 209.

18. George Graham to Mr. Collinson, February 17, 1740/1, *Colden Papers*, II, 207.

19. Jonathan Sisson to Cadwallader Colden, August 31, 1744, *Colden Papers*, III, 71–72.

20. Cadwallader Colden, "New Method of Printing" in the form of a Letter to Benjamin Franklin, *American Medical and Philosophical Register*, 1 (1811), 440.

21. Cadwallader Colden to William Strahan, November 1743, *Colden Papers*, III, 38.

22. William Strahan to Cadwallader Colden, May 9, 1744, *Colden Papers*, III, 58.

23. Cadwallader Colden to Peter Collinson, May 1743, *Colden Papers*, II, 261.

24. Cadwallader Colden to Mr. Logan, n.d., *Colden Papers*, I, 46.

25. James Logan to Cadwallader Colden, March 17, 1719/20, *Colden Papers*, I, 103.

26. Governor Hunter to Cadwallader Colden, July 11, 1720, Colden MSS, Box 11, #55, New-York Historical Society.

27. Cadwallader Colden to William Douglass, n.d., *Colden Papers*, I, 271.

28. Cadwallader Colden to George Shelrock, February 15, 1758, *Colden Papers*, V, 218; Cadwallader Colden to Peter Kalm, n.d., *Colden Papers*, IV, 260.

29. This was the "Several Species of Matter" of which Logan said: "It must necessarily have some further meaning in it than the language itself imports, otherwise I can by no means conceive the service of it." Benjamin Franklin to Cadwallader Colden, October 25, 1744, *Colden Papers*, III, 77.

30. James Alexander to Cadwallader Colden, February 15, 1743/4, *Colden Papers*, III, 49.

31. James Alexander to Cadwallader Colden, February 23, 1745/6, *Colden Papers*, III, 196.

32. Cadwallader Colden to Peter Collinson, July 8, 1746, *Colden Papers*, III, 224.

33. Peter Collinson to Cadwallader Colden, March 27, 1746/7, *Colden Papers*, III, 367–368.

34. Peter Collinson to Benjamjin Franklin, April 12, 1747, *Colden Papers*, III, 371.

35. Peter Collinson to Cadwallader Colden, August 3, 1747, *Colden Papers*, III, 410–411.

36. J. Betts to James Alexander, September 7, 1749, *Colden Papers*, IV, 137.

37. Cadwallader Colden to Dr. Betts, April 25, 1750, *Colden Papers*, IV, 204.

38. Benjamin Franklin to Cadwallader Colden, April 23, 1753, *Colden Papers*, IV, 384; Benjamin Franklin to Cadwallader Colden, October 25, 1753, in ibid. 413; *Gentleman's Magazine*, 22 (1752), 560–562.

39. Cadwallader Colden to Benjamin Franklin, May 20, 1753, *Colden Papers*, IV, 328.

40. Cadwallader Colden, *The Principles of Action in Matter, the Gravitation of Bodies, and the Motion of the Planets, explained from those Principles* (London, 1751), Preface. Hereafter referred to as *Principles*.

41. "Letter of Newton to Bentley, January 17, 1692/3, reprinted in "An Historical and Explanatory Appendix," Isaac Newton, *Mathematical Principles of Natural Philosophy*, ed. Florian Cajori (Berkeley, Calif., 1946), 634.

42. Isaac Newton, *OPTICKS, or a Treatise on the Reflections, Refractions, Inflections and Colours of Light*, 4th Edition (New York, 1952), Query 31, 351.

43. Cadwallader Colden to Benjamin Franklin, October 29, 1752, *Colden Papers*, IV, 352.

44. *Principles*, section 6, 19.

45. *OPTICKS*, Query 31, 397.

46. Colden, *Principles*, section 2, 5.

47. Ibid., section 5, 7.

48. Ibid., section 3, 14.

49. Ibid., section 2, 72.

50. Ibid., section 3, 74.

51. Ibid., section 4, 76

52. Ibid., section 7, 79.

53. Ibid., selection 4, 120; section 20, 129.

54. Cadwallader Colden, "The Essential Properties of Light," Colden MSS, New-York Historical Society.

55. Cadwallader Colden to Benjamin Franklin, May 20, 1752, *Colden Papers*, IV, 326.

56. Cadwallader Colden, "Of the Transmission and Reflection of Light in Solid Bodies," Colden MSS, New-York Historical Society, paragraph 21.

57. James Alexander to Cadwallader Colden, February 23, 1745/6, *Colden Papers*, III, 198.

58. Ibid., 199.

59. James Alexander to Cadwallader Colden, March 6, 1753, *Colden Papers*, IV, 375.

60. Benjamin Franklin to Cadwallader Colden, November 28, 1745, *Colden Papers*, III, 180.

61. Benjamin Franklin to Cadwallader Colden, July 10, 1746, *Colden Papers*, III, 326–327.

62. Ibid.

63. Benjamin Franklin to Cadwallader Colden, October 16, 1746, *Colden Papers*, III, 273; James Bernouilli, *De Gravitate Aetheris* (1683).

64. Ibid.

65. Benjamin Franklin to Peter Collinson, March 28, 1747, in Benjamin Franklin, *The Autobiography and Other Writings* (New York, 1961), 228.

66. Benjamin Franklin to Cadwallader Colden, June 5, 1747, *Colden Papers*, III, 397.

67. Benjamin Franklin to Cadwallader Colden, June 28, 1750, *Colden Papers*, IV, 218.

68. Cadwallader Colden to Benjamin Franklin, March 16, 1752, *Colden Papers*, IV, 316.

69. Benjamin Franklin to Cadwallader Colden, April 23, 1752, *Colden Papers*, IV, 319.

70. Ibid.

71. Cadwallader Colden to Benjamin Franklin, October 29, 1752, *Colden Papers*, IV, 353.

72. David Colden to Benjamin Franklin, September 18, 1757, *Colden Papers*, V, 184.

73. David Colden to Alexander Colden, September 23, 1757, *Colden Papers*, V, 185.

74. "David Colden's Reply to the Abbe Nolet," December 1753, *Colden Papers*, IV, 429–430. The reference is probably to Nollet's *Lettres sur l'Electricité*.

75. Benjamin Franklin to Cadwallader Colden, January 1, 1753, *Colden Papers*, IV, 359.

76. Benjamin Franklin to Cadwallader Colden, April 23, 1752, *Colden Papers*, IV, 321.

77. Ibid.

78. Cadwallader Colden to Benjamin Franklin, May 20, 1752, *Colden Papers*, IV, 327.

79. Ibid.

80. Benjamin Franklin to Cadwallader Colden, September 14, 1752, *Colden Papers*, IV, 343.

81. Benjamin Franklin to Cadwallader Colden, February 28, 1753, *Colden Papers*, IV, 372.

82. Benjamin Franklin to Cadwallader Colden, January 27, 1747, *Colden Papers*, IV, 6.

83. Cadwallader Colden to Benjamin Franklin, March 16, 1752, *Colden Papers*, IV, 316.

84. Peter Collinson to Cadwallader Colden, November 21, 1752, *Colden Papers*, IV, 355.

85. Ibid.

86. Cadwallader Colden to Benjamin Franklin, November 19, 1753, *Colden Papers*, IV, 414.

87. Cadwallader Colden to Peter Collinson, July 7, 1753, *Colden Papers*, IV, 395.

88. Cadwallader Colden to Peter Collinson, June 3, 1755, *Colden Papers*, V, 14.

89. Cadwallader Colden to Dr. Betts, December 9, 1755, *Colden Papers*, V, 44.

90. Peter Collinson to Cadwallader Colden, March 13, 1755, *Colden Papers*, V, 6.

91. Cadwallader Colden to Peter Collinson, November 1754, *Colden Papers*, IX, 147.

92. Colden letter [1758], attached to "Remarks on Mr. Melvill's Observations on Light and Colours," Colden MSS, New-York Historical Society.

93. Cadwallader Colden to Peter Collinson, July 7, 1753, *Colden Papers*, IV, 396.

94. Peter Collinson to Cadwallader Colden, October 18, 1753, *Colden Papers*, IV, 408.

95. Cadwallader Colden to Peter Collinson, December 5, 1753, *Colden Papers*, IV, 419.

96. Peter Collinson to Cadwallader Colden, March 10, 1754, *Colden Papers*, IV, 378.

97. Cadwallader Colden to Peter Collinson, May 28, 1754, *Colden Papers*, IV, 447.

98. "Criticism of *The Principles of Action in Matter*," unpublished translation of Kastner's remarks, Colden MSS, New-York Historical Society, section 1.

99. Ibid., section 2, 4.

100. Ibid., section 10, 11.

101. Peter Collinson to Cadwallader Colden, October 7, 1755, *Colden Papers*, V, 28.

102. Dr. J. Bevis to Peter Collinson, August 10, 1755, *Colden Papers*, V, 23.

103. Alexander Colden to Cadwallader Colden, September 30, 1756, *Colden Papers*, V, 93.

104. Benjamin Franklin to Cadwallader Colden, April 12, 1753, *Colden Papers*, IV, 382.

105. Alexander Garden to Cadwallader Colden, March 14, 1758, *Colden Papers*, V, 228.

106. Samuel Pike to Cadwallader Colden, July 10, 1753, *Colden Papers*, IV, 397.

107. Ibid.

108. John Hutchinson, *Moses's Principia. Of The Invisible Parts of Matter; Of Motion; Of Visible Forms; And Of Their Dissolution, and Reformation* (London, 1724), 27–28.

109. John Hutchinson, *An Abstract from the Works of John Hutchinson, Esq. Being A Summary of his Discoveries in Philosophy and Divinity* (Edinburgh, 1753), 157.

110. Hutchinson, *Moses's Principia*, 399.

111. William Jones, "An Essay on the First Principles of Natural Philosophy," in *The Theological, Philosophical and Miscellaneous Works of the Reverend William Jones* (London, 1801), 12 Vols., III, 14.

112. George Horne, *A Fair, Candid, and Impartial State of the Case Between Isaac Newton and Mr. Hutchinson* (Oxford, 1753), 26.

113. Leslie Stephen, *History of English Thought in the Eighteenth Century* (New York, 1962), 2 Vols., I, 331.

114. Robert Spearman, *An Enquiry after Philosophy and Theology* (Edinburgh, 1755), 77.

115. Samuel Pike to Cadwallader Colden, July 10, 1753, *Colden Papers*, IV, 398.

116. Cadwallader Colden to Samuel Pike, 1753 [?], Colden MSS, New-York Historical Society.

117. Cadwallader Colden to Benjamin Franklin, November 19, 1753, *Colden Papers*, IV, 415.

118. Cadwallader Colden to Samuel Pike, 1753 [?], Colden MSS, New-York Historical Society.

119. Ibid.

120. Benjamin Franklin to Cadwallader Colden, August 30, 1754, *Colden Papers*, IV, 462.

121. Cadwallader Colden to Samuel Pike, June 1755, Colden MSS, New-York Historical Society.

122. Ibid.

123. Samuel Pike to Cadwallader Colden, September 9, 1775, *Gratz Collection*, Historical Society of Pennsylvania.

124. Ibid.

125. Cadwallader Colden to Alexander Colden, n.d., *Colden Papers*, V, 148.

126. Dr. Robert Whytt to Cadwallader Colden, May 16, 1763, *Colden Papers*, VI, 218.

127. Cadwallader Colden to Dr. Robert Whytt, September 3, 1763, *Colden Papers*, VI, 273.

128. Cadwallader Colden to Peter Collinson, May 28, 1754, *Colden Papers*, IV, 447.

129. Cadwallader Colden to Dr. Robert Whytt, September 3, 1763, *Colden Papers*, VI, 273.

130. *OPTICKS*, Query 31, 404–405.

131. Cadwallader Colden, "An Introduction to the Study of Philosophy wrote in America for a Young Gentleman," Colden MSS, New-York Historical Society, section VII.

132. In his *Principles*, for example, Colden stated that a "lively imagination" is required for the creation of theory (168). Again, Colden remained largely unconcerned about the lack of empirical data in his treatise. His usual explanation was that experiments were of dubious value and expensive to perform. "A Treatise on Animal Oeconomy," Colden MSS, New-York Historical Society, 2. Colden remained convinced that a "a truly philosophic turn of mind can never want opportunities of improving in knowledge, without the expense of any apparatus for experiments." "An Introduction to Philosophy," section IV.

133. "[T]he motion of a planet cannot be from a projectile motion alone impressed in the beginning. . . . There must be some agent continually acting to give motion to the planets & to continue that motion." Cadwallader Colden, "Draft of Preface for a 2nd Edition of *Principles of Action in Matter*," Colden MSS, New-York Historical Society.

134. Edmund Whittaker, *A History of the Theories of Aether and Electricity* (London, 1958), 2 Vols., I, 8.

135. Cadwallader Colden, "Of the Transmission and Reflection of Light," Colden MSS., New-York Historical Society, paragraph 14, 15.

136. Colden, *Principles*, section 13, 26.

137. Alexandre Koyré, *From the Closed World to the Infinite Universe* (Baltimore, 1957), 101.

"New York in banderole in sky." Eno Collection #16. Anonymous. *New York* [engraving], ca. 1716–18. Courtesy of Miriam and Ira D. Wallach Division of Art, Prints and Photographs, The New York Public Library, Astor, Lenox, and Tilden Foundations.

1760

You are now my dear — going to the college to begin your studies in order to become useful to — and for — employment in the society — a knowledge of that knowledge which is necessary for that purpose. But it may happen that your time may be employed in a kind of learning which is of no real use. You may spend your time in acquiring a kind of learning which — so far from being useful that it renders the mind unfit to receive real knowledge & to grow really — you the greatest part of young mens time in the common method of teaching in the colleges is not employed to better purposes. For this reason I am desirous to give you some Principles of knowledge by which you may judge of what you learn & hear. Young men it is true ought to be diffident of their own judgement because they want that knowledge which others have. & they want likewise their experience, but it is not of so bad consequence to make a rash judgement as to form your judgement merely on the judgement of others. Never receive any thing as truth till you are fully convinced till then receive your masters dictates as probable & with no further submission to his opinion —

History informs us, that the Egyptian priests, the Chaldeans & Persian Magi had acquired great knowledge in Physics, long before the Christian era: such as exceeds the knowledge of the most learned among the moderns. It is certain that they had carried Geometry, Astronomy & Mechanics to the greatest perfection. The Greeks were only mere Scholars of the Egyptians. It may be questioned, whether they made any one discovery absolutely their own: & it is not improbable that, like mere Scholars they did not throughly understand the first Principles of the Egyptian Philosophy; & yet it is from them only that we have any knowledge of the Learning of these Ancients. Pythagoras was the first instructed of any of the Greeks in the Egyptian Learning. It appears from the few remains of his Doctrine that the Egyptians knew what of late times has been called the Copernican System, & that he knew the general apparent attraction between bodies; which has been rediscovered in the last century by Sr Isaac Newtone. But as we have nothing remaining of the Pythagorean Philosophy, except what is found in a few abstracts in much later writers we know very little of what were the true principles of that Philosophy. It may be that we are now regaining the Principles of Physics which were known many ages before the beginning of the Christian era.

War, & the irruptions of barbarous nations, into the countries where Learning flourished, have been the Destruction of knowledge in those countries. But nothing so much prevented the propagation & advancement of knowledge as the Craft of the pagan Priests, who, in order to secure their influence over the common people confined Learning to their own order; & communicated their —

Page one of Cadwallader Colden, "Introduction to the Study of Physics or Natural Philosophy." Cadwallader Colden, MSS Collection, Negative Number 56216. Courtesy of The New-York Historical Society.

Portrait of Cadwallader Colden by Matthew
Pratt, dated 1772. This portrait was commis-
sioned by the New York City Chamber of
Commerce in recognition of the granting of a
charter by Colden as lieutenant-governor of
the Province of New York. Courtesy of the
New York City Partnership and Chamber of
Commerce.

Chapter 4
AN ENQUIRY CONCERNING MATERIALISM

Philosophy is entirely distinct from religion, they have not the same objects and, therefore, a wise philosopher as such never opposes the religion of his country, but conforms to it so far as required by a good subject. On the other hand, Divines who oppose any speculation in philosophy from principles of religion act very unwisely: for thereby they injure religion in the minds of the people more than otherwise could be done.

Whatever the scientific merits of Colden's *Principles of Action in Matter* for his readers, it was its philosophical implications that were more apt to draw serious and sustained attention both from his contemporaries and from subsequent historians of the period. Colden's contention that the operations of the physical universe could be explained exclusively according to several material powers or "principles," together with his insistence that all matter is active, lends credence to his assigned status as a philosophical materialist.

One of the first historians of colonial philosophy to label Colden as a materialist was I. Woodbridge Riley. In his *American Philosophy: The Early Schools* (1907), he placed Colden in the company of a later colonial physician, Benjamin Rush.[1] While this suggests that there was at least one other notable representative of philosophical materialism in the American colonies of the eighteenth century, it says little about the distinctive features of Colden's particular theories.[2] Nevertheless, Riley's general classification has been reinforced by another writer's remark that "Colden made a pioneer contribution toward a mature phase of scientific materialism which deserves to be remembered."[3] The biographer of Thomas Clap, president of Yale College, asserts that Colden was "a downright materialist in philosophical conviction."[4] Another author claims that Colden is "the only important American materialist of the eighteenth century prior to the Revolution."[5] Finally, the suggestion has been made that Colden's philosophy represents "lines of investigation which were taken up by later materialists."[6]

To many of his contemporaries, evidently, Colden's philosophy would have appeared equally materialist. His constant attempts to obtain readers for his treatise—both in the colonies and in Europe—were primarily meant to solicit their views on its scientific value. Yet the attempts could just as often lead to comments on his philosophy rather than on the status of his physics. The previously cited comment of Professor Betts, which was directed to Colden's active material principles and "the unfathomable depths" that they could open in both philosophy and divinity is a case in point. In the process of trying to define and clarify his scientific theories, Colden was often forced into discussions on the implications of his theories for ethics, epistemology, and related topics. It was in terms of these issues that Colden's philosophical materialism became most relevant and was to remain a critical factor for some of its readers.

Much of the comment on his *Principles* that Colden received from Europe concerned its failure to improve on Newtonian physics. It remained largely the self-appointed task of a colonial philosopher, Samuel Johnson, to take the major responsibility of inviting Colden to consider the philosophical meaning and implications of his treatise. In so doing, Colden was gradually led to analyze the relationship of intelligence, that is, purpose or design, to those active material principles that were the basis of his natural philosophy.

One of the major reasons why Samuel Johnson of Yale was prompted to pursue this inquiry was that he himself had a definite philosophical position, which was distinctly opposed to that held by Colden. It was the visit of Bishop Berkeley to the American colonies between 1729 and 1731 that converted Johnson to philosophical Idealism, although he had begun to read Berkeley's *Principles of Human Knowledge* almost a year earlier.[7] Thereafter, Johnson went about the task of trying to induce others to embrace the bishop's philosophy. In Colden, however, he found a correspondent who was equally devoted to his own philosophical convictions and determined to demonstrate their validity to others. While this created a situation in which there was to be an interesting and revealing exchange of viewpoints, both men remained to the end nearly as far apart as ever. Colden's persistent espousal of the "truth" of his own theories and his tenacity in their defense made him more likely to endure, rather than welcome, Johnson's repeated efforts to instruct and guide him toward a position more compatible with Idealist tenets.

As early as 1743 Johnson sent Colden some books by Berkeley, including his *Introduction to the Principles of Human Knowledge* and *New Theory of*

Vision. He informed Colden that the purpose of the former book was to "banish Scholasticism and abstract ideas which have been the bane of all science of every kind."[8] Several years later, he sent Colden a copy of Berkeley's *De Motu*, together with his own piece on morals.[9] Colden responded by submitting to Johnson his treatise on "Fluxions" and, thereafter, *An Explication of the First Causes of Action in Matter*. By 1752, Colden also supplied Johnson with the revised and published version, *The Principles of Action in Matter*.[10] Thus, for nearly a decade, the two men continued to exchange some of their most important philosophical productions. All of this inevitably set the stage for a lengthy correspondence on their respective philosophical tenets.

Colden found it difficult to comprehend, much less appreciate, most of the books that Johnson sent him. He apparently did read Berkeley's *Essay Toward a New Theory of Vision* (1709), in which an attempt was made to demonstrate that the distance, size, and location of objects were dependent on a combination or "fusion" of sensations.[11] Thus, the notion of space— in which such objects were located—could be regarded as an association of ideas. Colden also read Berkeley's *Treatise Concerning the Principles of Human Knowledge* (1710), in which Berkeley refuted the common belief in the independent existence of a material substratum. Colden, however, regarded this work as merely a "subtle dissertation about the use of words."[12] He evinced even stronger feelings toward Berkeley's *De Motu* (1721), a book devoted to an examination of the status of abstract ideas in physics. For some time, Colden hedged with regard to giving his real opinions on this treatise but, when he finally responded to Johnson's "demand" for an answer, he felt he could tell him, "I think that the Dr. has made the greatest collection in this and his other writings of indistinct and undigested conceptions . . . that I ever met with in any one man's performance; that he has the art of puzzling and confounding his readers in an elegant style not common to such kind of writers; and that he is as great an abuser of the use of words, as any one of those he blames most for that fault."[13]

All of this may well have amazed Johnson, but it did not prevent him from telling Colden that he should not have to ask pardon for censuring Berkeley, for he himself was for an entire "Liberty in philosophizing."[14] At this early stage in their correspondence it was, perhaps, the only remark he could offer in response to Colden's categorical dismissal of Berkeley's theories. It certainly did not prevent them from continuing their mutual exchange of views, with Johnson remaining convinced that he could demonstrate to Colden that Berkeley's philosophical concepts were quite comprehensible and worth serious consideration. Colden, however, adamantly retained his critical attitude toward Berkeley's books and, for Johnson's benefit, emphasized his respective differences with Berkeley on such topics as the doctrine of fluxions, ideas, and the status of matter.

Fluxions were independently developed by both Isaac Newton and Gottfried Leibnitz, the German mathematician and philosopher, and became an important contribution to the development of mathematics in the eighteenth century. It was a branch of mathematics that attempted to describe the change in the ratio of two quantities, one of which was a function of the other—subsequently better known as calculus. The variable rates or flowing quantities were described as fluxions, and the process for determining that ratio was called differentiation.[15] There were, apparently, various ambiguities and contradictions in Newton's application of the fluxional method, such as his use of infinitesimals in his *De analysi*, or that of flowing quantities (fluxions) in the *Methodus fluxionum*, and finally, those concerning prime and ultimate ratios in his *De quadratura curvarum*.[16]

Perhaps what remained most controversial and subject to some confusion was Newton's application of the concept of the infinitesimal. Although he later developed reservations about the concept of the infinitely small, he apparently retained the notion of moments as somehow consisting of infinitely small parts.[17] In biology, too, the use of the concept of the infinitesimal or indivisible also had relevance for adherents of preformation theory, where the discovery of animalcula or spermatozoa suggested the divisibility of such forms to infinity.[18]

In *The Analyst: or, a Discourse addressed to a Infidel Mathematician* (1734)—possibly directed toward Edmund Halley—Berkeley pointed out some of the ambiguities surrounding the nature of fluxions and, more particularly, the issue of infinitesimal quantities that Newton had introduced in his *De analysi* (1711). The book subsequently prompted an English mathematician, Benjamin Robin, to introduce the concept of a limit to which a variable may be said to approach, and a Scottish mathematician, Colin MacLaurin, to place the entire subject of fluxions on a more coherent and systematic basis (in *A Treatise of Fluxions*, 1742).[19]

After he had read *The Analyst*, Colden was also prompted to write a rebuttal to Berkeley's criticisms, entitled "An Introduction to the Doctrine of Fluxions." To Johnson, he categorically stated that Berkeley did not understand the doctrine of fluxions as employed by mathematicians.[20] It remains questionable, however, whether Colden was able to contribute very much to this dispute. At least, that was the opinion of James Logan, who thought that Colden had not only failed to answer Berkeley's objections, but had not fully understood the correct method of determining fluxions.[21] In any case, Logan remained dubious about the value of Newton's mathematical fluxions.

It was not the first time that Colden had turned his attention to this topic. He had earlier devised a scheme for applying fluxions to physics, which he sent to John Rutherfurd, commander of the military garrison at Albany. The latter was a devotee of mathematics and philosophy and had invited Colden to correspond with him on these and related matters.[22] While Rutherfurd doubted that fluxions were relevant to physics—where knowledge was primarily derived from observation and experiment—he conjectured that they might lead to some truths in geometry, since "our knowledge in geometry we owe to reason alone."[23] He prefaced these remarks with the note that "fluxions help the imagination prodigiously," an indication, perhaps, of why Colden found them relevant to his own work in physics and defended their use to both Rutherfurd and Johnson. In any case, Colden did little to heed Rutherfurd's distinctions concerning such "reasonings" as applied to geometry and physics.

Apparently, Colden expected the doctrine of fluxions, or rather the concepts that he derived from this doctrine, to illustrate the emission theory of light. In this way, for example, he might be able to explain the intellectual conundrum of how the sun could lose an infinite times an infinite number of particles and yet insist that this would only amount to a very small finite quantity in any given finite interval of time. This conceptualized explanation is not unrelated to the retort that Colden gave to Franklin's query, previously cited, regarding the continual loss of matter by the sun.

Rutherfurd invited Colden to apply his notion of fluxions to other aspects of natural philosophy as well as light but emphasized that philosophers usually tended to dispute the nature of light and, to illustrate the point, recapitulated the views of Descartes, Malebranche, Newton, and Boerhaave on this topic. He added: "The Ancients wanting the advantage of later experiments I shan't mention their notions." He described Descartes theory as based on a "Materia subtilis" which filled space, whereas Newton introduced a kind of "Aetherial Medium" distinct from that of Descartes. He summarized Newton's doctrine of light as "real particles emitted with, as you call it, infinite force or motion, in infinite quantities, etc. from the Luminous body itself."[24] Rutherfurd's own preference, however, seems to have been for Boerhaave's version of a universal fire that could take the form of either heat or light and to which all motion could be attributed.

In a subsequent letter, Rutherfurd confessed that he still could not arrive at any distinct ideas of fluxions, in spite of Colden's endeavors to explain them and apply them to his own conception of light. Rutherfurd remained convinced that, on the basis of the particulate theory, the sun would be quickly exhausted. Part of the same letter was devoted to a further examination of Newton's philosophy for the purpose, as he told Colden, "to humble you a little further about Sir Isaac."[25] Neither on this particular subject nor on the limitation of fluxions was Rutherfurd able to do much to alter Colden's views.

To Samuel Johnson, fluxions remained, at best, a problematical issue. After Colden sent him his criticisms of Berkeley's *Analyst*, Johnson invited another mathematician to join him in comparing Colden's version of fluxions with that of Berkeley.[26] Several months later, Johnson informed Colden that, in their considered opinion, they did not believe that there were any major differences between Colden and Berkeley, and those that might yet exist, led him to aver, "I am persuaded that could you converse together & explain yourselves to each other, you would find the difference would come to little or nothing."[27]

This shortly proved to be a somewhat gratuitous assumption. Perhaps to disabuse Johnson of this opinion, Colden sent him his "Introduction to Fluxions," which was subsequently appended to his *Principles of Action in Matter*. The result was that Johnson next wrote to tell Colden that "the doctrine of fluxions cannot subsist with Dr. Berkeley's principles, that therefore the one or the other must be false."[28] This seemed to be sufficient justification for Colden to retort that any inconsistencies between the doctrine of fluxions and Berkeley's philosophy could only prove prejudicial to the latter; he went on to make the more inclusive comment that the Bishop's notions were "mere chimeras" and gave a strong suspicion of "sophism." Johnson thereafter may have been reluctant to continue this discussion, but he felt compelled to remind Colden that he remained unconvinced that any finite quantity could be infinitely divisible.[29]

A defense of his view on fluxions ineluctably led Colden into giving a *précis* of his doctrine of ideas. In a more literal sense, Colden proposed, an idea could refer to "the picture or representation of anything which we have received from our senses."[30] Yet an idea can be taken "in a more large sense for any kind of conception we form or perception we have of anything." Colden described the first category as "finite" ideas, apparently because they were derived from sense experience of particular objects. The second group of ideas might therefore be regarded as "infinite," by comparison, since they seemed to include all those conceptions that were not derived from or related to particular phenomena. Given this dichotomy, all ideas not of finite objects could be classified as infinite. This is what Colden would appear to have meant when he claimed that the latter encompassed "any kind of conception . . . we can have of anything which is not assigned to finite objects." Although Colden did not identify ideas other than finite as being necessarily infinite, he did employ the more inclusive term when he referred to conceptions we could form of "God" or "eternity." It was largely by proposing that the "infinite difference" between God and creature, or time and eternity, were conceivable that Colden was enabled to conclude that one could form infinite ideas or, rather, ideas of infinites.

He concluded the discussion by proposing that the mind could have "Ideas in the strict sense & conceptions or perceptions . . . in the large sense." It was Berkeley's failure to make this distinction, Colden maintained, that vitiated his philosophy. Here, however, when it came to explaining his mentor's doctrine of ideas, Johnson was audacious enough to assert that "I would only beg leave to make a short remark on the distinction between an Idea & a notion or conception of the mind which is very just & made by the Bishop himself; your not observing which convinces me that you did not (as the case was with me at first) give so exact an attention to what he says, as to enter thoroughly into his meaning." After explaining the basic differences between John Locke's theory of ideas and those of Bishop Berkeley, he advised Colden that, properly speaking, we can not have any idea of God or of any intelligent being, although we can form notions or conceptions of such entities. More pointedly, he added:

Nor does the Bishop define the term Idea in the sense as you do, *viz. a Picture or Representation of anything we receive from our Senses.* On the contrary, he takes what you call *pictures of things* to be the very things themselves, & that we do vainly and without any ground imagine any things intervening between the Divine Mind & ours, whereof our Ideas, of sense & imagination, are the supposed pictures. The Ideas of imagination may indeed be called pictures of the Ideas of sense, but he can have no notion of any original whereof that idea or objects of sense . . . can be said to be a picture.[31]

In itself, this may not have prompted Colden to reexamine his own doctrine of ideas, but at least it pointed out where and to what extent he differed from Berkeley and from Johnson. One such difference, at least, appears to be in regard to Colden's premise that ideas of infinites can—in some inexplicable manner—be derived from sense experience in much the same manner as ideas of finites. He may possibly have meant that such general ideas are simply abstract conceptions, but it would seem that Colden more properly treats them as perceptions, for he states that finite as well as infinite ideas are "the effects of essentially different agents."[32]

In his *Principles,* Colden claimed that the idea that one has of the Intelligent Being is related to its actions or operations and, thus, is much the same as the ideas derived from the activity of the material principles.[33] This can only strengthen the supposition that the Intelligent Being is known by its "effects." The ambiguous manner in which Colden discussed the Intelligent Being—both in his letters to Johnson and in his *Principles*—make the treatment of this subject seem somewhat more complex than it perhaps was meant to be. Colden had to determine, for instance, how material and intellectual "effects" could be differentiated; he had to resolve their comparative roles in the operation of the universe; and, finally, he had to show how the innate power or activity of matter would not conflict with the activity of Intelligence. While such issues invited further examination, it is relevant to note here that it was in terms of this basic dualism—matter and intelligence (or mind)—that Colden was required to discuss and defend his philosophical tenets.

In addition to their differences over the status of fluxions and ideas, it was the ongoing problem of defining the distinctions that applied to mind and matter that engendered much of the intellectual controversy between these two colonial philosophers. This issue was not, of course, unrelated to other topics, but it became the single issue most often raised by Johnson for repeated examination. Johnson was not sufficiently well informed in mathematics, as he repeated to Colden several times, to contest the latter's view on fluxions. Consequently, he limited himself to making only a few brief comments on this subject. Again, as far as the doctrine of ideas was concerned, he tried to resolve the problem by telling Colden that "the difference between you & the Bp. . . . is in great measure owing to your using the same words in different senses & not attending to each other's meaning."[34]

However that may be, such excuses could not hide the gulf that separated Colden and Johnson on the nature and reality of material substances. Not only did Colden have well-defined views on this subject but it was, of course, the one metaphysical assumption that Berkeley's philosophy was especially designed to refute. If any additional impetus were needed on Johnson's part to raise this particular issue, it is sufficient to note that by 1745 he had begun to read and by 1746 had become a convert to Hutchinsonian views.[35] Whatever the disparities between Idealism and Hutchinsonian philosophy, their combined effect could not but create a prejudice in Johnson's mind against someone who would assert not only the reality but, what was even more reprehensible, the innate activity of matter.

As early as 1744, Johnson must have received some intimation of Colden's materialism when he received the latter's observations on Berkeley's *Principles.*[36] Colden dismissed this work, like others by this author, as merely a "subtle dissertation" on words. At this point, Johnson limited himself to saying that this could only be the case if one meant by "matter" that which is immediately perceived by the senses. Thereafter, the subject seems to have faded into the background for about two years while both men went on to discuss their opinions on fluxions, ideas, and, incidentally, the virtues of tar water.

In the interim, Colden provided Johnson with a copy of his *Explications* in June 1746, having previously indicated to Johnson that it would be "on the subject of material agents which I hope may be of use to enlarge our knowledge in natural philosophy," and he promised that "As soon as it shall be printed, it will kiss your hands for that purpose."[37] It was to be primarily the contents of this treatise that initiated an ongoing debate regarding the activity of material agents in the universe.

Their discussion was antedated by the repercussions of the Great Awakening. This prompted Johnson to pen a short piece on the "Sovereignty & Promises of God," which he forwarded to Colden. Having read it, Colden, too, was prompted to consider such issues as prescience, liberty of choice, and will, which, he claimed, were within the purview of, and could only be assigned to, intelligent beings. These alone, he asserted, could be regarded as truly free. In order to explain his position, he deemed it helpful to make some brief observations on the differences that pertain to material and intelligent beings.[38]

Colden began with the proposition that all beings are either agents or acting principles. The conceptions or ideas that we are able to derive from such agents come from their effects, for "nothing without action can produce anything." This, of course, became an axiomatic presupposition in Colden's philosophy. It served certain epistemological as well as scientific requirements. Colden decided that all such agents could be divided "into two essentially different kinds of beings." One category includes all material agents that are determined by efficient causation and possess neither perception nor consciousness; the other is reserved for intelligent agents or beings. The latter are not only conscious of their own actions but "perceive the actions of all other beings which any way reach or affect them & which alters & determines its own actions according to the perceptions it has of its own & of other beings which surround it whose actions reach it & this allwise for some purpose or end, & therefore is of itself properly moved or determined only by final causes."[39] Colden summarized this as representing the inherent differences between matter and spirit. The most basic distinction between the two involves the role of causation in their activity. This alone gives "a real positive and essential difference."

Thus, even before he had seen a copy of the *Explications*, Johnson had been given a preview of Colden's metaphysical tenets and the kind of reasoning that allegedly confirmed them. After making an attempt to reconcile their personal differences on such issues by giving a patently symbolic interpretation of Colden's terminology—such as suggesting that material beings might be called "sensible" beings—Johnson had to confess, however, that "I should not have expressed myself exactly in the same manner as you do."[40] In his view, the term "material agent" was self-contradictory. The word *agent* "in strict philosophical verity, always imports a Being that has a principle of activity within itself & acts upon a design whereof it is conscious," he told Colden. Matter, then, can only mean "a meet passive thing, & to be so far from being capable of consciousness, that it has not the least glimpse of any principle of self activity." Johnson concluded: "I apprehend there are no such things as efficient causes in nature besides Spirits or Intelligent Beings (either Supreme or subordinate) who, as such, ever act from a principle of consciousness, design, & self activity."[41]

By uniting the material with efficient causality, Colden had blunted one of the standard distinctions in formal philosophical discourse; it should not be surprising, therefore, that subsequent readers of Colden's treatise would be more apt to agree with Johnson's orthodox position relating to matter and spirit. Colden rose to his own defense by inviting Johnson to give him "a definition of matter or any other being merely passive without any power or force. Such a being I cannot conceive & therefore for as to me does not exist."[42]

As already indicated, the interposition of Hutchinsonian notions at this juncture of the debate made it even more unlikely that Johnson would succeed in establishing a *via media* between their respective positions. He first discovered Hutchinson's novel philosophy from reading Duncan Forbes *Thoughts on Religion Natural and Revealed*. Forbes had, for Johnson, set the Hutchinsonian philosophy "in an agreeable light & earnestly recommended the study of [it] to all gentlemen of leisure, capacity, and learning." Perhaps it was to elicit Colden's interest in this philosophy that Johnson informed him—after having learned of Colden's intention to "improve" on Newtonian natural philosophy—that Hutchinson, too, "is said to have amended & even confuted some things in Sr. Isaac's System."[43] Johnson went on to list the titles of five Hutchinsonian works and devoted several paragraphs of his letter to giving a brief sketch of Hutchinsonian philosophy. A singular feature of the same, he told Colden, was the doctrine of an "infinitely subtle fluid," which exists in the sun as fire but emanates in the form of light and returns to the sun again as either air or spirit. On the basis of this cosmic circulation, Johnson contended that "the rotation of the orbs, both annual and diurnal, may be accounted for, with all the phenomena in each globe, without having recourse to Sr. Isaac's gravity or attraction, projection, etc."

By 1750, Johnson had not only read all the collected volumes of Hutchinson's works but also incorporated some of the latter's theories in his own *Elementa Philosophica*.[44] Even thereafter, Johnson continued to read all the books by other Hutchinsonian authors that he could obtain. These included the writings of Hodges, Bates, Pike, Patten, Horne, and Spearman. Colden's response to Johnson's latest overture was not encouraging; at least, none of his extant letters to Johnson make any mention of the subject. The only time that Colden did offer some opinions on Hutchinsonian philosophy was to Samuel Pike, as previously noted, following the publication of the *Principles* in England.

Unfortunately, Johnson did not respond to the publication of Colden's *Explications* with any equal measure of interest, much less enthusiasm. While he regarded the treatise as a "curious dissertation," he also added, "I have hardly furniture and force of mind enough to comprehend it." The fact that both Forbes's book and the *Explications* were coincidentally brought to Johnson's attention within a short period of time prompted him to tell Colden that there were some apparent similarities between the two works. As if to stress his own differences from Colden, however, he devoted the major portion of his letter to reiterating his opposition to the separation of consciousness and intelligence from self-activity. He wrote to say that "a blind senseless power or principle of activity appears to me repugnant and, if it were possible, it would [be so] far from being of any use in nature, that it would be mischievous without a mind to direct and over rule it." Consequently, he felt justified in concluding that all motion and activity in nature "must therefore be under the active management of a most wise and designing principle or cause; so that it seems to me repugnant to place intelligence and activity in or derive them from different principles; I can have no notion of action without volition. For, if you suppose a blind principle of action in matter, you must still suppose it under the over-ruling force of an intelligent and designing principle."[45]

Johnson also warned Colden that "it is not the part of the philosopher to multiply beings and causes without necessity." In spite of such evident reservations, Johnson divulged to Colden that he had written an ingenious theory on gravitation and considered the notion of an elastic aether as "the most probable hypothesis." All of this led him to believe that Colden had, indeed, improved on Sir Isaac Newton. Other than saying this, however, he remained at a loss regarding its scientific merits and, moreover, doubted that anyone in the colonies was sufficiently competent to offer an informed opinion, for "I do not think any this way can enter far into your reasonings."[46]

Johnson subsequently shared his copy of Colden's treatise with President Thomas Clap of Yale, whereupon Johnson could tell Colden that the president "can't understand your solution of gravity: for two balls in your aether will certainly be pressed as much by it on the sides between them, as on the opposite sides, unless it has some laws of motion that we have never yet been acquainted with."[47] Euler, as already noted, would later voice similar criticisms. For Johnson, however, such points may only have been academic, for his abiding concern was directed toward the metaphysical aspects of Colden's theories. He remained doggedly persistent in reminding Colden that "the actions which you ascribe to matter must be the actions of Mind, which alone can be the agent to whom such species of matter can be no more than a meer passive tool or instrument."

Johnson's concerns regarding Colden's active material principles must have prompted him to distribute the treatise to some of his colleagues at Yale. It was this philosophical issue—rather than its scientific content—that would continue to provoke critical comments. The result was that one of the fellows even went so far as to become "apprehensive of some tendency in it towards Atheism" but, to mitigate the charge, Johnson added, "I do not think he was capable of understanding it."[48] Of course, neither could Johnson. As much as he might have tried to excuse the remarks of another academic at Yale, the impression persists that Johnson remained keenly interested in learning Colden's response to this charge; otherwise, why mention it? His own inquiries were quite restrained, even polite, within an academic context; however, it is not unlikely that he had his own lingering suspicions concerning someone who persisted (notwithstanding Johnson's attempts to dissuade him) in assigning activity to matter.

If, however, Johnson expected Colden to take this latest allegation "philosophically," he was greatly mistaken. Colden certainly did not intend to allow this invidious remark to pass lightly. He could not consider such a comment as motivated simply by ignorance or misunderstanding. He interpreted it as a personal affront which, he added, was the fate of all those who offered something new in philosophy: "So Copernicus; so Galileo; Descartes; Leibnitz, etc have all been branded. They must have very weak minds who think they can do service to religion by aspersions of this kind on such like men. Men who have given any ground to be suspected of atheism have at the same time given proof of their ignorance in natural philosophy. And, I do not remember of any one man that has made any considerable discovery in natural philosophy, that has given any real ground to suspect him an enemy to true religion, but the contrary."[49]

At this time Colden had yet to learn the reaction of several European scientists and mathematicians to his treatise. Thus, he still felt some confidence that his treatise would someday place him in the company of those notable scientists and philosophers who had been vilified for their daring and startling theories. To Johnson, he implied that he was too well versed in the foundations and history of natural philosophy to allow his own treatise to give any suspicion of atheism. Far from regarding his philosophical precepts as antithetical to religious belief, Colden told Johnson, "from [them] a certain proof may be given of the existence of Spirits or immaterial beings." While he did not elaborate on his statement, this latest episode may well have been conducive to the inclusion of a section entitled "The Intelligent Being, and of the Foundation and Duration of the several Systems in the Universe" in the subsequent edition of his *Principles*.

It was not until the end of 1752 that Johnson finally received his own copy of *The Principles of Action in Matter*.[50] In the accompanying letter, Colden rather reluctantly admitted the ideological differences that separated both men and "for that reason I expect from you the strongest arguments that can be brought against it." Somewhat defensively, he tried to introduce several passages from Johnson's textbook in philosophy as a heuristic aid in bridging the gap between their positions. He noted, for instance, that Johnson had stated that "our perceptions cannot be produced in our minds *without a cause* (so far we agree); or, which is the same thing, by any *imagined, unintelligent, inert, or unactive cause*." Given this presupposition, Colden found another area of agreement in the mutual belief that "an unactive cause was synonymous with no cause."

Whereas for Johnson—insofar as he might argue as an Idealist—this meant that perceptions could only be attributed to a spiritual or mental cause, for Colden, on the other hand, only a material agent could be productive of such perceptions. Here, however, he did not quite put it in these terms; rather, he argued negatively by claiming, "I am not convinced that intelligence is an essential concomitant to all actions." More emphatic was Colden's declaration that the words *inert* and *inactive* could not be regarded as synonymous. His misunderstanding of Newton was again evident when he gave the latter's definition in the *Principia*, "Materiae vis inertia est Potentia resistendi, etc." as a defense of his own position. He added: "the word inertia . . . certainly cannot mean mere inaction" and concluded: "I shall say nothing more on these matters of speculation."[51]

It must have surprised Colden when his own attempt to find some common ground with his intellectual adversary led Johnson to propose, "I do not think we differ so much in the principles you set out with as you seem to imagine."[52] He now seemed somewhat resigned to accepting Colden's three material principles, in so far as they pertained only to natural philosophy. He thought the principles of resistance and elasticity could account for certain phenomena, but it is apparent that the real reason for Johnson's more positive attitude was the addition of the metaphysical principle, the Intelligent Being, to Colden's treatise. Even if it did not resolve all the remaining issues, it somehow made the notion of active matter less repugnant in Johnson's view. His preference remained to make the Intelligent Being a higher, more inclusive principle of unity so that it would "ultimately prove to be also the principle of the action."[53]

Not all issues were so readily dismissed. All that Colden had really done in his treatise was to make his distinctions between matter and intelligence dependent on the respective "idea" one could have of each. Thus, matter, though acting as an agent, that is, possessing self-motion, did not include in its "idea" anything of innate order or of a regular system. Matter could not, however, exist without or outside some system and, from observations derived from the planetary motions and stars, there was, Colden inferred, sufficient evidence of such a system. Consequently, the notion of a system, not innate to matter, must be granted to another "idea."[54] That "idea," of course, could now only refer to the Intelligent Being. While it stood in relationship to matter as ends to means and acted to fulfill final causes—or perhaps served as a teleological principle—it must do so, for Colden, without acting "in opposition to or contradiction to the material agents."[55] Obviously, even within this context, the latter still maintained their prerogative of self-activity.

Now, for Johnson, matter and its activity could only be dependent "on the constant free exertion of the divine will and power."[56] To assume then, as he did, that Colden could also be gradually led to accept this interpretation, or that their differences on this issue were reconcilable, was fatuous. The same is equally true of his attempt to have Colden modify his philosophy to suit certain Hutchinsonian tenets. All of this inevitably remained moot.

President Clap, having been given a copy of the revised and expanded version of the *Principles*, wrote to tell Colden that while it contained "curious thoughts," he had to admit that he, too, could not "unite the Idea of a Power or Principle of Self Motion, or Agency, to a non-Intelligent." While he agreed with Colden (as had Johnson) that they shared the same "fundamental principle, that we have no knowledge of substances or any Being or thing, abstracted from the action of that Being or thing upon us," he also disclosed that he had "always been inclined to Bp. Berkeley's scheme."[57] Colden's explanation for gravitational attraction left Clap unconvinced, for the latter argued that one could only conjecture by reason concerning gravitation and offered the opinion that it could only be due to an Intelligent agent.

On the basis of these last letters, written by Johnson and Clap, it is evident that Colden had done little to revise or adapt his philosophical position to meet the objections of his correspondents at Yale College. Clap, of course, never became as directly involved with Colden on the topic of material agents as Johnson had been. Hindsight might suggest that Johnson would perhaps have done better never to have troubled himself to convert Colden to an alternative viewpoint. The fact that he persisted for nearly a decade suggests that he may have found in Colden a challenging intellectual adversary in such speculative pursuits. Altogether, Colden's philosophical tenets may have been so different from those found among his more conventional colleagues at Yale that Johnson could not but become intrigued enough to examine their presuppositions. Then, too, there were so very few in the colonies with whom Johnson could engage in ongoing philosophical correspondence of any type.

Of the two, Johnson proved the more flexible regarding such philosophical matters. He had gone through several intellectual stages, as it were, and this may have made him more tolerant of alternative viewpoints. Although quite convinced of his own philosophical tenets, either as a convert to Lockean philosophy, Berkeleyian Idealism, or again to Hutchinsonian theories, he was able to adapt himself to each of these writers successively without much hesitation. Colden, by comparison, was both more stolid and inflexible. Once his basic presuppositions were formalized, he did little to reevaluate or compare them with conflicting philosophical concepts.

From his student days, Colden had developed an acquaintance with Newtonian literature and various scientific and medical works. While he continued to request such volumes from England, he was less widely read in, and exhibited little curiosity toward, the philosophical and quasi-theological titles that Johnson subsequently brought to his attention. Since they did not appear to relate directly to the contents of his treatise, he may have felt justified in virtually ignoring them. Thus, Johnson's and Colden's reciprocal interrogations and revisions probably did little to clarify, much less resolve, the merits of their respective theories to each other's satisfaction.

There were some philosophical issues on which they did agree. Colden could easily enough accept Johnson's doctrine of a "Supreme Governor" of the natural world who governed by "fixed, stable rules of his own most wise establishments, called the Laws of Nature."[58] To Colden this certainly did not mean—as Johnson had intended—that this being should "account for everything; whereas matter whereof we can have no Idea can account for nothing." To make all activity dependent on an "Almighty Spirit" was a kind of "Spinozism" or pantheism that Colden regarded as inimical to both morality and religion. Johnson's earlier suggestion that there might be "other inferior created spirits" which shared in this activity did little to improve this scheme in Colden's mind.[59] Largely for such reasons, Colden soon lost patience with the Idealists, regarding them as adhering to some exaggerated opinions that were hardly justified by common sense.

In his unpublished "Introduction to the Study of Philosophy," Colden candidly expressed his attitude to the Idealist school when he warned his reader of the dangers and absurdities of its influence in the colonies: "You will hardly believe, I suppose, that he [Berkeley] was in earnest when he wrote these things. Yes he was, he wrote a large and learned treatise in proof of this doctrine: and he has obtained disciples, who have formed a sect. . . . called *Idealists*, which has extended to America, where you will find men of sense advocates for it."[60]

By contrast, it was in matters of religion and morality that Colden and Johnson apparently found some basis for agreement. The first of these issues arose in conjunction with the coming of the Great Awakening to New England. It prompted Johnson to write a letter on the "Sovereignty and Promises of God" which he supplied to Colden. The letter contained Johnson's response to what he regarded as the pernicious and contentious effects of this religious movement. As a former Congregational minister who had converted to Anglicanism, he viewed the entire episode with some contempt although at its inception, at least, he anticipated that it might lead to a certain religiosity that could only redound to the advantage of the Anglican Church.

Speaking as an Anglican divine as well as one who participated in the work of the Society for the Propagation of the Gospel, Johnson felt compelled to describe to another correspondent, the Archbishop of Canterbury, the "hideous outcries of a set of itinerant preachers" and the convulsions and involuntary agitation which were inflicted on their listeners. Yet, he concluded, "The Church has not as yet much suffered, but has in many instances gained by these strange commotions."[61]

While there were a few precedents along these lines in the colonies, the Great Awakening was unique in terms of the intensity and extent of its influence.[62] It was an inter-colonial, interdenominational religious revival that appealed particularly to those segments of the population that might have felt largely excluded from, or disenchanted with, conventional church policies and worship. Its beginnings can be traced to the appearance of George Whitfield in Boston in 1740. A clergyman of the Church of England, Whitfield had experienced a sudden and dramatic religious conversion while still at Oxford. He subsequently associated himself with the work of John and Charles Wesley and—after being denied the use of pulpits in the Anglican Church—turned to open air preaching. It was the latter approach that he transferred to the American colonies and that thereafter became a precedent for other evangelists, such as Gilbert Tennent, James Davenport, and Samuel Davies, as they extended the Great Awakening throughout the middle and southern colonies.

Much of the success of the movement was directly due to the style of preaching adopted by these men. Instead of giving sermons devoted to lofty moral or philosophical themes, Whitfield and his followers stressed the necessity for a spiritual regeneration or New Birth. Hearers were made vividly aware of their personal depravity and helplessness before a wrathful God, as a means of preparing them for a sudden conversion that was invariably accompanied by extreme emotionalism. In 1741, for example, an observer could report: "their main design in preaching seems not so much to inform men's judgments, as to terrify and affright their imaginations, and by awful words and frightful representations, to set the congregation into hideous shrieks and outcries."[63]

By 1743, the movement was on the decline in New England and, by 1745, it had lost its vitality elsewhere in the American colonies. Yet its repercussions continued to ferment an ongoing debate concerning the role of emotions in religion, freedom of will, the depravity of man, and the sovereignty of God. Johnson examined some of these issues both in his treatise and in several letters to Colden.

The full title of Johnson's treatise was *A Letter from Aristocles to Authades Concerning the Sovereignty and Promises of God* (1745). The form of the treatise itself may have been partly adopted from Berkeley's *Three Dialogues*. In it, Aristocles expressed Johnson's own views, while Authades represented those who subscribed to the Calvinistic notion of God's sovereignty and absolute election. For Johnson, the latter was contrary not only to Scripture but "to the nature and attributes of God, because it appears plainly inconsistent with the very notion of his being a moral governor of the world . . . and leaves no room for either virtue or vice, praise or blame, reward or punishment, properly speaking."[64]

Apparently, Johnson had never been quite comfortable with Calvinist theology for in his *Memoirs* he noted, "He had always been embarrassed with the rigid Calvinistic notions in which he had been bred."[65] His disenchantment with Calvinism was reinforced by the arrival of the Dummer library at Yale College. It contained not only the works of Newton, but also such authors as Milton, Locke, Norris, Barrow, and Tillotson. After becoming a convert to Berkeley's philosophy, Johnson described the views of the Calvinists as founded on "the empty cobwebs of scholastical metaphysics (vain philosophy, science falsely so-called) together with some few obscure texts, not rightly understood."[66] Rather than entertain "hard and unworthy thoughts of God," Johnson argued that we must represent God as "an universal lover of the souls which he hath made, and sincerely and solicitously desirous of their happiness." To this end, God even grants mankind "all the aid and assistance necessary thereto." Consequently, God should be viewed primarily as a benefactor who judges man as a self-determining agent and "according to his conduct in the use of the talent that was committed to his trust."

Colden was quite pleased with the contents of Johnson's treatise, for he regarded it as "so much according to my manner of thinking." He thought of it as most timely and added that if only others could inform themselves on this topic, "Artful men would not have it in their powers to put such constructions on God's revealed Will . . . which [sets] religion in opposition to reason and morality." He then noted:

These principles are the invention and imposture of Popery & can only be defended on popish principles. . . . The Papists must allwise have the advantage against men of such principles, in support of their most absurd doctrines & the defenders of these principles (without knowing it) lead the people back as fast as they can to Rome. It is for this reason that the Popish Emissaries have directions to join with & promote all the enthusiastic sects & principles among the Protestants. The truth of this has appeared from several remarkable & uncontested pieces of history.[67]

Samuel Johnson equally shared the view that the papacy was an insidious force behind the Great Awakening. He regarded the itinerant preachers as "Dupes to the Jesuits" and part of a scheme that had been hatching for some time.[68] As evidence, he pointed to the recent rebellion in Scotland (1745) and informed Colden that "the Seceeders (as the Methodists are called in Scotland) have many of them joined with the papist Jacobites."

Aside from pointing out the more sinister aspects of the Great Awakening, Johnson's main concern, as he reminded Colden, was simply to defend common sense. He himself could never accept the "barbarous and unnatural notions" of its representatives as being the teachings of God. Indeed, he concluded, "in truth I would rather, if it were possible, believe there is no God, than to believe in such a Being."

In his letters to Johnson, Colden revealed relatively little regarding his own concept of God, except to say that foreknowledge did not necessarily imply predestination. If some were befuddled by such distinctions, he opined, it was due to their lack of proper notions in such matters. For Colden, every intelligent being was necessarily free to make proper choices. Religion itself ought to be founded on reason, rather than on any authority, "since there are no means to distinguish between true and false religion when we are not allowed to use our understanding in forming our judgment."[69] Colden was quite aware—particularly in terms of his scientific aspirations—of the deleterious effects of certain authorities. His attitude, in any case, was representative of the progressive expectations of the Enlightenment and its emphasis on free inquiry aided by rational criteria.

The presupposition not only that reason and religion were compatible but that the former could "inform" the latter explains Colden's aversion to excess emotionalism or, in the parlance of that age, "enthusiasm" in religion. There is little doubt concerning Colden's attitude to this topic in one of his smaller treatises intended more for private than public consumption. Since this treatise was nominally written for medical purposes, Colden also considered some of the physiological and pathological factors relating to enthusiasm. He would interpret enthusiasm, for example, as a kind of "madness" that could develop from thinking too long on any one subject and seemed to believe that it was not unrelated to "some particular kinds of folly that studious men are subject to." Here, for example, he argued that emotions, such as fear, were often induced through an association of ideas formed in childhood and that these almost always persisted into adulthood. He pointed to the common apprehension of the dark, or of being in cemeteries, as due primarily to the childish belief that these were inhabited by ghosts. He wrote: "If these connections of ideas have continued during a great part of our life, perhaps our best reason may not be able entirely to break it."[70] In time, these might become so dominant that the individual could be entirely unaware of their pervasive influence and unable to ascertain either the cause or the effect of such ideas. Whenever operative, however, they were likely to produce those excessive emotions, for example, terror or joy, which "weak judgments" often attributed to supernatural causes; for Colden, however, they were more likely due to hysteria.[71]

Colden transposed his discussion on to another plane when he undertook to demonstrate the political repercussions of enthusiasm in history. He limited his examination primarily to the major events relating to the Stuart sovereigns in England, Charles I and II. Enthusiasm, in this context, refers to those social instincts that are generally shared by all men and can be transmitted, as it were, from one individual to the next or, as Colden expressed it, "propagated like contagion through a large assembly" by means of mutual empathy.

The real distinction between enthusiasm in an individual and enthusiasm viewed in terms of its societal aspects is that it is not as likely to become equally habitual to the latter. Colden blamed the enthusiasm that developed during the Interregnum between the reigns of Charles I and Charles II on a number of enthusiastic preachers. Through the means of constant "denunciations of damnations [and] vociferation" they were able, he claimed, to propagate enthusiasm throughout the entire nation. Much the same interpretation was extended to the aftermath of the "Popish Plot" in the reign of Charles II. On the basis of such episodes, Colden set down the more inclusive theme that "Many parts of the English history show that popular orators and writers are dangerous tools in a free government. . . . Reason has no force with enthusiasts till by some other means the frenzy is removed. Enthusiasm is a mere animal habit & brutes acquire something similar to it, tho' it cannot properly be called enthusiasm in them because they cannot attribute it to any supernatural influence. This is a bad effect of reason in men from a faulty use of it."[72] In summary, therefore, enthusiasm violated man's dignity as a rational being and could also disturb the balance and harmony of the social order. Interestingly, Colden's antipathy to such social disorder, political conflict, and revolution—while primarily drawn from historical examples—may have had some subsequent relevance to his stance toward the events presaging the American Revolution.

Colden's description of enthusiasm and even the examples he employs to illustrate its repercussions are drawn primarily from Locke's *Essay Concerning Human Understanding* (1690). Although Colden does not specifically cite this author, he makes use of Locke's theory of the association of ideas to suggest how certain ideas coalesce over a period of time by force or custom. Somewhat similar views can be found in a later work, David Hartley's *Observations on Man, His Frame, His Duty and His Expectations* (1749). In this context, Colden cites the example of musicians who play tunes in succession without using notes or having any awareness of how this is done.[73] Not only can an identical account be found in Locke but so, too, a similar explanation of the childish fear of darkness.

In June 1746, Johnson disclosed to Colden that he had prepared a "little piece of morals" which was then being printed, and he promised to send Colden a copy for his perusal; it arrived within a month.[74] Even if Colden had to inform Johnson sometime later that he had been unable to give it the attention it deserved, it is evident that he must have read at least part of Johnson's treatise on morals with considerable interest.[75] Not only would he subsequently submit his own treatise on morality to Johnson, but he even offered some suggestions for a planned second edition of Johnson's treatise.[76]

Philosophical issues relating to ethics remained an evident Enlightenment concern. In the colonies alone, during the early part of the eighteenth century, moral treatises were written not only by Colden and Johnson, but also by such individuals as Thomas Clap, Jonathan Edwards, James Logan, and Benjamin Rush. For Colden, at least, the intent may have been to deal with a topic that had not been included in his other philosophical writings. His natural philosophy was not directly relevant to such queries; indeed, it might even have left the reader wondering, as it probably did Johnson, if that philosophy could be expanded to include a meaningful discussion on the possibility of a moral universe.

The title of Johnson's first treatise on ethics was *A System of Morality* (1746). A revised and enlarged edition was subsequently published as *Elementa Philosophica*. This work was divided into two sections: *Noetica* and *Ethica*. The first dealt with Johnson's speculations on the mind, whereas the second part contained his views on moral behavior. Published by Franklin in 1753, this work became the first such textbook to be printed in America and was used by students at King's College in New York City during Johnson's tenure as its president.

The views expressed in this work can be regarded as complementary to those contained in Johnson's *Letter . . . Concerning the Sovereignty and Promises of God*. In the latter, Johnson had described God as a Being concerned with man's felicity and eventual salvation. To that end, man was given the freedom to exercise those talents with which he had been endowed by his Creator. Such a doctrine supplied Johnson with the means for reconciling the sovereignty of God—central to Calvinistic teachings—with conventional notions of moral responsibility. His intention, as he stated in his *System of Morality*, was "to endeavor to give a just notion of [morality], and the reasons on which it was founded, and to show its extent and importance, and what connection there is between it and Christianity."[77]

For Johnson, ethics are founded on the first principles of nature. Since the object of ethics is the "art of living happily," it is dependent on a knowledge of virtue, or, what is identical, truth and goodness. In society, morality is expressed in the principle of benevolence. This provides an "intuitive evidence of the fit, the fair, and decent in behavior" and acts to promote universal harmony and happiness. The function of reason in this scheme is "to make a right judgment how we ought to affect and act, and conduct ourselves to the best advantage of our happiness." In addition, reason is useful to discover truth and regulate the passions.[78]

Similar notions were expressed by many eighteenth-century writers on ethics. The pursuit of happiness is aptly confirmed in the number of works devoted to that topic and, of course, would later find political expression in the American Declaration of Independence.[79] Again, a belief in man's capacity for benevolence was meant to counteract psychological egotism as presented, for example, in the writings of Thomas Hobbes.[80] Rather than basing ethics on an authoritarian conception of the moral law, or on abstract principles, eighteenth-century writers such as Shaftesbury and Hutcheson argued that man is, by nature, a social animal.

Being part of the social order would suggest that the individual ought to bring his natural affections, such as self-love, into harmony with society. It is only by doing so that he can achieve the good of both. To do otherwise, of course, would only alienate the individual from society and render him miserable.[81] The moral sense, then, may be said to be informed by, and designed to conform to, enlightened self-interest. In his *System of Moral Philosophy*, for example, Francis Hutcheson asserted that from reason and reflection we can know that God intended universal happiness; the same should equally be our own intention. Actions that serve the most general good are not only approved by the moral faculty, but also give "the noblest enjoyment." Ultimately, it is the "calm, stable, goodwill to all" that becomes the highest expression of moral behavior.[82]

Colden's own treatise on ethics, *Of the First Principles of Morality or of the Actions of Intelligent Beings* (n.d.), incorporated similar views. Like Johnson's treatise, it testifies to the general vogue of these ideas by the mid-eighteenth century and their pervasive influence on ethical theorists. While

Colden does not refer to any particular authors in this treatise, it is known, of course, that he did correspond with Johnson on ethics and had received a copy of the latter's *System of Morality*. It is difficult to ascertain to what degree this may have guided Colden in forming his own theories in ethics, but it must have exerted some influence.[83] Colden's treatise, by comparison, is less a philosophical treatment of ethics than a series of related observations on the theme of moral behavior. It extends and refines some of the conceptions that Colden had initially proposed in his *Explications*, and is consistent with the views expressed in the section on the "Intelligent Being" that he appended to his *Principles*.

Colden begins his treatise, in a somewhat scholastic manner, with certain definitions, such as the term "morality" which, he claims, is derived from the Latin *mores* and signifies manners. Since this involves activity, ethics may be said to be a science for "Action in general is the subject of all knowledge." Now, it is evident that ethics only deals with certain kinds of activity, that is, of those beings that are self-determining or free agents. That such beings do exist can be known from "ideas or perceptions which arise from their impressions."

While this statement is certainly consistent with Colden's general epistemology, he seems to imply that such perceptions are not only derived from other active beings, but also from our own existence or, from the "power of determining or altering our own actions of ourselves without the force or compulsion of any thing external to it."[84] Thus, the individual's own apperceptions provide the best demonstration of the capacity for self-determination. Once the ego or self has realized the dimensions of this process, it properly assigns or extends the same qualitative mode to all other entities within its class; in short, the self becomes aware of the status of other such existing "Intelligent Beings." This is achieved by comparing "our own actions with those of other men [by which] we are convinced that they in like manner must have perception & knowledge & that they regulate their own activities in the same manner that we ourselves do."[85]

Only intelligent beings can be the subject of ethics, since they alone are both self-determined and conscious of their own and others actions. Here, again, Colden introduces another distinction: when the term "intelligent being" is generally employed, it refers to spirits; when applied to mankind, it is known as soul or mind. Colden is careful to give not only this distinction, but also the more fundamental one between intelligence and matter by rejecting the contention that one is reducible to the other. Even if matter, *per se*, is unknowable, we can still know something of its qualities—such as extension and figure—from the ideas we form of it. This is, of course, reminiscent of the Lockean doctrine of ideas, although Locke suggested that there was nothing contradictory in the supposition that God could add to matter the power of thought.[86]

Such ideas, Colden proposed, are due to a "complication or combination of the actions of resisting & moving" in matter. To combine, compare, and relate these ideas is the inherent function of mind. This, too, is related to its reasoning faculty and becomes productive of knowledge.[87] Yet something more is involved: not only does the mind establish or procure knowledge, but it also is concerned with the ends or purposes of such information. Colden writes:

As the view of purpose in all actions or operations of the mind is the motive or cause by which the mind is set to work, by which likewise its actions are directed or determined, as to this or that manner of acting or thinking, the actions of the mind are determined & altered by Final Causes, or the end or purpose for which it acts or thinks. Here is the essential difference between the action of Matter & Spirit.[88]

The mind, therefore, is not simply a passive recipient of sense information; it both organizes and directs the information obtained from such sources to certain ends. Precisely how this is done, Colden does not say: he confesses himself ignorant on such issues. He does, however, go on to make the more inclusive comment that all operations of the mind involve some view or purpose, and that this is "the first principle or final cause of all the actions of the mind in general." From self-introspection, together with observations of what usually motivates others, Colden asserts that the first principle consists in the "avoiding of pain or the procuring of pleasure." He added: "This is something essential to all the actions of the Mind and distinguishes them from the actions of Matter."[89]

Distinctions are again in order as Colden decides that pleasure can be divided into two categories: intellectual and sensual. While the former are altogether more "numerous, exquisite and lasting" than the latter, he does not deny the importance of sensual pleasures. They are innate and necessary for the preservation of life, for the continuation of the species, and as a guide to obtain the comforts of life. Such pleasures, when combined with knowledge (an intellectual pleasure), provide the proper means for procuring happiness.

Morality, then, is defined as the "Art & Science of living so as to be happy." Happiness, in turn, consists in enjoying the greatest amount of pleasure with the least measure of pain.[90] Of course, Colden recognizes this as an ideal state, for the general circumstances in which men find themselves will hardly permit them to regulate their lives at all times to such ends. There are, as Colden termed it, "accidents of fortune" which cannot be avoided, and over which it may not be possible to exercise any direct control. Yet the manner in which they are received directly depends on the individual and his ability to remain resolute enough to bear "external actions." What is recommended, in effect, is a kind of Stoic indifference or inner fortitude for "it depends much on himself whether [the actions of the mind] be calm & regular or violent & disorderly."[91]

What is equally important, in the view of this moralist, is to achieve a balance between the various pleasures. Elsewhere, for example, Colden mentions some of the adverse effects of too much study; here, he warns against allowing any one pleasure to dominate the others. The exclusive pursuit of any one pleasure—such as glory or riches—can not only create anxieties and cares for the individual, but render him incapable of enjoying that pleasure of benevolence which "Moral men feel in doing good to mankind in general or to the Society in which they live or to particular persons."[92]

The ability to achieve this rather encompassing view, so that the individual can calculate what actions benefit others as well as himself, seems to depend directly on the amount of knowledge that he possesses. Ultimately, then, Colden returns to the intellectual pleasures as being not only more refined but more useful than the sensual pleasures. While it might be reiterated that, for Colden, a man must have a full share of both the intellectual and the sensual pleasures, it remains the function of knowledge to guide and direct such pleasures—particularly those that pertain to the intellectual—to certain ends.

Given the premise of a connection between knowledge and happiness, Colden is able to introduce certain further distinctions regarding the various kinds of knowledge within the compass of man's mind. These include

Knowledge of the relations between God (the Infinite Intelligent Being or Mind of the Universe) & his creatures, as he is the Supreme Governor of them. Next, the knowledge of ourselves or of Mankind in general, & this knowledge is of great use to the purpose of procuring happiness, as men are social creatures & thereby contribute to or obstruct the happiness of each other. And, lastly, the knowledge of those things that are necessary for life, or make it more comfortable and pleasant, or are hurtful to life, or render it painful & uneasy.[93]

Knowledge of the first of these, or the relations that pertain to God and His creatures, is contained in natural religion, which is the "Will of God as far as it can be discovered by Reason." It presupposes that God, an infinitely wise and benevolent Being, desires the happiness of his creatures and has given them the sense of pleasure (intellectual and sensual) for this purpose.[94] These permit man to procure happiness as long as such pleasures are subservient to reason—an evident Enlightenment theme.

When reason is unaccompanied by reflection, it is commonly called either "instinct" or "habit" and explains why animals as well as man produce certain actions without conscious volition or design. When put into this context, it suggests that the mind is not always aware of its various perceptions. It may be said, therefore, to operate on two levels: the conscious, when it is concerned with knowing and thinking, and the subconscious, when it directs and guides the operations of the body toward the avoidance of pain and the gratification of pleasure. That these two activities are not completely autonomous is indicated when Colden appends the warning that certain habits can become "vicious" if they dominate other pleasures or become ends in themselves. For this reason, it is necessary that the individual periodically "reflect" on his habits to insure that they do not become prejudicial to his general behavior.

By supplying a unity within the animal system, the Intelligent Being or, more properly, the soul, acts as a capstone of that system. Although matter and intelligence are different "Genera of Beings," the Intelligent Being is dependent on the activity of matter for perception and, in turn, excites motion or resistance "in the parts of that system of which it constitutes the soul or mind." Another distinction between matter and the Intelligent Being is that while matter can be thought of as being divisible and having shape or figure, no such conception can be associated with the Intelligent Being. Yet insofar as each soul or mind is distinct, if not unique, there must be a plurality of intelligent beings. Colden attempts to meet this difficulty by proposing that our conceptions of the Intelligent Being must be analogous to our conceptions of space.[95]

Space, of itself, has neither shape, figure, limits, nor bounds; but it does contain, and can be contained within, separate material entities. In much the same manner, the idea of intelligence, *per se*, can be combined with that of matter to form the idea of separate and distinct intelligent beings. For Colden, this problem initially arose because the Intelligent Being, in his view, could not be regarded as quantifiable. It may be said, however, that the Intelligent Being is individualized through its conjunction with matter in much the same way, for example, that matter is actualized by Form in Aristotelian philosophy. It is, then, only by the combination of these two substances—matter and intelligence—that all the numerous systems in the universe are made possible. Colden's cosmology was such that he could now write:

On attentive consideration we shall discover, I think, that the whole universe consists of a collection of systems from the minutest animal or vegetable to the solar system. And if our means of knowledge were sufficient, it is probable we should discover that everything so far as it is properly distinguishable from any other, forms a peculiar system. That the lesser systems are all part of the greater & that this composition goes on infinitely.[96]

In this vast scheme, there must be some point or center that unifies this infinite number of systems and supplies "that connection between its parts as to form a regular or permanent being." Although it may not be possible for man to know the point [*terminus ad quem*] toward which all such systems tend, their perfect harmony, proportion, and fitness are evident. It is here that Colden introduces the argument from design as sufficient proof of intelligence, knowledge and wisdom which is, he adds, "discovered in the universe and in every part of it."[97]

This, of course, raises the issue of the relationship of the Intelligent Being, as a cosmic entity, to that universe. Colden had previously limited himself largely to discussing the manifestation and activity of intelligence in particular animal systems. In order to expand on this parallel, he now proposed that as intelligence or mind perceives the actions of matter in finite systems so, too, does the infinite Intelligent Being perceive all actions within the infinite systems of the universe.[98] Again, in the same way that intelligence may be said to guide or direct a particular material system, it can also be said that the infinite Intelligent Being directs the material systems of the universe, for it excites "such actions as serve to the preservation & well being of the universe and every part of it."[99]

There is an important proviso, however, that circumscribes the meaning of this passage. In spite of Colden's insistence that the Intelligent Being exercises guardianship over the universe, it must do so without coming into opposition to matter. Having already restricted the role of the Intelligent Being by asserting that it does not, strictly speaking, "cause" the activity of matter, Colden adds the further constraint that it must always act in harmony with matter. Such preordained harmony, if anything, seems to share some of the precepts found in Leibnitz's *Monodology*. If the universe required constant corrections or "amendments," Colden avers, that would then be inconsistent with its original design.

With a view to his *Principles*, perhaps, Colden does allow that there may be certain small "corrections" that the Intelligent Being is permitted, indeed required, to make. Such, for example, is the case when either the moving or resisting powers are equal, or when the direction of the moving power has to be determined. Under these conditions, the Intelligent Being intervenes to resolve this dilemma and give direction to these material principles. These minor exceptions can hardly mitigate the very circumscribed role to which the Intelligent Being is otherwise relegated, and almost suggest that its periodic interventions are introduced, almost as a *deus ex machina*, to resolve some of the conundrums implicit in the *Principles*. This conception of the Intelligent Being—at least to the degree that it is consonant with some of the theological attributes of God—is quite at variance, for example, with Newton's attitude toward the "Divine Being." For the latter, God continually sustained and directly upheld His creation.

It remains doubtful, however, that Colden accepted this doctrine of creation. In his treatise on ethics, he appears to accept a belief in the eternality of the universe, primarily on the philosophical assumption that actuality is preferable to potentiality. Thus, a universe that exhibits wisdom and design for an infinite time is a more perfect example of the work of the Intelligent Being than one that does so merely from some point in time.[100] The same argument would require that matter is coeternal with the Intelligent Being—a point that Colden admits in his *Principles* and one, incidentally, that was also expressed by Locke.[101] Such a doctrine was condemned by the early

Church as being inimical to the notion of Biblical Creation, and certainly appeared equally suspect to most of his contemporaries—Samuel Johnson, of course, is a case in point. While it confirms Colden's philosophical materialism, he may have thought it defensible in regard to his distinction between the truths of revelation and the truths of reason. In one of his later treatises, Colden contends, "Philosophy is the object of reason" and goes on to suggest that "The Divine and the Philosopher may each of them pursue their several objects without interfering with each other or doing any injury to each other. This was the practice of both the clergy and the philosopher in ancient times."[102]

It is, of course, quite legitimate to disagree with Colden's view, for it represents a somewhat overcompartmentalized scheme of intellectual investigation. Aside from the latitudinarian attitude toward the content of religious dogma, Colden's statement regarding the separate spheres of religion and philosophy is quite consistent with those distinctions and divisions that would prevent any one activity or mode of knowledge from usurping any other. It is this intellectual schematic, for example, that was the basis for his *Principles.* While it may have been one method of seeking intellectual clarity in his natural philosophy, it would appear that here, at least, it was intended to protect the mutual claims of religious teachings and those of free rational inquiry. In this way, then, neither can be said to preempt the other or become, in effect, the "touchstone" of the other.

Colden's "liberty of philosophizing" may have been intended largely as a means of defending himself against the charge of atheism, but his discussion of the Intelligent Being was also consonant with the deism of the eighteenth century, with its view of God derived primarily from natural philosophy, rather than exclusively based on divine revelation. Again, the proviso that moral virtue is in proportion to knowledge induced Colden to adopt the Socratic thesis—which also had some relevance to the period—that "vice and immorality must proceed from ignorance & error & that a vicious course of life is the strongest proof of its folly."[103]

While Colden's materialistic stance may have put him into a distinct minority in the American colonies, he would undoubtedly have found some company among English writers who expressed similar views. In his *Inquiry into Human Understanding*, for example, David Hume suggested that matter had certain powers that produced effects, while John Toland, in his *Letters to Serena* (1704), proposed that action was essential to matter.[104] Someone like Governor William Popple would even contend that Colden had not gone far enough in his doctrine of matter. He had high praise for Colden's philosophy and informed him that "the eternity of the universe or rather the non-Creation of it is no absurd notion."[105] Quite frankly, he saw no reason why Colden should introduce an Intelligent Being, since it might well be that our ignorance of matter and all its properties accounted for the reliance on an Intelligent Agent. In effect, then, perfect knowledge of the operations of matter might make the role of intelligence, *per se*, largely irrelevant. For Popple, matter could act without intelligence or even, if necessary, be defined as including intelligence as one of its essential properties. In a series of suggestive comments, he could tell Colden at one point, "Why then exclude Thought, Mind, Intelligence from being a general property of matter because it is not in every part of matter[?]"[106]

Popple was perhaps not so much trying to disprove the existence of an Intelligent Being as to argue that the only knowledge man could have was of material, sensible objects. To introduce the Intelligent Being into philosophical discourse was, for him, quite inappropriate in terms of the available evidence. He noted: "the mind of man acts by material organs and not by any power but what it has in itself." Again, "Matter . . . without any extraordinary invention of a Creator brought forth every thing by its own powers." Consequently, he concluded, "to assume and give God an action, which he never discovered in the reason of man, nor expressly revealed in his works, from where man deduces it, is a presumption which, I confess, I think too great for man."[107]

Colden, in turn, would probably contend that there was some minimal evidence of the actions of an Intelligent Being, and he refused to reduce the operations of the universe or that of the mind to strict material causation. The Intelligent Being was "knowable" in the same way as the actions of those material principles that were, for Popple, the beginning and end of man's limited knowledge.

Another Englishman, Joseph Priestley—a migrant to the United States late in the eighteenth century—would cite somewhat similar arguments to those found in Popple. In his *Disquisitions Relating to Matter and Spirit* (1782), Priestley defined matter as "a substance possessed of the property of extension, and of powers of attraction or repulsion," and went on to query the necessity for two substances in man (material and mental) that had nothing in common.[108] Thus, the primary object of the treatise was to show that the mind was not merely interrelated or even dependent on the body, but that "the human mind is nothing more than a modification of [the body]." After giving extensive consideration to the arguments that would support such a proposition, Priestly was led to conclude:

Man is possessed of the powers of *sensation* or *perception*, and thought. But if, without giving the reins to our imagination, we suffer ourselves to be guided in our inquiries by the simple rules of philosophizing . . . we must necessarily conclude, as it appears to me, that these powers also may belong to the same substance, that has also the properties of attraction, repulsion, and extension, which I, as well as others, call by the name of *matter*.[109]

Both Colden and Priestley evidently shared the opinion that matter is essentially power, force, or activity. While Priestley's conceptions may appear more "modern," and his use of the term was more consistent, he did have the advantage of reading certain authors that apparently remained unknown to Colden. Whether a fuller acquaintance with such authors would have, in time, altered Colden's philosophical position remains a moot point. It would appear, too, that both men combined a philosophical materialism with a belief in God.[110] It is not certain that that would include for Colden, as it did for Priestley, an acceptance of Divine Revelation, since Colden did not positively declare himself on this topic.[111] As he once noted, it was sufficient for a philosopher to "pretend" to some religion.

The fact that Colden did not intend to incorporate Popple's suggestions in any subsequent edition of the *Principles* suggests that his own philosophical position on this topic was more muted, or approximately situated perhaps between the positions of Popple and Johnson. Basically, Colden remained a dualist. He refused to go to the extent of assigning all activity in nature to matter or, alternatively, to mind or intelligence. In his natural philosophy, therefore, he reserved a place for both activities as the prerogative of distinct substances. Whether Colden originally intended to introduce a discussion on the Intelligent Being into that philosophy is not certain. If not, then the Idealists must be credited for carrying on a dialogue with Colden on the metaphysical implications of his treatise. Even if he remained too intellectually obstinate to alter the original structure, he did make certain qualifications or additions that may have been designed to satisfy the approbation of his readers and, more particularly, to allay any suspicions of an implicit atheism regarding its contents.

It must be recognized that Colden's main intellectual concerns had always been to analyze and describe the material operations of the physical universe. When it came to such broader philosophical questions as mind, ideas, design, personality, consciousness, liberty, and so on, he was neither as self-assured nor as fully committed to exploring these topics. This perhaps explains why his statements on such issues tend to be somewhat derivative, perhaps even commonplace. His discussion on the Intelligent Being certainly lacks the conviction and intensity of argument that marks the expansive treatment he gives to other aspects of his natural philosophy. It need hardly be repeated here that, within that philosophy, the Intelligent Being has a severely restricted role and is seemingly devoid of any personal dimension. He neither directly creates nor upholds the universe. Thus, His singular task is to assure its harmonious and balanced operation and this became, for Colden, the testament of His existence and activity.

NOTES

1. Vincent Buranelli, "Colonial Philosophy," *William and Mary Quarterly*, 16 (1959), 347.
2. Ibid., 349.

3. Merle Curti, *The Growth of American Thought* (New York, 1969), 91.

4. Louis L. Tucker, *Puritan Protagonist: President Thomas Clap of Yale College* (Chapel Hill, N.C. 1962), 99.

5. Max Savelle, *Seeds of Liberty: The Genesis of the American Mind* (Seattle, Wash., 1965), 172.

6. Louis L. Gitin, "Cadwallader Colden as Scientist and Philosopher," *New York History*, 16 (1935), 175.

7. Theodore Hornberger, "Samuel Johnson of Yale and King's College," *The New England Quarterly*, 8 (1935), 387. Johnson was not the only Idealist in eighteenth-century America, but he was the only individual to be directly converted to that philosophy by Berkeley's appearance in the colonies. Graham P. Conroy, "Berkeley and Education in America," *Journal of the History of Ideas*, 21 (1960), 215.

8. Samuel Johnson to Cadwallader Colden, November 21, 1743, *Colden Papers*, III, 40.

9. Samuel Johnson to Cadwallader Colden, July 24, 1746, *Colden Papers*, III, 228.

10. Cadwallader Colden to Samuel Johnson, December 20, 1758, in Herbert and Carol Schneider, eds., *Samuel Johnson, President of King's College: His Career and Writings*, 4 Vols. (New York, 1927–1929), II, 299.

11. Cadwallader Colden to Samuel Johnson, March 26, 1744, in Schneider and Schneider, II, 287.

12. Samuel Johnson to Cadwallader Colden, April 18, 1744, in Schneider and Schneider, II, 289.

13. Cadwallader Colden to Samuel Johnson, November 19, 1746, *Colden Papers*, III, 283.

14. Samuel Johnson to Cadwallader Colden, January 12, 1746/7, *Colden Papers*, III, 331.

15. W.W. Rouse Ball, *A Short Account of the History of Mathematics* (New York, 1960), 343.

16. Roy N. Lokken, "Discussion on Newton's Infinitesimals in Eighteenth-Century Anglo-America," *Historia Mathematica*, 7 (1980), 144.

17. Carl B. Boyer, *The History of the Calculus and Its Conceptual Development* (New York, 1959), 202.

18. Boyer, 213; Elizabeth B. Gasking, *Investigations into Generation, 1651–1838* (Baltimore, 1967), 46.

19. Ball, 386.

20. Cadwallader Colden to Samuel Johnson, March 26, 1744, in Schneider and Schneider, II, 287.

21. Benjamin Franklin to Cadwallader Colden, October 25, 1744, *Colden Papers*, III, 77.

22. John Rutherfurd to Cadwallader Colden, January 10, 1743, *Colden Papers*, III, 1.

23. John Rutherfurd to Cadwallader Colden, March 2, 1742/3, *Colden Papers*, III, 6–7.

24. Ibid., 7.

25. John Rutherfurd to Cadwallader Colden, April 19, 1743, *Colden Papers*, III, 21.

26. Samuel Johnson to Cadwallader Colden, October 20, 1744, *Colden Papers*, III, 76.

27. Samuel Johnson to Cadwallader Colden, June 26, 1745, *Colden Papers*, III, 120.

28. Cadwallader Colden to Samuel Johnson, September 3, 1745, *Colden Papers*, III, 146.

29. Samuel Johnson to Cadwallader Colden, July 10, 1745, *Colden Papers*, III, 127.

30. Cadwallader Colden to Samuel Johnson, September 3, 1745, *Colden Papers*, III, 147.

31. Samuel Johnson to Cadwallader Colden, October 5, 1745, *Colden Papers*, III, 161–162.

32. Cadwallader Colden to Samuel Johnson, September 3, 1745, *Colden Papers*, III, 147.

33. "[W]e may have ideas of the actions or operations of intelligence, as we have of the actions of matter, or as we have of motion or resistance." *Principles*, section 11, 162.

34. Samuel Johnson to Cadwallader Colden, October 5, 1745, *Colden Papers*, III, 162.

35. Hornberger, 393.

36. Samuel Johnson to Cadwallader Colden, April 18, 1744, in Schneider and Schneider, II, 288.

37. Cadwallader Colden' to Samuel Johnson, June 2, 1746, *Colden Papers*, III, 212; Cadwallader Colden to Samuel Johnson, April 12, 1746, *Colden Papers*, III. 205.

38. Cadwallader Colden to Samuel Johnson, April 12, 1746, *Colden Papers*, III, 204.

39. Ibid.

40. Samuel Johnson to Cadwallader Colden, April 22, 1746, *Colden Papers*, III, 207.

41. Ibid.

42. Cadwallader Colden to Samuel Johnson, June 2, 1746, *Colden Papers*, III, 212.

43. Samuel Johnson to Cadwallader Colden, October 5, 1745, *Colden Papers*, III, 163.

44. Hornsberger, 394.

45. Samuel Johnson to Cadwallader Colden, June 23, 1746, in Schneider and Schneider, II, 291.

46. Samuel Johnson to Cadwallader Colden, October 31, 1746, *Gratz Collection*, Historical Society of Pennsylvania.

47. Samuel Johnson to Cadwallader Colden, January 12, 1746/7, *Colden Papers*, III, 331.

48. Samuel Johnson to Cadwallader Colden, October 31, 1746, *Gratz Collection*, Historical Society of Pennsylvania.

49. Cadwallader Colden to Samuel Johnson, November 19, 1746, *Colden Papers*, III, 282. In the same letter, Colden asserted: "I am persuaded that whatever reception this piece may have in my life time, the docrine I deliver will be received when I am dead & rotten & perhaps forgot."

50. Cadwallader Colden to Samuel Johnson, December 20, 1752, in Schneider and Schneider, II, 299.

51. Samuel Johnson to Cadwallader Colden, February 19, 1753, in ibid., II, 302.

52. Samuel Johnson to Cadwallader Colden, February 19, 1755, in ibid., II, 302.

53. Ibid., 303.

54. Cadwallader Colden, *Principles*, section 5, 158.

55. Ibid., section 14, 163.

56. Samuel Johnson to Cadwallader Colden, February 19, 1753, in Schneider and Schneider, II, 303.

57. Thomas Clap to Cadwallader Colden, July 1, 1755, *Gratz Collection*, Historical Society of Pennsylvania.

58. Samuel Johnson to Cadwallader Colden, April 15, 1747, *Colden Papers*, III, 374.

59. Samuel Johnson to Cadwallader Colden, June 6, 1747, *Colden Papers*, III, 399.

60. Cadwallader Colden, "An Introduction to the Study of Philosophy, wrote in America for the use of a young Gentleman," Colden MSS, New-York Historical Society, section III.

61. The letter was written in September 1741. Quoted in Claude E. Newlin, *Philosophy and Religion in Colonial America* (New York, 1961), 103.

62. Earlier developments that contributed to the Great Awakening are found in the appearance of Theodore Frelinghuysen in New Jersey during the 1720s and Jonathan Edwards in New England in the 1730s.

63. Newlin, 78.

64. Ibid.

65. Quoted in Schneider and Schneider, II, 169.

66. Quoted in Newlin, 110.

67. Cadwallader Colden to Samuel Johnson, April 12, 1746, *Colden Papers*, III, 202.

68. Samuel Johnson to Cadwallader Colden, April 22, 1746, *Colden Papers*, III, 205.

69. Cadwallader Colden to Samuel Johnson, January 27, 1747, Schneider and Schneider, II, 293.

70. Cadwallader Colden, "The Reading of an elaborate Treatise on the Eye by the learned & ingenious Dr. Porterfield was the occasion of the following Reflections," Colden MSS, New-York Historical Society, 22.

71. Ibid. Colden may have derived some of his views on the claims and dangers of enthusiasm from Shaftesbury's "Letter on Enthusiasm," in which the notion that enthusiasm was related to any supernatural influence was rejected and, again, the argument was made that enthusiasm might directly benefit the Church of Rome. Leslie Stephen, *History of English Thought in the Eighteenth Century* (New York, 1962), 2 Vols., II, ix, 23.

72. Colden, "Treatise on the Eye," 23, 24.

73. Ibid., 22.

74. Samuel Johnson to Cadwallader Colden, June 23, 1746, in Schneider and Schneider, II, 292; Samuel Johnson to Cadwallader Colden, July 24, 1746, *Colden Papers*, III, 228.

75. Cadwallader Colden to Samuel Johnson, January 27 1746/7, in Schneider and Schneider, II 293.

76. Ibid., 294. Samuel Johnson to Cadwallader Colden, April 15, 1747, *Colden Papers*, III, 372.

77. Quoted in Newlin, 111.

78. Quoted in ibid., 117.

79. The titles of many such books are recounted in Paul Hazard, *European Thought in the Eighteenth Century* (Cleveland, Ohio, 1954), 14.

80. E.M. Albert, T.C. Denise, and S.P. Paterfreund, eds., *Great Traditions in Ethics* (New York, 1953), 142.

81. Harald Höffding, *A History of Modern Philosophy* (New York, 1955), 2 Vols., I, 394; L.A. Selby-Bigge, ed., *British Moralists* (New York, 1965), 2 Vols., I, 64–65.

82. Francis Hutcheson, *A System of Moral Philosophy* (London, 1755), 69.

83. That Colden's treatise was written sometime during the 1740s and most likely after 1745 is suggested by its inclusion with other pieces of this period, such as "Reflexions . . . on Tar Water" and "Fluxions," in a "Copy Book" that Colden intended to bequeath to his children. It might be added that Johnson was "very much pleased" with the treatise. Samuel Johnson to Cadwallader Colden, April 15, 1747, *Colden Papers*, III, 372.

84. Cadwallader Colden, "Of the First Principles of Morality or of the Actions of Intelligent Beings," 126: hereafter cited as "Principles of Morality." The treatise is in the possession of the Rosenbach Museum and Library (Philadelphia).

85. Ibid.

86. John W. Yolton, *Thinking Matter* (Minneapolis, 1983), 4.

87. "Principles of Morality," 129.

88. Ibid., 128.

89. Ibid., 130.

90. This doctrine, together with the distinction between intellectual and sensual pleasures, can be found in Epicurean philosophy. Henry Sidgwick, *Outlines of the History of Ethics for English Readers* (London, 1960), 85.

91. Ibid., 131.

92. "Principles of Morality," 132.

93. Ibid., 133.

94. For Colden, a religious or virtuous life "must be the life of the greatest pleasure." Consequently, he could not fathom any religion that denied "most if not all the pleasures of life." Such a notion could only be derived from a false opinion of God, for "he has so ordered the constitution of his creatures that the same means which tend to their eternal happiness likewise serve to make them happy in this life." Ibid., 135.

95. Ibid., 137–138. "Since the effects of intelligence are discovered everywhere, it may be concluded that some intelligent being is universally present: for, as you will observe, nothing can act where it is not . . . It has most generally obtained the name of *Nature*, sometimes that of universal Mind or of Anima & some occasions it is called Instinct." Cadwallader Colden to Dr. William Porterfield, May 19 1760, Colden MSS, New-York Historical Society.

96. "Principles of Morality," 145.

97. Ibid., 146.

98. Ibid., 145. Colden may have derived this notion from Newton's conception of space as the sensorium of God. Isaac Newton, *OPTICKS, or a Treatise on the Reflections, Refractions, Inflections and Colours of Light.* 4th edition (New York, 1952), query 28.

99. "Principles of Morality," 146.

100. "[I]t cannot from reason be discovered why the infinitely intelligent being should not have produced the universe from eternity." Ibid., p. 147.

101. Colden, "Principles of Action in Matter," section 16, 165.

102. Colden, "Treatise on the Eye," 3, 31.

103. "Principles of Morality," 134.

104. Yolton, 100–101.

105. Governor William Popple to Cadwallader Colden, December 20, 1762, *Colden Papers*, VI, 203.

106. Ibid., 206.

107. Ibid., 207.

108. Joseph Priestley, *Disquisitions Relating to Matter and Spirit* (Birmingham, 1782), 2 Vols., I, "Preface," ii–iii.

109. Ibid., 45.

110. Priestley stated: "I hope that *materialism* will be . . . perfectly consonant . . . to the scheme of revelation." Ibid., xxiii. Even Popple asserted, "I hope I shall not be esteemed an Atheist." William Popple to Cadwallader Colden, December 20, 1762, *Colden Papers*, VI, 207. Colden's own belief in God can only be culled from his philosophical utterances, but there is no evidence that would controvert such a belief.

111. Stephen, in his *History of English Thought* (I, 64), represents Priestley as a "theological materialist" and as a vigorous believer in a "miraculous revelation."

Chapter 5

AN AMERICAN *PHILOSOPHE*

Le philosophe est donc un honnête homme qui agit en tout par raison, & qui joint à un esprit de réflexion & de justesse les moeurs & les qualités sociables.[1]

To apply the term *philosophe* to a colonial scientist and philosopher, such as Cadwallader Colden, may at first seem somewhat inappropriate. The *philosophe* movement is historically relevant to Europe, primarily France, where it received its form and expression through the efforts of those men who wished to reform and enlighten their society by popularizing certain ideas and attitudes. Through such means, they also hoped to remove or lessen remnants of ignorance, oppression, and excessive authority by holding them up to constant ridicule and criticism.

While no similar coterie of men, comparable literature, or agenda was directly relevant to the American colonies, *philosophe* views were apt to find expression in the broader context of the Enlightenment that was shared within the trans-Atlantic community of the eighteenth century. This would be particularly the case with those colonists who, through birth, background, or education, continued to maintain their intellectual and cultural connections to the Old World. Moreover, the urban centers that represented the Enlightenment for the American colonies were generally found in London or Edinburgh, rather than in Paris or, more notably, in the fashionable French salons that attracted the *illuminati* of that age. Yet it was precisely in those kinds of settings that someone like Benjamin Franklin, while in

France, would be regarded as an *exemplar* of that "honnête homme" promoted by the *philosophes.*

A comparable description of a *philosophe,* as supplied by the French Academy, for example, was someone who was a student of the sciences, pursued a "quiet life," and exercised free thought (*libertinage d'esprit*) at some distance from the constraints or obligations of civil life.[2] In both his scientific and philosophical work, Colden gave expression to several of the themes that would have been applauded by the *philosophes*—including the emphasis on rational precepts, the rejection of authority or received opinion, the belief in knowledge as a form of virtue, the antipathy toward excess emotionalism or enthusiasm, the necessity for improvement of society, and so forth.

It would be primarily in his smaller treatises and some occasional, almost ad hoc, writings that Colden more directly assumed the role of a *littérateur,* wherein he attempted to instruct, guide, or advise his reader. These less extensive, more pointed productions aptly reflect Colden's insights, prejudices, and attitudes on life, knowledge, history, religion, and social behavior. It is here, then, that one can view something more of the man and his personal dimension, rather than in those abstruse speculations that generally served as his primary intellectual pursuit; such informal writings also give expression to that broader "esprit de réflexion" noted by the *philosophes.*

Two such treatises that were primarily written as guides or abbreviated manuals containing personal advice were Colden's "Essay on the Art of Right Living" and, "An Introduction to the Study of Philosophy wrote in America for a Young Gentleman." The latter was written for his grandson, Peter DeLancey, and it is probable that the "Essay" was intended for a similar purpose. In both instances, Colden may have been motivated to offer some meaningful insights and personal observations garnered from his readings, largely of English writers, and such experience as he had gained in a public capacity over a long lifetime.

The "Essay" concerns the topic of education in its broadest sense. For a man who was so keenly devoted to scientific pursuits and who desired, above all, to be remembered for his attempts to improve Newtonian physics, Colden provided an unusual critique of the scientific aspirations of the age. In the opening paragraph of the "Essay," for example, he advised his reader, "The present and last age seems to have very much neglected the study of morality, or the conduct of human life while they have been extremely industrious in improving the sciences as if it were more consequence to us to understand astronomy or geometry than to know how to live happily."[3]

There were, of course, no lack of ethical guides in the eighteenth century, but what evidently concerned Colden was something less abstract or theoretical and something more practical in scope and emphasis. This became, as it were, a matter of instructing the whole man, of acquainting him with the arts as well as the sciences, so that education would best serve both social and intellectual goals.[4] Colden's statement suggests that he remained uneasy with the emphasis on scientific progress and the advance of knowl-edge without some corresponding attention to man's ethical behavior. His concern was to restore a balance so as to permit man to live happily by providing those rules or guides that were most relevant to the conduct or the art of life. The quest for happiness, as already noted, was an enduring theme of eighteenth-century literature and, in this relatively short treatise, Colden attempted to examine the issue by evaluating the role of educational precepts and their relevance to society.

Unlike that notable social critic, Jean-Jacques Rousseau, however, Colden was not really concerned with making education more "natural," that is, removing some of the constraints and artificiality of civilization, but rather with the means whereby man can best act to fulfill his part in society. Col-den's concept of an educated individual was apparently one who had both knowledge and social graces and one able to converse and express himself in public. Such a person would avoid any pretense to impress or impose on others the merits of his knowledge, for example, but realize that true esteem comes not only from being learned, but from being of good reputation or character.

One might be tempted to suggest that Colden's "Essay" might just as easily have been subtitled, "Advice to a young gentleman." To a certain degree, Colden was disposed to provide a guide to deportment in society, which was, he claimed, the distinguishing mark of a gentleman. It was this, be believed, that separated the latter from a buffoon or "the man from the beast." To live well, in his opinion, was to train the young to enjoy "all the pleasures of a healthy, lively and vigorous constitution" in conjunction with those rules that would prevent such pleasures from becoming—as he ex-pressed it—"unruly, ungoverned and unskillful."

Somewhat similar advice was offered by the Earl of Chesterfield in his letters to his son. His main concern in these letters was to outline a pattern of education that would permit the young man to take his place in society or, in other words, to present a suitable figure in the world at large. Ches-terfield at one time entertained ambitious hopes that his son would enter politics and eventually assume a high administrative position in the state. While many of his admonitions were designed to enable his son to succeed in these goals, his general attitude involves a philosophy of life that, as one writer has aptly remarked, is "the creed of Mr. Worldly Wise."[5] In such a scheme, needless to say, it is external appearance that becomes of almost paramount importance. This is revealed, quite bluntly, in Chesterfield's sug-gestion that, for the sake of one's own interest and character, it would be most helpful to "pretend to some religion."[6] Colden's apparent deism would probably prompt him to subscribe to similar views. At least this would en-courage a certain latitudinarianism that would retain religious beliefs more for their moral or instructional value than as absolute truths.

One of the more important subjects that Chesterfield recommended to his son was the study of history. In his view, it was not only the preferred topic of conversation in polite society but—perhaps more to the point—it furnished some worthwhile clues as to what enabled men to succeed in society and affairs of state. Yet whatever one's preferred subjects might be, one should never try to boast or impose upon others the extent of one's learning, for this was "unwelcome and tiresome pedantry." The mark of a true gentleman was to be an agreeable conversationalist: eloquent, polite, and modest. Such qualities were more the result of an individual's education than of his nature, for the former was "the cause of that great difference we see in the characters of men."[7]

In terms of his interest in education and its role in the formation of character, Chesterfield reflected the general influence of Lockean psychology in the eighteenth century.[8] The didactic use of history was also included by Locke as one of the perennial sources from which one could derive invaluable insights regarding the affairs of mankind. As Locke expressed it: "nothing can be more necessary than the knowledge of men; . . . though it be had chiefly from experience, and next to that from a judicious reading of history."[9] For Chesterfield, such pragmatic considerations were also paramount. The study of any subject, in itself, was "of no use no where but in a man's own closet; and consequently, of no use at all." For Locke, too, the study of history could be both useful and instructive but, "if it be studied only for the reputation of being an historian, it is a very empty thing."[10]

Colden's approach to history was selective and, for instructional purposes, also employed various historical references to illustrate the necessity of a balance between the passions and the appropriate "rules" in the educational process. Using a kind of calculus of numbers, Colden argued that the greater the number of people who were educated according to certain "rules," the greater the possibility of that nation becoming happy and wise and, consequently, attaining great achievements in wealth, learning, and military power. It was when "vain and conceited study of subtleties and ornament" were introduced that factions appeared, government fell into confusion, and the nation became prey to external enemies.

After applying this summary judgment in the first instance to the civilization of classical Greece, Colden next analyzed the fall of the Roman Empire. Here, he blamed the loss of living well on "the pursuit of riches, luxury, and pleasures, without any restraint or rules to govern themselves by." In time, Rome also failed to maintain its former status as an empire and subsequently fell victim to internal dissension and, inevitably, tyrannical rulers. In this case, Colden did not stress the external factors as much as the internal forces of decline, and suggested that the situation was much the same even in his own day because Rome was "still ruled by crafty wicked priests who make themselves great by the oppressing [and] robbing of the poor inhabitants."[11]

In the interval between the fall of those civilizations associated with clas-

sical antiquity and the eighteenth century, Colden could find no other relevant examples to give his reader regarding the terrible fate that awaited
those societies that did not adhere to proper rules. These rules, of necessity,
were often the determining factor as to whether nations rose or fell. It was
the lack of European examples, however, that compelled him—like several
other writers of his age—to turn to the Orient, even if he regretted that he
had to select such foreign and remote examples. Here, Colden did not necessarily place the rules of Confucianism on a higher plane than those of
Western Christianity, but he remained adamant that one of the reasons
China had been successful in keeping its cultural civilization intact was that
its rules were taught strictly and consistently to "all the youth who hope to
make any figure in their country."

These rules become particularly significant to all those who anticipate any
preferment in the state. With the education of its future leadership based
on a sure foundation, the stability of the country is assured. Such education
must be imbibed early in youth, so as to train the mind, order the passions,
and set forth ideals for public service. Only in this way can the laws of the
country be enforced for the common good, for "The happiness of this people under this education appears by the long continuance of the same form
of government having subsisted upwards of 2000 years, and consequently
that they have been free of all that bloodshed, confusion, and desolation
which necessarily follow revolution and changes of government."[12]

In Japan, furthermore, could be found equal evidence of the advantages
of morality because here, too, Colden argued, the teachings of Confucius
were taught and observed. It was, Colden explained, the "fashionable education of the young gentry" and its positive benefits were demonstrated,
he argued, in the large population, the extensive agricultural improvements,
and the fact that the Japanese nation could be held up as an example of "a
school of charity and good manners." Colden did not describe or define
any specific rules, but he noted that these generally tended to preserve and
enhance the existing social structure.

In his own day, Colden lamented, "how difficult is it to reform nations
grown old and habituated to vice." Although he may have hesitated to
specify which nations he meant, he certainly regretted that Christianity in
Western civilization had not had the same effect as, say, Confucianism in
the East. Apparently, he was less concerned with their comparative teachings
or religious beliefs than with the necessity of having some cohesive model
that would be fundamental in the educational schemes of societies. In any
case, he appeared more confident about his historical judgments than about
contemporary developments when he wrote, "May this encourage some
great soul to attempt the like in our plantations." Only when such reforms
had been instituted would happiness—the aim of true education—be transmitted "to their latest generations."

If the intention of the "Essay" was to suggest the importance of a sound

education and of proper rules for a society, then the purpose of the "Introduction to the Study of Physics or Natural Philosophy" was to set forth
Colden's ideas regarding the basis for a proper education.[13] The treatise was
written as a guide for a student beginning his college career. There, Colden
remarked, one can learn those principles by which one might acquire knowledge and, thereafter, "be enabled to distinguish your self in every part of
your life, either in public employments, or in private life, or that you may
become an useful member of the commonwealth and of a private family."[14]
Education, then, was also a means of self-improvement. It not only acquainted the student with past knowledge, but also prepared him for subsequent learning and the experiences of life. Through such means, he would
be enabled to make a more suitable contribution to his society.

Nevertheless, Colden regarded much of the education of his day as irrelevant, since the methods of teaching did not do much more than "fill young
people's heads with useless notions and prejudice." Colden's plea was that
"real and useful knowledge" should be taught. Before defining or describing
what he meant, Colden found it necessary to launch into a historical parable
to determine what past civilizations could teach the present age. The fact
that Colden eventually developed the treatise into a brief exposition of his
own natural philosophy perhaps indicates the kind of knowledge that he
himself regarded as "real and useful."

Had Colden been asked to write an overview of Western science he would
not have begun his historical account with the important scientific achievements of the seventeenth century nor, indeed, even with the notable contributions of the classical Greeks. Instead, in chronological order, he made
the ancient Egyptian priests and Persian magi the true founders of this discipline. Colden assured his reader that history fully substantiated his view
that these societies "had acquired great knowledge in physics before the
Christian era, such as exceeds the knowledge of the most learned of the
moderns. It is certain that they had carried geometry, astronomy, and mechanics to a great perfection."[15]

Such a statement, in itself, may not be sufficient evidence that, in the
seventeenth century academic dispute known as the "Battle between the
Ancients and the Moderns," Colden would necessarily opt for the former.
Yet he had no hesitation in arguing that these early societies and kingdoms
possessed remarkable scientific knowledge that, presumably, was lost and
never fully recovered, even by the "moderns" of the Scientific Revolution.
This suggests that, for Colden, the subsequent scientific history of the West
has been, in effect, a process of recovering and regaining that which had
once been known only in past eons.

Again, there is an undeniable implication in all this that science was once
the preoccupation of certain religious leaders or "wise men"—such as priests
and magi—who either had a special source of knowledge or possessed a
superior intellect. Their social, religious, and intellectual leadership presum-

ably gave them a unique ability to pursue scientific investigations into the mysteries of nature; to put it another way, the social basis of science during its formative period was the preserve of men of extraordinary insight who were themselves members of an aristocratic cult. As such, scientific knowledge was restricted to the initiates of a particular sect or religious order in these ancient civilizations.

Having given an encomium for scientific discovery to the Egyptians, it is predictable that, in Colden's scheme, the Greeks would occupy only a minor footnote in the history of science. They were, he claims, "meer scholars" of the Egyptians—and no phrase better expresses Colden's disdain for bookish and pedantic learning. The Greeks may not even have understood what they inherited, and it is not likely that they made any discoveries on their own. Their major role, he proposed, was to preserve and transmit the learning of the ancients, so that everything one can know of Egyptian civilization was channeled through the Greeks.

The only Greek who was suitably instructed in Egyptian learning, Colden maintained, was Pythagoras. From Pythagoras's writings, he averred, one can be certain that the Egyptians knew the Copernican system and the "general apparent attraction between bodies, which has been rediscovered in the last century by Sr. Isaac Newton." In this scheme, the Scientific Revolution was less of a revolution and more of an evolution toward, and gradual recovery of, the great scientific achievements of the ancients. It is this interpretation that leads Colden to conclude: "It may be that we are now beginning the principles of physics, which were known many ages before the beginning of the Christian era."

Predictably, Colden made the advent of the Christian era the chronological division between the achievements of the ancients and the loss of these achievements to the West. It was largely the successive wars and barbarian invasions of the medieval period that were responsible for this lapse. Yet nothing would explain this diametrical contrast in scientific achievements between the two epochs as the rise of a priestly class that prevented free inquiry and reserved knowledge only to themselves. This was, Colden suggested, done to maintain their direct control and influence over the laity. Although Colden blamed some "pagan priests" for the trial and death of Socrates, his real animosity was directed against the modern priests of the Christian religion.

Nothing, in later ages, so much obstructed the advancement of knowledge as the craft of popish priest[s], when they, in imitation of the pagan priest, founded the power of their dominion on the ignorance and credulity of the laity, by which they established a tyranny in the Pope and the clergy over Kings and Princes, as well as over private persons, under pretence of their being entrusted with the keys of heaven and hell, and exerted their power more absolutely than ever had been done by any potentate before their time.[16]

They were able to achieve their ends, Colden continued, by removing all those books that might propagate any "real or useful knowledge" and by empowering the Church to censor all literature. Through these means, the collective knowledge of antiquity was lost although, Colden sarcastically added, "the lascivious poets are transmitted to us entire."

Like others of his age, Colden took a dim view of the medieval period, regarding it as an era when religious authority and barbarism combined to eradicate the cultural and intellectual legacy that could have contributed to the scientific and intellectual development of European civilization.[17] Though critical of both war and revolution—since it invariably disturbed learning and social tranquility—Colden could nevertheless regard these as historical events often beyond the control of man. It was the Church, in his opinion, that had purposely calculated the means to suppress the learning of the ancients and would have continued to do so as long as it could control the rulers of states.

Given this historical overview, it was the appearance of the Protestant Reformation that once more freed men's minds from the terror and ignorance that had held sway in the past for, as Colden noted, "Had not the reformation in religion taken place about that time, and several nations thrown off the authority of the Pope, the learning and knowledge of the present age had been nipped in the bud, and we should at this day have been in barbarous ignorance."[18] Since it was its educational control over youth that permitted the Church to maintain its ascendancy, it was only through the reform of education that the mind of man could be freed.

Thus, Colden now reverted to the subject that was the initial motivation for writing the "Study of Philosophy" by arguing that the choice must be made between the school learning of the clergy and the "real knowledge of things." The former involved a logic that required "the art of continuing an argument or dispute without end, and without convincing or being convinced, without design to discover truth, but to cover ignorance, and defend error." As such, it served equally well the Church, various religious sects, and the "chicanery of the law."[19] In this context, at least, Colden had no hesitation in blaming the legal profession for much of the "fraud, villany and perversion of justice." By implication, there was also the hint that their knowledge was neither useful nor productive to the common good; moreover, they were less ethical in their pursuits than someone who was presumably committed to "real knowledge."

If the Reformation broke the temporal and spiritual dominion of the papacy, it was with the subsequent appearance of René Descartes that an interest in new discoveries was introduced. This gave the final blow to Scholastic philosophy with its propensity to "divert the inquisitive mind." While Colden did not provide any synopsis of Cartesian philosophy, he did find two faults with Descartes' approach: first, "He carried the humour of doubting a little too far" and, second, his distinction between matter and spirit was incorrect. In Colden's opinion, "Extension . . . can make no distinction between matter and spirit."

Colden, in other words, was looking for a definition with a distinction. Consequently, such a classical philosophical distinction was inadequate. Neither was he prepared to accept the Scholastic distinction between matter and spirit as based on inactivity and activity. Although this was certainly Newton's view, Colden rejected it because (as he made abundantly clear in his natural philosophy) he regarded passivity or inactivity as a "nothing" and, consequently, as "a definition of nothing."[20] All of this, while not perhaps new, demonstrates Colden's undaunted persistence in promoting his philosophical concepts and his ongoing attempt—even in this informal work—to argue that knowledge of these powers was fundamental to man's well-being.

After rejecting Scholasticism, which was based on "the imaginations of idle useless monkish men," Colden spoke of those powers or forces "on which our well being depends. Our life and health, our pleasures and pain, all depend on the powers of other beings, which constitute the human system, and on the powers of other things, which are continually acting on it. Not only the speculative sciences, the explaining of all the phenomena which strike our senses, depend on the knowledge of these powers; but, likewise, all the practical arts depend on them."[21] Here, Colden was apparently giving expression to the "New Learning" promulgated by Francis Bacon in the sixteenth century.

The inquisitive mind should concern itself with those things that can improve knowledge and serve the needs of mankind. In this way, both intellectual satisfaction and public utility are served. Scientific investigation may be the *nexus* between the two, but Colden's real concern was also that the individual be as "rounded" as possible, so as to make an easy transition between his private and public roles. The educated individual, the gentleman, should not necessarily be a specialist in any one field, but he should have broad knowledge that makes him useful to his society. For Colden, "The meer scholar, the meer physician, the meer lawyer, musician or painter, take them out of their way, and they are often more insipid, than the meer plowman." Education, therefore, has a multifaceted role: it instructs and guides for purposes of virtue, it informs and trains the mind toward the pursuit of "real knowledge," and it establishes a model and an incentive for becoming useful in one's society.

Colden provided a more practical basis for a suitable educational curriculum in his correspondence with Benjamin Franklin. The latter had prepared a document entitled *Proposals Relating to the Education of Youth in Pennsylvania*, which was published in 1749 and later revised in the *Idea of an English School* (1751). Having been primarily trained as a tradesman, Franklin approached Colden on this topic, and also Samuel Johnson, largely due to their university background. In his *Proposals*, Franklin acknowledged that he had derived his views from various sources, but it was John Locke's treatise on education that apparently proved—as it evidently did for Colden—the most relevant and influential work. [22] The intent of the *Proposals* was to point out the need and opportunities for a college in Pennsylvania. Franklin was aware of the strides several other colonies were making in higher education, and became determined that his own should not lag behind them in this important area. Thus, his *Proposals* were meant to publicize this issue and obtain the necessary attention and support of the government and people in Pennsylvania.

It may have been Franklin's own pragmatic temperament or his realization that he had to demonstrate the benefits to be attained through such an institution that prompted him to begin his argument with the observation that the happiness and wealth of a nation are often directly related to the education of its youth. Much of the present prosperity of the colonies, he remarked, was due to those first settlers who "had received a good education in Europe."[23] He then went on to plead for the formation of a corporation, with a suitable charter, whose purpose would be to establish an academy and furnish it with a library, maps, mathematical instruments, prints, and "an apparatus for experiments in natural philosophy."

As far as the curriculum was concerned, Franklin proposed that everything that was "useful" and "ornamental" should ideally be taught. However, since "art is long and . . . time is short," only the most useful and ornamental subjects should be presented to the students.[24] The ornamental part of the curriculum could include such lessons as learning to write legibly, speak clearly and, eventually, acquire the ability to form a proper style. Most important of all was the study of history. This was the kind of "useful" knowledge that would lend itself to the examination of government, public religion, civil constitutions, and the effects of oratory in past societies. Franklin also recommended the study of the histories of nature and of commerce; the former so that the students would be enabled to make observations of nature and the latter to give them a proper appreciation of the role of the arts, trade, and manufacture in the development of the nation.

At all times, he hoped to encourage the students' interest in these fields by having them read the best authors and by exciting their natural curiosity. In his *Idea of an English School*, Franklin also stressed the necessity for the student to gain some understanding of moral philosophy and logic. In both cases, he recommended Dr. Johnson's treatises, such as the *Ethices Elementa* and the *Noetica: Or the First Principles of Human Knowledge*.[25] Altogether, Franklin's educational scheme was intended to be both practical and balanced, at least as far as the popular subjects of the day were concerned. It blended classical and modern literature with the latest books on science and the study of ethics with modern languages. After Franklin completed the *Proposals*, he sent Colden a copy. It was one of those polite rituals both men followed; Colden probably expected that Franklin would want to solicit his opinions on this work.

In his *Proposals*, Franklin had made a brief reference to the necessity for including agriculture in the curriculum, but Colden went further. He wrote to tell Franklin, "I am pleased with you mentioning agriculture as one of the sciences to be taught, because I am of the opinion [that] it may be made as much a science as any of those that are not purely mathematical, and none of these deserve so much to be taught as this—at least none more, since it is truly the foundation of the wealth and welfare of the country, and it may be personally useful to a greater number, than any of the other sciences."[26] Such a view presumably reflects the Physiocratic doctrine, especially prevalent in eighteenth-century France, regarding the importance of land and agriculture as a primary source of national wealth.

Colden was apparently critical of the alternative mercantilist contention that "the power and strength of a nation consists in its riches and money." While Colden admitted that "money can do great things," he once more felt compelled to turn to history to establish the thesis that a nation is not necessarily made strong in proportion to its wealth, but "by the knowledge and virtue of its inhabitants." When Colden went on to emphasize that poor nations, possessing virtue, had often been able to conquer others "abounding in silver and gold," he may have been referring to the Dutch or, more likely, to the English military supremacy over the Spanish Empire. He could express, at times, such a phobia about the deleterious effects of inordinate wealth that he seems to have believed it was almost a historical law that a wealthy nation would invite invasion and, in any case, since wealth created luxury (with its attendant moral decline), it would eventually become an easy prey.[27] In one of his treatises, Colden had cited the fate of Rome as an appropriate example of this theme—a variant on a cyclical view of history.

Colden's ethical injunctions regarding the use of time and being useful in society may well have reflected a residual Calvinist trait. He was particularly critical of the leisure achieved through excessive wealth, which he always regarded as a temptation to indolence and self-gratification. His historiography was replete with examples that provided illustrations of the extent to which such excesses often determined the fate of nations. In his own day, too, Colden assumed the role of a social moralist and critic by pointing out the need for those whose social prerogatives were based on wealth to employ their advantages for the benefit of mankind.

Perhaps no better illustration of this precept can be found than in Colden's letters to Lord Macclesfield. The latter had often supplied astronomical findings to Colden that he had gathered through his private observatory in England. Colden appended some of these to his *Principles* in the expectation that they might serve to illustrate the application of his natural philosophy to such scientific phenomena. He expressed his deep gratitude to Macclesfield by dedicating the 1751 edition of the *Principles* to him.

Colden evidently meant to encourage Macclesfield in pursuing such observations by telling him that science, particularly astronomy, required such great expense that only "persons of considerable fortune" could hope to continue in such a field. The provision of instruments and proper buildings and the expense of maintaining two observatories, as in this case, would certainly be beyond the means of less wealthy individuals. If those, however, who were more fortunate in this respect used such advantages for the good of the community, Colden suggested, then poorer citizens would neither envy nor complain of this wealth, for the scientific contributions of the rich would ultimately bring both honor and prosperity to the nation.

Since the wealthy could choose to contribute so directly to the progress of the nation, their failure to do so could only be regarded as reprehensible. It would serve as a judgment both on their privileged status in society and on their misuse of wealth. Colden firmly believed that "aristocratic leadership" was dependent on accepting the responsibility to direct and guide the nation. Such individuals, in his view, were best able to pursue science, establish ethical standards, and give the highest example of human dignity. Any shortcomings in attaining these standards would certainly make them greater objects of scorn than would be the case with lesser mortals. As he did not hesitate to instruct his patron, Colden wrote to tell him, "if a rank of men thus exalted above others should debase their honor, either by indolence or by employing their wealth in vicious pursuits to the hurt of the community, they must become the aversion of the rest of mankind, and they will not be able to maintain any dignity, and consequently their superiority must fall and sink under the general contempt which unavoidably attends such misbehavior in exalted stations."[28]

How far such views influenced Colden's determination to exercise an intellectual leadership of his own in the colonies is not certain. He evidently believed that it was important to set a comparable example, in addition to any gratuitous advice he was apt to offer. In this regard he may have tried, in a more limited role, to duplicate some of the social consciousness and sense of public responsibility that were often exhibited by members of the English aristocracy. In any case, Colden certainly did not hide his conviction that society should be ordered according to rank, and that it remained the responsibility of an aristocracy to set definite standards of taste, deportment and social leadership.

Colden corroborated Franklin's inclusion of agriculture in the proposed curriculum when he urged that agriculture be given proper scientific status and, for this purpose, recommended that a professor be appointed whose primary responsibility would be to make suitable experiments with regard to improving crops.[29] Further evidence of Colden's high regard for agriculture is seen in his suggestion that the college be situated in the country so that the student could continue his education by combining formal academic work with farming, planting, and animal husbandry.

However, having the college in the country served another, equally important purpose, which was to prevent the young scholars from "temptations to idleness and some worse vices that they meet with in the City." As appears to have been the case with Thomas Jefferson, Colden was suspicious of the urban environment and its emphasis on commercial enterprise. Thus, it would be preferable for the student to remain close to nature, observing and studying its beauty, rather than moving to the city and being exposed to some of its worst features. For such reasons, Colden at one time had urged the establishment of a college near his estate at Newburgh.[30] Of course, Colden realized that having the students live in the country was not an unmixed blessing and that lacking access to an urban milieu had at least one disadvantage. He admitted that the scholars might not have (as he termed it) "the advantage of behavior and address" that could only develop in a more sophisticated and cosmopolitan environment. As part of their education, for example, Colden himself sent some of his children to the city so that they could obtain "some education that they cannot have in the country and to rub off some of that country awkwardness."[31]

In order to avoid any rustic traits, Colden told Franklin that "this I think may be remedied by obliging them to use the same good manners towards one another with a proper regard to their several ranks, as is used among well bred gentlemen, by having them taught dancing and other accomplishments, an easy carriage and address in company, and other exercises usually taught gentlemen."[32] Again, to remove any "bashfulness," the students would also be required to "dispute" and "act plays." Colden was concerned that the curriculum should serve not only the intellectual or academic but equally the social or public needs of gentlemen, so that they would become informed, articulate, and well mannered. There is apparently a conservative emphasis in Colden's proposals regarding the recognition and retention of social rankings and equally, the transposition of an essentially British model of public education to the American colonies.

It may be surprising, however, to learn that in keeping with his former disputation against useless or bookish learning, Colden agreed with Franklin that he would not have the students learn either Greek or Latin. He went even further, to say that neither a knowledge of these languages nor, indeed, any foreign language should be required as a prerequisite for entry into college. All courses, he proposed, could be equally well taught in English, especially the sciences, since it was the most useful for their future careers. "Our own language," he told Franklin, "ought to be our principal care."[33]

Thus, Colden's educational scheme was guided by idealistic as well as more mundane, practical criteria, although it might appear rather archaic to direct education toward an appreciation of social rank and the other accoutrements of a gentleman. Still, Colden was quite practical when he urged that English and science be made the core of the curriculum, since they were most useful for the individual and society. Like Franklin, he minimized the importance of the classics, advocated the elimination of instruction in religion, and emphasized a general rather than a specialized educational program. While Franklin would have applauded these suggestions, he might have been less likely to share Colden's emphasis on the social goals of a college curriculum.[34]

Neither in their educational schemes nor in the ensuing discussion between Colden and Franklin was any provision made for the education of women. Colden's attempts to popularize botany for his daughter suggest that he was concerned that women be given some acquaintance with the sciences. And, although he never set forth any specific proposals for the education of women, he was at least aware that the deportment of the "gentle woman" was important enough to warrant some discussion of this topic with his granddaughters.

His intention—as he diligently advised them—was to instruct and instill in them that "one virtue . . . which in a woman ought to be the leading principle in the conduct of life." As in the development of a society or that of a man so, too, for a woman, the necessity of virtue was constantly stressed by Colden. It became, for him, the guiding principle in judging the life of a nation as well as that of an individual. For a woman, in particular, the virtue of modesty was most important. It would make her actions appear "natural and easy," give her grace and dignity, and permit her to indulge herself "in any moderate gaiety and innocent amusements of pleasures."[35]

Modesty in a woman, Colden affirmed, was "a firm and steady resolution in all our actions to preserve the dignity of our natures as rational beings and of that rank which we hold in society." This was especially necessary since it was certain that "our appetites and passions are often too strong for our reason." Consequently, these had to be ordered toward certain ends. For Colden, it was reason that lent the individual dignity and that should be exercised by all those who claimed any rank in society. In a footnote, Colden briefly explained what he himself would regard as "a just sense of our own dignity." It was, in his opinion, "the middle between having too high an esteem of our selves and having too mean thoughts of our own worth."[36] Here, again, there is the same endeavor to find a balance between two extremes that is evident in Colden's thoughts on education. In his "Study of Philosophy" and numerous letters, Colden emphasized the symmetrical development of the self, so that both reason and the "appetites" would be given due recognition within their respective spheres.

Such education as was provided for women—and Colden's daughters would have received theirs at home—was directed primarily to the domestic arts and household management including, for example, cooking, preserving, sewing, and managing servants. Some sense of what was deemed worthwhile and necessary for a gentlewoman's education is suggested in the program of a school that was established in New York in the 1740s. A notice in a local paper stated that "a school is opened to teach young ladies reading

and writing, all sorts of needlework, and the making of artificial flowers."
Each girl was expected to make a sampler, articles for the home, and many
of the decorative items she would wear.[37]

In his role as *paterfamilias*, not only was Colden prepared to share his
views on the rules and deportment that were important to the education of
women, but he did not hesitate to give pointed advice on domestic issues
to one of his daughters, Elizabeth DeLancey. In a long letter written shortly
after her marriage—intended to serve as a guide to her new role as wife and
mistress of a household—Colden began by telling her: "You know, my dear
child, how much I love you and I don't flatter you when I say you deserve
all the love a Father can give; you have been a dutiful child to your parents;
your natural disposition will incline you in like manner to be dutiful and
affectionate to your husband."

Perhaps with reference to his own domestic situation, he advised her that

The husband's business generally leads him abroad, and is often accompanied by
fatigue of the body, or more painful cares of the mind. He has to do with all sorts
of men, and cannot, as the wife may, confine himself to those he likes best; he often
comes home disgusted with fools, or provoked with knaves. He comes home in the
hope of having all his inquietudes soothed in the endearments of an affectionate wife;
to forget his cares and pains, and to have the pleasure of unloading his own breast
into the bosom of a faithful and affectionate friend where he hopes to find relief and
comfort.[38]

If, instead, the husband encounters a wife who is fretful and peevish, or
finds that "his wife is in the dumps, sullen and waspish," then "the husband
must shun his own house as he would a place of torment." He added:
"When a man has no comfort, he will, of course, seek it somewhere else;
this drives more married men to taverns and to gaming, makes them careless
of their affairs and families, and it will be no wonder if he avoid the company
of a wife that on all occasions disgusts him and takes up with a mistress who
endeavours to please him."

Although he emphasized that he did not think it necessary to advise his
daughter in all such matters, given her natural disposition and dutiful behavior as a child, he concluded: "The art, certainly, of pleasing a husband
deserves the wife's constant study more than anything else;—can any study
be more coming in a lady, or gain her more honour, and yet how few make
it their study. It is this art that I now endeavour to teach you."[39]

Several years later, based on what he had learned from his son, Cadwallader, who had recently returned from a visit to his sister in New York City,
Colden told Elizabeth that her present situation in dealing with the children
and servants had prompted him to write some further "reflections" on the
often trying circumstances facing a mother and mistress of a household.

Regarding her two sons, Warren and Peter, Colden suggested that they should not be allowed to stay at home where they would continue to give her "unease" and could only acquire idle habits and a "love of diversion." Instead, he proposed that they "be put under a master who would be more apt to restrain any unruly appetites." Each of the children, he noted, should eventually be directed to a different career, so that they would not compete with each other but become useful in promoting their mutual interests. It was for one of Elizabeth's sons, Peter DeLancey, that Colden penned his smaller treatises on education and philosophy. Peter not only had Samuel Johnson as a tutor, but would later attend King's College (later Columbia University) where Johnson had been appointed the first president.

The apparent "unease" which the domestic situation was evidently causing his daughter was particularly noted by Colden and led him to advise her:

My dear child, as your cares grow upon you, I am concerned that you do not fall under a misfortune, which they who are the most careful are in the greatest danger, that is, of acquiring an angry or peevish & fretful temper. I beg of you to guard against it as much as possible, as nothing will make your life more disagreeable to yourself & others, or endanger the esteem of a husband, who must often see & hear the disagreeable effects of such a temper. Nothing will make you lose your authority of your servants so much as this will. It will, in short, either destroy or give a bitterness to all your pleasure. A calm reproof or chastisement, mixed at other times with a benevolent aspect & kind treatment will certainly do more than perpetual chiding, for this last certainly begets distaste & disregard, & perhaps hatred, & may produce all the wicked consequences of malice. Chiding does not deter but irritates, whereas the other begets love & respect.[40]

Whether Elizabeth welcomed such unsolicited personal advice is unknown, but at least the letter suggests some of Colden's paternal precepts regarding the model role for a wife in a genteel eighteenth-century household.

Although Colden did not offer any further comments on Franklin's recommendations on the study of history as he had done, for example, in regard to the inclusion of agriculture in the academic curriculum, there can be no doubt that Colden remained a keen student of history. His interest in non-Western or pre-Christian societies is reflected in his several treatises, and is consonant with related themes of that age—an evident *philosophe* trait.[41]

His own reputation as a historian would be based on that which proved close at hand: the Indian tribes that inhabited the hinterland of the colony (province) of New York. Here, he believed, he had "living specimens," as it were, of mankind's beginnings. The connection between these primitive tribes and more recent society is revealed in Colden's judgment that "We are fond of searching in remote antiquity, to know the manners of our earliest progenitors: if I be not mistaken, the Indians are living images of them."[42] Thus, an examination of these Indian tribes and their mode of life proved as relevant to Colden's interest in history as the ancient civilizations of Greece and Rome or, moreover, those of China and Japan.

Colden could more readily come into his own as a historian in this case, since relatively little was known or had been written about these tribes. Whether he actually met all the tribes that constituted the Iroquois Confederacy is questionable, but he did travel to and lived for an interval with the Mohawks in his capacity as surveyor general of the province.[43] He had also been adopted into one of their clans and given an Indian name as a token of friendship.[44] Colden maintained an ongoing interest in Indians and Indian affairs. He participated in several conferences between representatives of the Indians and provincial officials.[45] Although he never fully understood their language—which made it necessary for him to rely on an interpreter—he was impressed with their astuteness in trading and their oratorical abilities when treaties were negotiated.[46] Such meetings, too, could not but convince him of the many instances of deception and fraud perpetrated upon the Indians by traders, merchants, and landowners. Many of his letters mention this topic and contain recommendations for reform.

In his capacity as surveyor general and member of the provincial council, Colden was often required to prepare reports and submissions on colonial matters, including papers on the climate or trade of New York, that were subsequently forwarded to the Lords of Trade. In 1732, for example, Colden wrote a noteworthy document entitled "On the Lands of New York." He used this opportunity to demonstrate that the pattern of land grants in the colony was contrary to the instructions provided by the ministry; that they were proving inimical to the settlement and development of the colony; and that such grants had often led to the illegal appropriation and dispossession of the native Indians.

Colden traced this issue as originating in the extravagant landholdings that had been established in the seventeenth century by governors who had used such grants to curry political favor or to reward associates. He noted that many of the grants were left deliberately vague in regard to the exact amount of land deeded. This often encouraged a patentee to make subsequent claims of from five fold to one hundred fold increases in their holdings. In the absence of proper surveys, boundaries were often described using Indian terms for identifiable physical features, such as brooks, hills, or waterfalls, even if the Indians themselves were apt to give the same names to several sites. Thus, it would not be difficult to find some feature that could easily be used to support a more favorable interpretation of the extent of a grant. And, as Colden noted, it was not unknown—in return for the gift of a blanket or some rum—for an Indian to corroborate such an interpretation.[47]

Colden obviously recognized that this system could not be abolished outright, since it was too deeply entrenched in provincial politics where large landowners often used their influence in the assembly to thwart any major reforms. Instead, he suggested that the taxes, or quit-rents, nominally imposed on large land grants be revised and vigorously collected, particularly on unimproved lands. He anticipated that such a step would not only reduce the number of extravagant grants, but would also provide the government with an assured source of income. This particular issue would become a constant point of contention between the governors and the assembly and often led to the gradual diminution of the executive powers that Colden noted in his comments on provincial politics.

Colden's ongoing attempts to improve the status of the Indians led him to make several useful suggestions. Based largely on his experience as surveyor general, Colden proposed that all lands deeded by the Indians be surveyed in their presence and that the terms of any contract be carefully and fully explained to them.[48] In a separate paper, Colden urged the passage of a law that would guarantee legal protection for the Indians. He cited many of the delays and undue costs that were imposed on Indians seeking redress in provincial courts, but then also noted that the evidence or testimony of an Indian was not admitted in court. He added: "Can these people who are treated in this manner be supposed to be under the protection of the King of Great Britain, or can they be supposed to be treated like friends, or like rational or human creatures? It is but too obvious what the consequences of this treatment must be."[49] Finally, he proposed that a commissioner for Indian affairs be appointed, with an annual salary, so that the office would not be under the influence of avaricious traders and merchants. This was something that the Indians themselves had suggested on numerous occasions. Here, again, Colden cited the French model in which a single council was incorporated to direct Indian affairs, in contrast to the heterogeneous and largely ad hoc approach that was prevalent throughout the American colonies.

Similar proposals had previously been made by Archibald Kennedy in an article entitled "The Importance of Gaining and Preserving the Friendship of the Indians to the British Interest, Considered." A member of the provincial council, Kennedy published his views in 1751 and supplied Colden with a copy. This furnished Colden with some of the material that he incorporated in his "Present State of the Indian Affairs" (1751). The two men shared an imperial outlook and were acutely aware of the many abuses associated with illegal land seizures and trade with the Indians, and of the necessity for developing some concerted means to protect the interests of the Indians at a time when they were likely to prove particularly crucial to the outcome of the Franco-British military conflict.

Kennedy was particularly critical of what he described as the Anglo-Dutch traders and their "harpies or handlers" who had so abused the Indians that few were left who could be depended upon. He noted, for example, that "without a proper regulation of the trade, all other endeavors to gain and preserve the friendship of the Indians will avail but little . . . those poor Indians have for many years been under the direction of the people of Albany, whose interest it was to deceive and defraud them."[50] Kennedy proposed a unified Indian policy by having it taken out of the hands of the traders and placing it under a single person, acting as a superintendent of Indian affairs, who would be directly responsible to the governor and council. He urged that the colonies assume greater responsibility in managing such policies, adding that it was "high time we should look to our own security, and most unnatural to expect, that we should hang forever upon the breast of our Mother-Country."[51] Such views evidently met a response from the British ministry and, at its urging, were to find expression in the Albany Congress that was held in 1754. A direct result of this congress was the appointment of William Johnson as superintendent for Indian affairs.

In his own paper on Indian affairs, Colden had already cited Johnson as having been indispensable in retaining the alliance of the Indians. Born in Ireland, Johnson had immigrated to the colonies in 1738, bringing several families with him to settle on his uncle's land in the Mohawk River valley. He became a merchant—primarily in the fur trade principally centered at Fort Oswego—and eventually amassed large landholdings as well as founding the community of Johnstown. It was his enduring reputation with the Indians that eventually made him their primary spokesman in colonial political affairs.

Johnson remained an avowed imperialist in his views of Indian affairs. As one means of bringing the Indians closer to British interests, for example, he encouraged their conversion to the Church of England. To Colden, he could write that the Jesuits were a dangerous society, and that he hoped that Protestant missionaries would "greatly promote the interest of his Majesty and soon increase the number of his protestant subjects."[52] To the Reverend Henry Barclay, who served as a representative of the Church of England at Fort Hunter and who would supply Colden with ethnographic details regarding the Indians, Johnson could write, "I cannot omit mentioning my opinion of the great necessity there is for some Ministers of the Established Church to reside in these parts, as well for the Whites, as Indians, without which the former must in a short time become altogether Presbyterians, which I have observed seldom betters them."[53] Indeed, Johnson even suggested that it might be practicable to establish the headquarters of the Anglican Church in America in proximity to his property.

Although he was eventually appointed to the provincial council, it was Johnson's military rather than political career that would enhance his reputation. After receiving a military commission in 1746 as a colonel of forces raised out of the Six Nations and having been later promoted to brigadier general and finally major general, Johnson was instrumental in defeating the French garrison at Lake George in 1755, for which he received a baronetcy. He also took part in the battle at Fort Niagara in 1759. Finally, in 1760, he successfully raised a large contingent of Indians to assist Jeffrey Amherst, the commander-in chief, in the campaign against Montreal. This resulted in the capitulation of Canada by France, which was subsequently ratified by the Peace of Paris in 1763.

While imperial concerns certainly demonstrated why the Indians had to be retained as indispensable allies—especially in the province of New York— it was their role in the fur trade that formed the immediate background to Colden's initial involvement in Indian affairs. In 1724, Colden had a series of papers published in New York that dealt with the commercial and military factors of the Indian trade.[54] The first of these papers concerned a petition by a group of London merchants asking that an act passed by the Assembly of New York be rescinded. The intent of that act, put into effect in 1720, was to prohibit all trade in Indian goods between the inhabitants of New York and the French in Canada.[55] Initially, the Act was limited to a probationary period of three years. By 1724, the London merchants believed that there was sufficient evidence to argue that the act had actually proven beneficial to the French and prejudicial to British trade to New York. It had, in their words, "greatly promoted that mischief which it was intended to prevent."[56]

They brought their grievance before the King's Council, which transferred the matter to the Lords Commissioners for Trade and Plantations for further examination and adjudication. Before making any final decision, however, the Lords Commissioners decided to solicit the opinions of Governor Burnet. It was in the governor's meetings with his council that Colden, a supporter of Burnet's imperial policies, was given the opportunity to argue that the extension of the act was necessary for the continued safety and economic viability of the province.

The report of the provincial council demonstrated that the London merchants had only a vague knowledge of the geography of the province and of the various Indian tribes living in the triangle between Albany, Niagara, and Montreal. There can be little doubt that Colden, in his capacity as surveyor general and due to his abiding interest in the Five Nations, was of direct benefit to the members of the council in pointing out such defects. To provide some illustration of these matters, Colden appended a map of the province and the surrounding territory to his *Papers Relating to the Indian Trade*.

On this map, the location of the Indian tribes, the Great Lakes, and the course of the principal waterways were clearly delineated. The map demonstrated, for example, that there were no other Indian tribes between New York City and the area west of Albany, except for the Five Nations Confederacy, and that there were no other major tribes between the Iroquois Confederacy and French Canada, contrary to what the London merchants had contended. As if to ridicule such notions, the report added, "to say that these Indians cannot come to trade at Albany, but by going down the River

St. Lawrence, and then into a lake . . . is to the same purpose as if they should say, that one cannot go from London to Bristol, but by way of Edinburgh."[57]

The fears of the London merchants, namely, that restrictions on the Indian trade would force the Indians to turn to the French, were uniformly discounted by the members of the council. Not only were all the goods that were of use to the Indians, such as strouds, made in Britain, but they could also be supplied considerably more cheaply at New York than at either Montreal or Quebec. The fact remained—as the council insisted—that the act had increased the control of the English over the Indians in the province by damaging French commercial interests and by drawing the colonists and the Indians into pacts of trade and friendship that often developed into military alliances.

To the various petitions and reports of the merchants, the Lords Commissioners of Trade and Plantations, and the provincial council, Colden attached a paper of his own, entitled *A Memorial Concerning the Fur Trade of the Province of New York*. In it, Colden dealt primarily with the economic advantages enjoyed by the province in the purchase and sale of furs. The *Memorial* is presented almost as if it were a military reconnaissance report in response to the perceived French intent to encircle English settlements along the Atlantic seaboard. Colden prefaced his report by noting that he had, "for some time past, endeavored to inform myself from the writings of the French, and from others who have traveled in Canada, or among the Indians," as to the climate, geography, and terrain that the French had to contend with.

While Colden recognized that the French had the benefit of an extensive inland water system, he added that this was largely offset by the greater distances over which the furs had to be transported, not only to Montreal, but also thence to France. In comparison, the distance between New York and Albany was relatively short and the Hudson River, unlike the St. Lawrence, was easily navigable and relatively ice-free for most of the year. Colden described the St. Lawrence River, for example, as beset by "tempestuous weather and thick fogs," as well as many strong currents and tides. Consequently, the French "never attempt to sail in the night, though the wind be fair and the weather good." And, although the French might be closer to Europe than the English colonies were, he added that they were only able to make one trip each year to either Europe or the West Indies, whereas merchants in New York could easily make at least two such trips annually.[58]

Of some significance, too, were the cheaper goods that could be made available at New York for the Indian trade. These included such items as "strouds, duffels, blankets and other woolens . . . which are only made in England and must be transported into France before they can be carried to Canada." Rum was another item that the French could not supply "by rea-

son they have no commodities in Canada fit for the West Indian market."
After pointing out the ease of transportation and shorter distance afforded
by the Hudson River—in comparison to the St. Lawrence River—he concluded:

Whoever then considers these advantages New-York has of Canada, in the first buying
of their goods, and in the safe, speedy, and cheap transportation of them from Britain,
free of all manner of duty or imposts, will readily agree with me, that the traders of
New York may sell their goods in the Indian countries at half the price the people
of Canada can, and reap twice the profit they do. This will admit of no dispute that
know that strouds, the staple Indian commodity, this year sold for ten pounds a piece
at Albany, and at Montreal for twenty-five pounds, notwithstanding the great quantity of strouds said to be brought directly into Quebec from France, and the great
quantities that have been clandestinely carried from Albany. It cannot therefore be
denied that it is only necessary for the traders of New York to apply themselves
heartily to this trade, in order to bring it wholly into their own hands, for in every
thing besides diligence, industry, and enduring fatigues, the English have much the
advantage of the French. And all the Indians will certainly buy, where they can at
the cheapest rate.[59]

Colden, however, could express grudging admiration for the French and
the extent to which they had tried to acculturate the Indians by sending
explorers, traders, and, most importantly, missionaries into their midst.
Many of the latter, he added, "have spent their lives under the greatest
hardships, in endeavoring to gain the Indians to their religion, and to love
the *French Nation* while, at the same time, they are no less industrious to
represent the *English* as the *Enemies of Mankind*."[60] Moreover, he credited
the French with being "indefatigable in making discoveries, and carrying on
commerce with nations, of whom the English know nothing but what they
see in the French maps and books." In effect, Colden transformed what
might have remained a document primarily for official purposes into an
expanded presentation that was researched in depth and gave him an opportunity to express his imperial vision and the role of the Native Americans
in this broader scheme.

Collectively, the *Papers Relating to the Indian Trade* confirm Colden's
early concerns with the Indians at a time when they were largely ignored,
taken for granted, or worse, mistreated by the colonists. He did not hesitate
to accuse the government—both in the colonies and in Britain—of failing
to acknowledge the real potential of the Indians for the expansion of empire
and trade at a time when these two were virtually synonymous. The *Papers*
also achieve an importance, in retrospect, because they served as a basis for
Colden's subsequent *History of the Five Indian Nations*, the confederation
composed of the Mohawks, Oneidas, Onandagas, Cayugas, and Senecas. In
1722, the Tuscaroras joined these tribes after they were evicted from their
territory in the Carolinas.

As he explains in its "Introduction," Colden's intention for writing a work on this subject was to acquaint a wider audience—particularly in England—with the economic and strategic importance of the Iroquois Confederacy to the province of New York.[61] The work was first printed in New York in 1727 and the five hundred copies that had been printed were quickly sold. After Colden made Collinson's acquaintance, the latter encouraged Colden to continue his account.[62] Several years later, Colden submitted to Collinson a revised and enlarged edition that was eventually published in London in 1747.[63] An interesting feature of this particular edition is that it contained the previous *Papers Relating to the Indian Trade* as one of its appendices.

In the "Introduction" to the *Indian History*, Colden also cited a letter sent to him by the Reverend Henry Barclay, who had done missionary work among the Indians for several years.[64] Since Colden had been limited in his opportunity for observing the daily life of the Indians, he welcomed the letter as a primary source document, as it were, for his own work. In his letter, Barclay remained generally impressed with the qualities of the Indians and remained optimistic that they could be "easily civilized." He told Colden that some might make "good mechanics . . . doubtless many of them [would be] very capable of a liberal education." He also regarded them as "good natur'd & hospitable, especially those who live farther distant from Christian settlements."[65] He went on to describe some of their customs and mores, such as the Indians' motivation for and practice of war, their system of marriage, means of employment, funeral arrangements, religious beliefs and worship, moral behavior, and use of language.

Barclay mentioned to Colden, for example, that the Indians' chief inducement to war was the quest for glory, while their main occupation was hunting. Such an arrangement made it necessary for the women to perform most of the manual tasks, such as planting, tilling, and harvesting of corn.[66] Nevertheless, Indian society remained essentially a matriarchal system, since the man normally remained with the wife's family; again, the children were generally regarded as part of the wife's possessions. The rite of marriage was quite simple and was essentially a declaration of intent, with an exchange of gifts, before the chiefs of the tribe.

Divorce, Barclay added, was "very common on the most trifling occasions" and was nothing more elaborate than either the husband or the wife leaving the other partner. While the Indian had a vague notion of a "Master of the Universe," there was no public worship or other religious practices, except in times of calamity. The Indians' language, according to this account, was limited to a few words; new terms were basically compounds of several common words.[67]

At the end of his stay with the Indians, Reverend Barclay believed that he had been able to introduce a "gradual reformation." He blamed the European, rather than the Indian, for the latter's moral corruption and cruelty in war. Such sentiments would certainly have found a response with

Colden, since they are similar to the views he expressed in his *History of the Five Indian Nations.*

Unfortunately, the second edition of that *History* did not sell as well as the publisher had originally expected. At first, the publisher told Colden that "The Book was received in the world with the greatest reputation," yet he ruefully discovered that, out of five hundred copies, he could only sell three hundred.[68] He eventually decided to dispose of the unsold copies at an appreciable financial loss.[69] This move soon proved to be somewhat premature. The purchaser of the remaining stock brought out another edition of Colden's work in 1750 and, in 1755, Osborne, the original publisher, also decided to introduce a new edition, but only after making extensive and unauthorized revisions.[70]

Although Colden had nothing to do with the editions of 1750 and 1755, Colden did, in fact, complete a third part, which brought his account down to 1720.[71] The second edition had ended with the Peace of Ryswick of 1697 and the third part began at 1707. Apparently, he had hoped to bring out on his own an authorized third edition that would include all three parts, as separate chapters, in one book. This plan, however, was never realized.[72]

In all three parts, Colden made extensive use of the various speeches given by colonial officials and their agents and those given by the Indians as they negotiated their differences on treaties of war, peace, or trade. Although he apologized that this might make his account less pleasing to some readers, he believed that "it is better to run the risk of being sometimes tedious, than to omit anything that may prove useful." Some histories, he explained, might be written "with all the delicacy of a fine romance" but this only made them "like French dishes" which may prove initially satisfying but, in the long run, lack depth and insight.

Finally, he remarked, "An historian's views must be various and extensive, and the history of different people and different ages, required different rules, and often different abilities to write it."[73] Here, Colden was suggesting that the historian must not approach his subject with bias or indulge in making any absolute judgments. Instead, wide knowledge and understanding were required in order to study each society within its own terms and individual features, namely, geography, religion, social organization, mores, and so on.

It is within these terms that Colden expressed his literary ambition to rectify the image of the Indian in the minds of his European readers. He remained convinced that nothing was more unfair than to view them simply as barbarians or as savage murderers intent on "thirsting after human blood." Instead, he offered the opinion that—although they could be fierce and formidable enemies—they possessed a nobility and honesty that often surpassed that of the European settler. The latter had, he believed, often victimized and debauched the Indians and was primarily responsible for acquainting them with all the treachery and deception that the Indians often resorted to as a means of self-defense.

Moreover, if Colden went on to make classical allusions concerning the Indians' bravery and endurance, it was due to his firm conviction that these were often equal to anything that could be found, for example, in the histories of Rome. In addition, he hoped that by studying the Indians' social and political organizations, one could find the "Original Form of all Government." Such a study would surpass anything written on this topic by the "most curious speculations of the learned," which, indeed, were "no better than hypotheses in philosophy, and as prejudicial to real knowledge."

It was with these themes in mind that Colden introduced his historical account of the Five Indian Nations by writing that

The Five Nations are a poor barbarous people, under the darkest ignorance, and yet a bright and noble genius shines through these black clouds. None of the greatest Roman hero's have discovered a greater love to their country, or a greater contempt for death, than these barbarians have done. . . . Indeed, I think our Indians have outdone the Romans in this particular.

But what have we Christians done to make them better? Alas! We have reason to be ashamed, that these infidels, by our conversation and neighborhood, are become worse than they were before we knew them. Instead of virtues, we have only taught them vices that they were entirely free of before that time. The narrow views of private interest have occasioned this, and will occasion greater, even public mischief's, if the governors of the people do not, like true patriots, exert themselves, and put a stop to these growing evils. If these practices be winked at, instead of faithful friends that have manfully fought our battles for us, the Five Nations will become faithless thieves and robbers, and join with every enemy that can give them the hopes of plunder.

If care were taken to plant in them, and cultivate that general benevolence of mankind, which is the true principle of virtue, it would effectually eradicate those horrid vices occasioned by their unbounded revenge; and then the Five Nations would no longer deserve the name of barbarians, but would become a people whose friendship might add honor to the British Nation, tho' they be now too generally despised.

The Greeks and Romans, once as much barbarians as our Indians now are, deified the hero's that first taught them the virtues, from whence the grandeur of those renowned nations wholly proceeded; but a good man will feel more real satisfaction and pleasure from the sense of having any way forwarded the civilizing of barbarous nations, or of having multiplied the number of good men, than from the fondest hopes of such extravagant honor.[74]

Colden's interest in the Indians as exemplars of the "Original Form of all Government" led him to note that each nation was an "absolute republic," that authority and power were derived, in effect, from the consent of the governed, and that honor and esteem were their most esteemed traits, while military leadership was based on courage and conduct in battle. Moreover, any presents or plunder obtained were distributed by their leaders "so as to leave nothing to themselves."

Because the book was largely devoted to Indian history from the latter half of the seventeenth century, Colden had to rely primarily on secondary sources, one of which, he admitted, was the *Histoire de L'Amérique septentrionale par Mr. De Bacqueville de la Potherie*. Colden commented, "I know of no accounts of them published in English, but what are meer translations of French authors."[75] This material was extensively supplemented by speeches taken from "The Minutes of the Commissioners for Indian Affairs." Consequently, the reader had to go through much of this documentary account—as Colden had noted—to learn something of the historical episodes affecting the fate of the Indians and the elaborate rituals and protocols they could engage in while negotiating treaties.

Franklin had a high regard for the book, agreeing at one time to sell all the copies that remained unsold by its English publisher. As he told Colden, " 'tis a well wrote, entertaining and instructive piece, and must be exceedingly useful to all those colonies who have anything to do with Indian affairs."[76] He might, however, have been less apt to accept some of Colden's literary pretensions regarding the Indians' innate dignity or nobility. At one point, after observing them quite inebriated, Franklin made the perhaps uncharacteristic remark; "indeed if it be the design of Providence to extirpate these savages in order to make room for cultivators of the earth, it seems not improbable that rum may be the appointed means."[77]

In any case, Franklin was well aware of the continuing importance of the various Indian tribes, particularly the Iroquois, and he published numerous Indian treaties that resulted from negotiations with provincial representatives relating to strategic and land issues affecting the Pennsylvania colony. One of the more notable of such representatives during this period was Conrad Weiser, whose father had originally emigrated from Germany to settle on the New York frontier. Here, the son lived for several years in a Mohawk village and would eventually develop an intimate knowledge of Indian language and customs. After the family moved to Pennsylvania, Weiser was appointed by James Logan, in 1731, to serve as an Indian agent and interpreter, and he was also to form a close friendship with Franklin. Over the next two decades, Weiser was instrumental in serving as an intermediary between the colony and Indians through his role in negotiating various treaties and land purchases.

While the interest in Indian affairs in the colonies would continue to be largely dominated by economic and strategic considerations, an interest in primitive tribes was not an uncommon feature of eighteenth-century literature. In general, it tended to reinforce the notion of the noble savage living close to nature, largely unfettered by the restraints and artificialities found in European society.[78] It was these characteristics that were emphasized by Colden in his own *Indian History* and that made it possible to transfer the qualities of the ancient Greeks—such as their oratory or stoicism in battle—to a more modern context.[79] Such themes, for example, also found expression in such works as the *Jesuit Relations* and Lafitau's *Moeurs des sauvages Américains comparés aux moeurs de Premier Temps* (1724).

Evidence of the Indian's singular status in popular fiction is well attested by the number of works on this topic. While too numerous to cite, an indication of their role in propagating Enlightenment views is suggested in Smollett's *Expedition of Humphrey Clinker* (1771). Here, the Indian captivity theme is developed when one of the captives is adopted as a sachem in an Indian tribe and, after his release, tells the tale of two French missionaries who arrived among the Indians in order to convert them to Christianity. In attempting to explain some of the mysteries and revelations central to this religion, the missionaries recount how Christ was born as a human being, only to be subjected to humiliation, suffering, and crucifixion. Thereafter, the priests explained how their God could be recreated "to swallow, digest, revive, and multiply *ad infinitum*," which the Indians only regarded as impious and then demanded to be shown some miracles to prove such magical abilities.

Although the missionaries were ordered to leave the Indian camp, they persisted in remaining and engaging in prayer, mass, and baptizing. Finally exasperated, the Indians put them on trial as "impious imposters" and the missionaries were condemned to the stake "where they died singing *Salve Regina*, in a rapture of joy, for the crown of martyrdom which they had thus obtained."[80] That the Indian also assumed an important place in eighteenth-century drama is suggested in representative works of the period such as Francis Hawling's *The Indian Emperor* (1728), James Bacon's *The American Indian: or the Virtues of Nature* (1795) and Josiah Arnold's poem, *The Warrior's Death Song*.[81] It was within this context that Colden's *Indian History* served an enduring interest in the ethnography of the Native American and his habitat—particularly among its European readers—as well as embodying several implicit tenets found in Enlightenment historiography.

Colden's more informal treatises on philosophy and education may not occupy quite the same importance in his *oeuvre* as his natural philosophy, for example, but such writings and his occasional letters on related subjects provide some insights into the opinions, attitudes, and convictions that he could not express in strictly scientific or philosophical terms. It is from such writings, however, that it is possible to appreciate the extent to which Colden shared in some of the prejudices and aspirations of his age, as is evident in his antipathy toward Scholasticism, the role of the priesthood, the dominance of the Church during the medieval period, and "bookish learning." It was primarily in his letters and informal treatises that he was more fully prepared to discuss his views on education, science, the use of reason, the pursuit of happiness, the role of aristocratic leadership, and various ethical themes.

Colden's status as an American *philosophe* is assured through his interest in science and history, devotion to intellectual pursuits, commitment to the improvement of society, and concern with "real and useful" knowledge in education. Representatives of the *philosophe* movement would assuredly have commended his social consciousness and emphasis on the wise use of time and talent. While he could express at times a degree of impatience, even a sense of frustration, with the lack of scientific or intellectual advancement— compared with material progress—in the American colonies of the eighteenth century, he himself remained dedicated to such improvements, particularly in relating education to scientific progress and ethical instruction. Such a program illustrates not only the degree to which he had absorbed the values of the Enlightenment but, perhaps equally important, the extent to which he was committed to impressing them on succeeding generations.

NOTES

1. M. Diderot, ed., *Encyclopédie, ou Dictionnaire Raisonné Des Sciences, Des Arts et Des Metiers* (Geneva, 1777–1779), 36 Vols, XXV, 669.

2. Preserved Smith, *The Enlightenment, 1687–1776* (New York, 1968), 309.

3. Cadwallader Colden, "Essay on the Art of Right Living." Colden MSS, New-York Historical Society, n.d., n.p.

4. The role of education in teaching virtue, rather than merely transmitting knowledge, was also expressed by Locke in *Some Thoughts Concerning Education.* "It is virtue," he argued, "direct virtue, which is the hard and valuable part to be aimed at in education." Quoted by J.A. Passmore, "The Malleability of Man in Eighteenth-Century Thought," in Earl R. Wasserman, ed., *Aspects of the Eighteenth Century* (Baltimore, 1965), 21–22.

5. F.L. Lucas, *The Search for Good Sense* (London, 1958), 147.

6. Philip Dormer Stanhope, Earl of Chesterfield, *The Elements of a Polite Education* (Boston, 1801), 226.

7. Ibid., 201.

8. "No one was more serious than Chesterfield in his recognition of the implications of the *tabula rasa* theory, that birth is irrelevant, and that knowledge can be acquired only by experience and learning," Kenneth MacLean, *John Locke and English Literature of the Eighteenth Century* (New Haven, Conn., 1936), 38–39.

9. Sterling P. Lamprecht, *Locke: Selections* (New York, 1928), 4.

10. John Locke, *Of Study* (1677), in James L. Axtell, *The Educational Writings of John Locke* (Cambridge, 1968), 409.

11. Colden, "Essay."

12. Colden, "Essay."

13. Cadwallader Colden, "Introduction to the Study of Philosophy wrote in America for a Young Gentleman." This treatise was apparently written sometime in the early 1760s. It is an unpublished manuscript in the possession of the New-York Historical Society, attached to a letter, "To my son, Alexander, July 10, 1760." A previous draft was entitled "An Introduction to the Study of Physics or Natural Philosophy for the Use of Peter DeLancey the Younger."

14. Colden, "Introduction to the Study of Philosophy," Section 1.
15. Ibid.
16. Ibid.
17. For a discussion of this particular topic in terms of Enlightenment historiography, see Herbert Weisinger, "The Middle Ages and the Late Eighteenth-Century Historians," *Philological Quarterly*, 27 (1948), 63–70. The selective treatment of the past by Enlightenment historians is found discussed in S.B. Barnes and A.A. Skerpan, "Historiography under the Impact of Rationalism and Revolution," *Research Series* 1, 40 (1952), Kent State University, Kent, Ohio.
18. Ibid.
19. Colden's letters are filled with vituperation against the legal profession. At one point he wrote that "a domination of lawyers was formed in this province ... founded on the same principles and carried on by the same wicked artifices that the domination of priests formerly was in the times of ignorance in the papist countries." "State of the Province of New York," *The Colden Letter Books*, 2 Vols., New York Historical Society, *Collections*, II, 71.
20. Colden, "Introduction to the Study of Philosophy."
21. Ibid.
22. Lawrence A. Cremin, *American Education: The Colonial Experience (1607–1783)* (New York, 1970), 376–377.
23. Jack P. Greene, ed. *Settlements to Society* (New York, 1966), 309.
24. Ibid., 310. A similar argument can also be found in Locke's *Of Study*.
25. "Benjamin Franklin on Education," in David Hawke, ed., *U.S. Colonial History–Readings and Documents* (New York, 1966), 341.
26. Cadwallader Colden to Benjamin Franklin, November 1749, *Colden Papers*, IV, 157.
27. According to one account, it was a popular literary work of the eighteenth century, John Brown's *Estimate of the Manners and Principles of the Times* (1757), that set the stage for an ongoing attack on luxury. Leslie Stephen, *History of English Thought in the Eighteenth Century* (New York, 1962), 2 Vols., II, 168.
28. Cadwallader Colden, "The observations annexed made in the Earl of Macclesfield's Observatory at Sherburn Castle," *Letters to Lord Macclesfield and Observations Made in His Observatory, 1749*. Colden MSS, New-York Historical Society.
29. Cadwallader Colden to Benjamin Franklin, November 1749, *Colden Papers*, IV, 157.
30. David C. Humphrey, "Urban Manners and Rural Morals: The Controversy Over the Location of King's College," *New York History*, 54 (1973), 8.
31. Cadwallader Colden to Elizabeth Hall, October 23, 1732, *Colden Papers*, II, 84.
32. Cadwallader Colden to Benjamin Franklin, November 1749, *Colden Papers*, IV, 157–158.
33. Ibid., 158.
34. David Tyack, "Education as Artifact: Benjamin Franklin and Instruction of a "Rising People," in Peter Charles Hoffer, ed., *An American Enlightenment* (New York, 1988), 215.
35. Cadwallader Colden to his Granddaughters, n.d., *Colden Papers*, VII, 305.
36. Ibid., 308.

37. Esther Singleton, *Social New York under the Georges, 1714–1776* (New York, 1902), 334.

38. Cadwallader Colden to Mrs. Elizabeth DeLancey (1737), *DeLancey Papers*, Museum of the City of New York.

39. Ibid.

40. Cadwallader Colden to Elizabeth DeLancey, n.d., *Colden Papers*, IV, 339–40.

41. See, for example, Donald F. Lach, "China and the Era of the Enlightenment," *Journal of Modern History*, 14 (1942), 209–223. Also, Adolf Reichwein, *China and Europe: Intellectual and Artistic Contacts in the Eighteenth Century* (London, 1925).

42. Cadwallader Colden, *The History of the Five Indian Nations Depending on the Province of New York in America* (Ithaca, N.Y., 1964), Preface, x. Hereafter referred to as *Indian History*.

43. Cadwallader Colden to ———, August 7, 1745, *Colden Papers*, III, 137; Benjamin Bissell, *The American Indian in English Literature of the Eighteenth Century* (New Haven, Conn., 1925), 12; Alice M. Keys, *Cadwallader Colden: A Representative Eighteenth-Century Official* (New York, 1906), 5. To Collinson, Colden wrote: "I have trusted myself alone with [the Indians] in the woods . . . & never any person took more care of their dearest relation that they did of me." Cadwallader Colden to Peter Collinson, May 1742, *Colden Papers*, II, 260.

44. Martha J. Lamb, *History of the City of New York: Its Origin, Rise, and Progress* (New York, 1877), 2 Vols., I, 611.

45. Colden's *Account of the Conference between Gov. Burnet and the Five Nations*, 1721, *Colden Papers*, I, 128–134; "Propositions made by his Excellency the Honorable George Clinton, Esq. . . . to five of the six united Nations of Indians," October 1745, *Colden Papers*, III, 166–177; "Propositions made by his Excellency the Honorable George Clinton, Esq.," 1746, *Colden Papers*, III, 247–259; "Colden's Conference with the Five Nations," *Colden Papers*, IV, 50–60.

46. Cadwallader Colden to Peter Collinson, May 1742, *Colden Papers*, II, 259; Cadwallader Colden to Dr. John Mitchell, August 17, 1751, *Colden Papers*, IX, 105.

47. Cadwallader Colden, "On the Lands of New York (1732)," in E.B. O'Callaghan, ed., *The Documentary History of the State of New York*, 4 Vols. (Albany, N.Y., 1849–1851), I, 383.

48. Cadwallader Colden, "To the Honorable George Clarke," *Colden Papers*, XIV, 159.

49. Cadwallader Colden to George Clinton, "The present state of the Indian affairs . . . with some observations thereon for securing the fidelity of the Indians to the Crown of Great Britain and promoting trade among them," E.B. O'Callaghan, ed., *Documents Relating to the Colonial History of the State of New York*, 15 Vols. (Albany, N.Y., 1856–1857), XIV, 383.

50. Archibald Kennedy, *The Importance of Gaining and Preserving the friendship of the Indians to the British interest, considered* (New York, 1751), 11.

51. Ibid., 7.

52. William Johnson to Cadwallader Colden, January 27, 1764, in *The Papers of William Johnson*, ed. Alexander C. Flick (Albany, N.Y., 1925), IV, 306.

53. William Johnson to Henry Barclay, March 30, 1763, in ibid. 73.

54. [Cadwallader Colden] *PAPER Relating to an ACT of the ASSEMBLY of the Province of New York, For Encouragement of the Indian Trade, etc. and for Prohibiting the Selling of Indian Goods to the French, viz. of CANADA* (New York, 1724). Hereafer referred to as, *Papers Relating to the Indian Trade.*

55. Ibid., 1.

56. Ibid., 2.

57. Ibid., 8.

58. Ibid., 19.

59. Cadwallader Colden, *A Memorial concerning the Fur Trade of the province of New-York. Presented to his Excellency William Burnet* (1724). Ibid., 20.

60. Ibid., 17.

61. Cadwallader Colden to Peter Collinson, December 1743, *Colden Papers*, III, 43. Colden's *History of the Five Indian Nations* was the first book to be written on this topic. Indeed, it would remain the only such history for another 178 years. George T. Hunt, *The Wars of the Iroquois* (Madison, Wis., 1980), 185.

62. Peter Collinson to Cadwallader Colden, March 5, 1740/1, *Colden Papers*, II, 207.

63. Cadwallader Colden to Peter Collinson, April 9, 1742, *Colden Papers*, II, 250. He told Collinson, "I may truly say that it is owing to you that ever it had a birth, by your giving me your approbation of the first part & desiring it to be continued as a work which you thought may be useful, for I had for several years laid aside all thoughts of it."

64. "From Rev. Henry Barclay, Missionary of the Society for the Propagation of the Gospel," December 7, 1741, *Colden Papers*, VIII, 279–285.

65. Ibid., 282.

66. Ibid., 282.

67. Ibid., 284.

68. Thomas Osborne to Cadwallader Colden, June 6, 1746, *Colden Papers*, IV, 64.

69. Thomas Osborne to Cadwallader Colden, July 20, 1751, *Colden Papers*, IV, 271.

70. Lawrence C. Wroth, *An American Bookshelf, 1755* (Philadelphia, 1934), 91–92.

71. [Cadwallader Colden], "Continuation of Colden's History of the Five Indian Nations, for the years 1707 through 1720," *Colden Papers*, IX, 359–456.

72. Ibid., 359, n.

73. Colden. *Indian History*, Preface, xi.

74. Ibid., vi–vii.

75. Ibid., vii.

76. Benjamin Franklin to Cadwallader Colden, January 27, 1747, *Colden Papers*, IV, 6.

77. *Benjamin Franklin: The Autobiography and Other Writings*, L. Jesse Lemisch, ed. (New York, 1961), 133.

78. Roger P. McCutcheon, *Eighteenth-Century English Literature* (London, 1958), 118; Hoxie M. Fairchild, *The Noble Savage: A Study in Romantic Naturalism* (New York, 1928).

79. Benjamin Bissell, *The American Indian in English Literature of the Eighteenth Century* (New Haven, Conn., 1925), 5.

80. Tobias Smollett, *The Expedition of Humphrey Clinker* (Oxford, 1930), 238–239.

81. Ibid., 184.

EPILOGUE

On Mr. DeLancey's death, the government devolved upon Doctor Colden, who immediately came out from his rural retreat in Ulster County,
and at the age of 73 took up his residence at the province house in the
fort, as president of the Council.

In his *History of the Province of New York*, William Smith, Jr., a lawyer and
historian, noted Colden's assumption of a public office in 1760 that
thereafter would also include, at times, the office of lieutenant governor,
and sometimes acting governor, of the province of New York. Colden wrote
to inform Peter Collinson of this "unexpected change" in his circumstances,
stating that although he had expected to spend the remainder of his life in
"such amusements as best fitted my age & were most agreeable to my in-
clinations," he was now obligated to "take the rein of government in his
hands, which has produced as great a change with respect to myself as well
could happen."[1] In any case, Colden remained hopeful that the administration would be made "easy" for him—especially at his increasing age.[2] Such
hopes, however, proved short-lived.

The office of president of the council was usually reserved for the oldest
of its members and, in this case, its longest-serving individual. As such,
Colden had not only gained a wide experience in provincial affairs that confirmed the opinions originally impressed upon him by Governor Hunter,
but had often taken positions or expressed views during his public career

that invariably brought him into direct conflict with one or more of those "factions" that usually dominated the assembly.

Over time, those factions had evolved into rudimentary political parties, and the two that dominated much of New York provincial politics were primarily divided between the DeLancey and Livingston families. Each could serve as either the "court" or the "country" party, depending on specific issues or on the policies and personal prejudices of a particular governor. Intermarriage and shifting alliances might often blur such distinctions, however, with the result that it remains difficult to discern any consistent pattern in the politics of the period, other than one largely based on perceived self-interest.[3]

Colden, of course, had never been entirely removed from administrative or political matters, even with his retirement to his estate. He remained a member of the provincial council, although his attendance was often sporadic, whereas someone like William Johnson, due to his location at a distance from the city, apparently never attended at all. It was under Governor George Clinton (1743–1753) that Colden was drawn out of his semiretirement, and thereafter he became more fully embroiled again in public affairs for a time. It was a period when he was still preoccupied with work on his treatise relating to natural philosophy and he may have been reluctant to put that aside. Yet, Franklin advised him, "I wish you all the satisfaction that ease and retirement from public business can possibly give you. But let not your love of philosophical amusements have more than their due weight with you," and went on to suggest that affairs of state often must take precedence at times.[4]

Governor Clinton had a military background with little experience in political administration, and seemingly had a need to find someone as a personal confidant who could assist and guide him in administrative matters. His first choice for this role was James DeLancey. A member of a New York mercantile family, DeLancey had through marriage and political connections risen through a series of appointive positions, including those of member of the provincial council and chief justice of the Supreme Court of New York. In 1747, he was appointed New York's lieutenant governor. Several years after Clinton's arrival in the colony, however, the two men parted company. As a result Clinton turned to Colden while DeLancey, as might have been expected, joined the opposition. Colden took up his responsibilities by advising Clinton on such matters as Indian policies and military proposals. He wrote many letters, speeches, and responses on behalf of Clinton to English correspondents or those relating to the assembly.[5] In effect, he served as an *éminence grise* to Clinton, something that was not lost on the opposition. As one caustic observer remarked, "Give him [Clinton] plenty of wine and Colden, and he'll come out all right."[6]

After their break, it was DeLancey's intent to belittle Clinton as a public figure, by making Clinton look ridiculous and making Colden appear a liability to Clinton's administration.[7] Philip Livingston, a member of another prominent family, would also hold Colden responsible for the "pernicious advice" he had given to Clinton.[8] The assembly, where such political figures could wield considerable influence, went so far as to describe Colden—after some acrimonious exchanges—as one who "had attempted to infringe their rights, liberties, and privileges, violate the liberties of the people, and subvert the constitution of the colony and therefore was an enemy to its inhabitants."[9]

While this episode may have done little to enhance Colden's public *persona*, he had by this time already alienated two groups that were associated with the assembly's political leadership. His *Memorial on the Fur Trade*, for example, was directed against the mercantile interests in the colony, who were primarily identified with the DeLancey faction, whereas his role as surveyor general—investigating the abuses associated with land distribution and acquisition—put him in opposition to the landowning oligarchy which was represented by various members of the Livingston family, among others. If the *Memorial* served as an indictment of the mercantile interests, it was Colden's report, *State of the Lands in the Province of New York*, written in 1732, that pointed out these abuses and included recommendations for reform.

It was a topic that, of course, had relevance to Colden's interest in Indian affairs, but it was the social and political repercussions of the land grants that Colden emphasized in his report. Such grants had not only discouraged an increase in immigrants, as compared to other colonies but, as Colden noted, "every year the young people go from this Province, and purchase lands in neighboring colonies." Again, the large grants were generally left uncultivated and did not produce the nominal quit-rents that could be used to support the government. Enforcing the collection of such quit-rents would reduce excessive holdings and the income from such payments would also free the executive from a dependency on those "humours of the Assembly they are now under for their daily support." Needless to say, Colden's recommendations were largely ignored, and he subsequently told a correspondent that his attempts at reform only met with such resentment that his preference was to try and avoid any public forum on the issue, even adding: "There are some in this province capable of everything Caesar Borgia was."[10] Later still, he would confess: "It had no other effect than to be prejudicial to myself."[11]

That this situation had continued largely unabated is confirmed in an official report Colden prepared for submission some five years after he had initially taken over the "rein of government," as it were, in 1760. Entitled "State of the Province of New York," it was intended to provide the Lords of Trade with an analysis of New York's several social rankings or classes. Preeminent among those were, as Colden observed, the proprietors of large tracts of land—ranging from 100,000 acres to over one million. Many of these grants were based on fraudulent claims and left deliberately vague, both as to quantity and boundaries, so that, he added, it "turns greatly to the advantage of the owners of these great tracts by the artifices they make use of to enlarge their claims perpetually."[12] Also, small farmers who had improved or cultivated their land often found themselves forced to defend their holdings against such vague claims and in the process were often ruined by legal costs—for, as Colden noted, the acquisition of the unimproved land was comparatively inexpensive, whereas its cultivation considerably increased its value.

Second in importance in this classification were the representatives of the law who, Colden suggested, were "of the most distinguished rank in the policy of the province." The merchants in the city constituted the third class, with many having risen to prominence chiefly from the fortunes made, as Colden noted, from illicit trade during the French and Indian War (1754–1763). The fourth and final ranking was reserved for the small farmers and merchants who, in his view, "comprehends the bulk of the people, & in them consists the strength of the province," adding that they were both the most useful and the most moral. However, it was this group that also invariably served as "dupes" of the others and "often are ignorantly made their tools for the worst purposes."[13]

What seems particularly noteworthy is that, in this scheme, Colden specifically cited the legal class or "rank" as significant enough to add to the traditional roster of the landowners and merchants as one of the preeminent groups in the province. The 1750s were to witness the rise of a legal fraternity that increasingly dominated political affairs in the colony. When he assumed public office, in 1760, Colden would hold them responsible for many of the problems he encountered in his own administration and thereafter made them the particular object of his loathing and scorn. Indeed, either through descent or intermarriage, many of them were related to the landowning or merchant classes that had dominated much of provincial politics throughout Colden's appointive career. James DeLancey, Jr., for example, was the son of a chief justice and lieutenant governor who had died in office, while William Livingston joined with two other lawyers, William Smith, Jr., and John Morin Scott, to form a well-known legal triumvirate in the colony. Of these, William Smith, Jr., would prove one of Colden's most entrenched adversaries.

In his "Introduction to the Study of Philosophy," Colden had observed how the book learning of the clergy or Scholasticism was largely based on "the art of continuing an argument or dispute without end . . . without design to discover truth, but to cover ignorance and error" and suggested that this kind of logic or sophistry served not only the Church but the "chicanery of the law." As noted, he would conclude that the legal profession was itself responsible for much of the "fraud, villany and perversion of justice" in the province.

By the time Colden prepared his submission to the British ministry in which he enumerated the various ranks or classes in the province, he had had some personal experience of dealing with members of this group and could only conclude that "In general, all the lawyers unite in promoting confusion, prolonging suits, and increasing the expense of obtaining justice," all of which made it difficult, if not impossible, for the average citizen to defend his rights or obtain justice.[14] And, while many might complain about this state of affairs, no man wished to offend the lawyers and, consequently, people were "deterred from making any public opposition to their power and the daily increase of it."

In a more political context, Colden cited the experience of Governor Clinton who, being "good natured," had acquiesced in the lawyers' goal of securing certain commissions only to find that, upon his refusal to further meet their demands, "they served him as the haughty priest in former times served their greatest benefactors when they opposed the priestly lust for power." For his part, Colden had taken it upon himself as lieutenant governor to reform legal abuses and the power of lawyers, but that this only "drew upon him the most virulent & malicious resentment of the lawyers," so as to demonstrate that "by the ruin of the only man who has ventured publicly to oppose them, all others may be deterred."[15]

Colden had received his political education, as it were, from Governor Hunter. Through him, Colden became acquainted with the factionalism of provincial politics, the problems of dealing with the assembly, the necessity for compromise on the part of the executive in obtaining funds to meet government expenses including salaries, and, finally, the dire prediction that such compromises, if left unchecked, might eventually lead to a general rebellion against the mother country. Now, almost as if it all had come full circle, Colden was himself in a singular position to exercise the largely self-appointed task of retaining, if not enhancing, the residual aspects of the executive prerogative that had gradually diminished over time.

Admittedly, he had criticized the exercise of certain prerogatives by Governor Cosby (1732–1736) when he himself was part of an informal opposition. By 1760, however, he could only regard the assembly as having gone too far in diminishing the powers of the executive office, so that the office itself appeared largely titular, and its occupant was even subject to personal affronts. Clinton was a case in point. He believed himself to be so humiliated, especially in public, that he requested to be recalled. Although family problems evidently had a role, Clinton's successor, Sir Danvers Osborne, having witnessed Clinton's treatment at his own reception and being more fully informed of the workings of provincial politics, committed suicide the day after his inauguration.[16]

It was in his initial period as lieutenant governor, from 1760 to 1762, that Colden asserted certain prerogatives that had fallen largely into disuse. One of these related to the appointment of judges to the provincial Supreme

Court. These had usually been regarded as permanent positions or, as it was phrased, appointed "during good behavior." Instead, Colden now insisted that these be made subject to subsequent review and/or recall, as connoted by the alternative phrase, "during the King's pleasure." At issue, too, was Colden's attempt to attach a permanent salary to the office so as to remove it from the undue influence of various political groups, just as he had supported a fixed income for the governor from quit-rents for the same purposes. The assembly would not agree to the salary proposal, however, and the attempt to bring in an independent judge from outside the province to serve in this capacity also met such resistance that it was quickly abandoned. The matter was not resolved until an order arrived in 1762 from the British ministry that such appointments should, indeed, be made "during the King's pleasure" only.[17]

More dramatic developments awaited Colden in his second stint as acting governor, from 1763 to 1765, when he occupied the office largely as a substitute for Governor Robert Monckton. The latter resided only sporadically in the province and later became preoccupied with directing a military mission to the West Indies. As his paper on the "State of the Province" suggests, Colden remained adamant on the topic of the large land grants, making further submissions to the ministry, including maps and supporting documents, in 1764 and 1765.[18] Previous attempts to deal with this issue in the province had been unsuccessful, and the problems associated with some of the major patents were resolved only through intervention from Great Britain. This was more the exception than the rule, however, as most holdings remained unchanged.

In what would become a *cause célèbre*, Colden became involved in a legal proceeding in 1764 that raised a procedural issue relating to the nature of appeals. Historically, appeals to the provincial council had been permitted only on the basis of an alleged error in the court's proceedings. In the case that was brought to Colden's attention, *Forsey v. Cunningham*, the latter— having been held personally liable for legal costs and compensation—had appealed the verdict. It was here that Colden lent his direct support to move the proceedings from a lower court to the provincial council and, thereafter, for possible submission to the Privy Council itself. The legal community was outraged by Colden's decision, regarding it as a novel and dangerous precedent and, moreover, as an arbitrary intrusion in legal affairs. Colden was now accused of undermining trial by jury—as enshrined in English common law—and, equally, of establishing, without warrant, a new court.

For Colden, however, the issue was simply one of protecting the prerogative and restricting the dominance of the legal fraternity in the province. It may also have been part of an agenda for a subsequent legal review of the large land grants that so far had eluded any real reform.[19] In any case, Colden defended his decision as adherence to his instructions, as duty required, and argued that "he conceived of this being the only legal method

by which the King's rights & authority in the colonies can be secured &
the people can be protected from iniquitous & oppressive verdicts and judgments."[20] Colden also cited a political context relating to this issue when
he noted that without the right of appeal to the Crown, he remained persuaded that "the dependency of the colonies cannot be preserved." Nevertheless, the general uproar over this issue in the colony finally convinced
the British ministry to void the appeal process.

The opposition of the legal community only convinced Colden that he
had proven his case, that the allowing of appeals "will weaken or destroy
their associations & domination." He admitted that through his actions he
had incurred their hatred and malice, which, he added, he bore with patience. The legal community reacted by publishing in the New York *Weekly
Post Boy* a series of columns entitled "Sentinal" that were later also printed
separately and widely distributed.[21] Colden described the articles as filled
with "the vilest & most abusive invective" and intended to render him odi-
ous to the people. Colden regarded the "people," largely those of the fourth
rank, as generally decent and responsible, but now made "dupes" primarily
by the lawyers who resorted to any means to hold him up to ridicule and
make his support of the prerogative tantamount to a threat to their liberties.
Caricatures of Colden were also drawn and distributed. He suspected that
there were "two or three lawyers" behind this campaign. He wrote: "Were
the people freed from the dread of this dominion of lawyers, I flatter myself
with giving general joy to the people of this province. I never received the
least opposition in my administration except when I opposed the views of
this faction."[22]

It was against this immediate background that the Stamp Act crisis developed in the colonies. The stamps arrived in New York in October 1765.
Personal threats and attacks against their distributors in other colonies, notably in New England, and a meeting of the colonies at a convention in
Massachusetts to develop a common plan to deal with this issue, had made
Colden cautious about the best means for their storage and delivery in the
province. He decided to temporarily retain them at the fort pending their
eventual distribution. While he might have waited for the newly appointed
governor, Sir Henry Moore, to arrive to deal with this contentious issue,
the governor's delay in arriving prompted Colden to renew his oath of office
in the interim and thereby assume sole executive responsibility for enforcing
the Stamp Act.

There had already been a fairly serious incident when the ship carrying
the stamps had arrived in port and a mob gathered and threatened to destroy
both the ship and the cargo if the stamps were not delivered to them.[23] The
stamps were thereafter transferred to a British frigate and eventually brought
to the fort. For a time, at least, the crisis seemed to have abated, as Colden
observed. It would prove to be only the lull before the storm. On November
1, 1765, an anonymous letter was delivered at the fort telling Colden that

his oath to enforce the act made him "the chief murderer" of the rights and privileges of its citizens, and any attempts to proceed with their distribution would make him a martyr to his own "villainy." Moreover, the letter contained the threat that he would be hanged and anyone who assisted him in this task would also be put to death.[24] Gradually, a large mob gathered in front of the fort that evening, carrying a portable gallows on which they had placed two effigies: one of Colden with a stamped paper in his hand and on his back the sign of "The Drummer"—a reference to his alleged role in the 1715 rebellion in Scotland. The other effigy was of the devil whispering in Colden's ear. The crowd made their way almost to the gate of the fort and taunted the soldiers on the ramparts to fire. When they refused to react to this provocation, the mob gradually dispersed only to force open Colden's coach house outside the fort, remove his carriage, sledges, and stable furniture, and take them and the effigies to a nearby field where they were destroyed in a large bonfire.[25]

While the fort was given additional reinforcements the next day and Colden put members of his family on a British vessel as a precaution, he also called a council meeting to try and defuse the situation. On the council's advice, he agreed not to distribute the stamps, but wait to deliver them to Governor Moore, who had yet to arrive in the colony. While Colden noted that this gave "satisfaction to great numbers," there were still those who demanded that the stamps be removed from the fort and placed on board a ship in the harbor. When the captain of the ship refused to become a party to this proposal, it was decided to turn the stamps over to the mayor and corporation of the city. It was only when this was done that, Colden observed, "the mob entirely dispersed, and the City remained in perfect tranquility."[26] The following April, the Stamp Act was repealed by Parliament.

It had proven an ugly incident for Colden, and one in which he had some cause to fear for his life. When he subsequently tried to obtain some compensation for the property that had been destroyed by the mob, the hostility shown him was confirmed when the assembly not only refused to consider his request, but went so far as to hold him accountable for any losses he had suffered. From Great Britain, too, he was censured for his inconsistency in carrying out his responsibilities with regard to the Stamp Act.[27]

With the arrival of Governor Henry Moore, Colden also found himself out of favor. The new governor tried to distance himself from Colden and held him largely responsible for any sporadic unrest thereafter. The new governor tried to placate the population by removing the additional fortifications that been installed in the fort, inviting the public in for tours, and making himself accessible by frequent socializing with the population at large. Moore's behavior was such that, as Colden put it, could not "but chagrin a person who had immediately preceded him in the chief command." It left him with only one option. As he wrote to a correspondent, "I thought it proper to retire to the Country."[28]

The "country" this time, however, was not to be Coldengham, but a property consisting of 120 acres in the vicinity of Flushing, Queens, at a distance of some fifteen miles from the city. Having purchased the property in 1762, Colden built a home with a garden that would serve as his country place for such times when he was not required to be in residence at the fort, or for use in the summer months as a bucolic escape from the city. Known as "Spring Hill," Colden's home still stands and in its features replicates some of those found at Coldengham. According to one report, at least, "the workmanship displays the care and characteristics of Colden in its construction. The foundations are solid thick walls, with the largest of the beams hand hewn. The halls and rooms are spacious with high ceilings."[29]

In other respects, however, 1762 was an unhappy year in Colden's personal life. His wife of nearly forty-seven years, who had assisted him so ably in the management of his estate that it had been feasible for him to pursue his myriad scientific and philosophical interests or "amusements," died in January of that year. After a long illness, one of his younger daughters died later the same year. Joining him at Spring Hill was his son, David, who thereafter served largely as his personal secretary, together with David's wife. It was their son, Cadwallader D., who would be born in the house and later serve in various political offices, including those of mayor of New York, congressman, and state senator.[30]

On Governor Moore's death in 1769, Colden became acting governor prior to the arrival of John Murray, Earl of Dunmore, in 1770. By this time, Colden might have appeared as a perennial figure in provincial politics, periodically materializing, as it were, to take over the government, as he would do again for a brief period in 1774–1775. Keeping Governor Monckton informed about these later developments, one writer could report: "He [Colden] fairly lives himself into office, being, they tell us, as hearty as when you knew him . . . the old man seems to be the Son of fortune in his advanced years."[31]

When Colden left government in 1770, the occasion was marked with numerous presentations made by the merchants of the city, including members of the Marine Society for whom Colden had procured a charter, and with various representatives of the Anglican Church also present. Colden later reported that "since I left the town I have been informed that other distinguished bodies designed to have made me the like complements had I not left the place sooner than expected."[32] Things remained relatively quiet thereafter, perhaps because of a growing reaction to the excesses associated with the opposition to the Stamp Act.

Something of his physical appearance at that advanced age is conveyed in a formal portrait that was painted circa 1772, showing him seated with his grandson, Warren DeLancey, standing nearby. His arm circles the child, and placed on a table in the painting are various objects—including a globe, a book and an astronomical diagram—all of which may have symbolic reference to Colden's scientific pursuits and his intent to inculcate these interests in his progeny. In its formality, the portrait shows him as serene, dignified, and composed. It probably was the way he would have wished to appear in public, but the contrast between his private and public *personae* was quite distinct. As a contemporary writer observed, Colden "had no friends but a few personal ones, and no enemies but a few public ones."[33]

At least one contemporary described Colden as having a "cheerfulness of disposition."[34] In his own family he was recognized as an affectionate and caring *paterfamilias*, concerned with his children's upbringing and education and, where he might, using his office to advance their public careers, a not uncommon practice in the colony. As exemplified in some of his writings and letters, he also took a continuing interest in the education and upbringing of his grandchildren. Again, through his extensive correspondence, he encouraged and supported the scientific activities of others in the colonies. He was a gracious host and generous in giving his time to visitors to his estate at Coldengham. Individuals such as John Bartram, Alexander Garden, and Samuel Bard all testify to the especial value they placed on their mutual friendship with Colden. Living in a remote location, he lacked that scientific fellowship for which he tried to find some compensation through the proposals he made for various societies to both William Douglass in Boston and Benjamin Franklin in Philadelphia. In short, he was involved in a continuing search for some broader community that would sustain and mutually share in its members' endeavors. Finally, an evident humanitarianism and general sense of benevolence are certainly conveyed in such literary productions as his *Indian History* and in his dedication, for example, to the improvement of medicine in the colonies to benefit his fellow man.

By comparison, a personal characterization based exclusively on Colden's public *persona* would remain largely one-dimensional. In this context, at least, contemporaries generally described him as "curt," "dogmatic," and "stubborn" in his views. His biographer notes that "he had many excellent social qualities" but then, in a more critical tone, adds that "the moment his mind touched on politics . . . his sympathy, his plasticity, his humanity even, dropped from him and he became a martinet, an intolerant theorist, an implacable stickler for the letter of the law, while tact and common sense became qualities to him unknown."[35] His physical appearance was unprepossessing: "He was diminutive, and somewhat more than high-shouldered," according to a contemporary account; there was a considerable "contrast between the wealth of his mind, and the poverty of his outward appearance."[36] He never attempted—indeed, he found it impossible—to cultivate a following or to engender any rapport with one or more of the factions in the political landscape of the colony. It is perhaps this that led Colden himself to lament: "But what can a man do who has no hands?"[37]

He evidently failed to perceive the temper of the times, and acted strictly on the basis of his entrenched views and fundamental political beliefs. He saw himself as a loyal servant of the Crown and, accordingly, as one of its officials who remained committed to preserving the prerogatives of its representatives in the context of a "mixed government." In his view, it was only through such means that a balance was preserved between the "democratical," monarchial, and aristocratic elements of society—at least insofar as this model could be replicated in the province within an imperial context. Moreover, increasing age only exacerbated such views, often prompting him to take an adversarial stance that promoted antagonism and confrontation. As one witness testified, "the Old Gentleman, tho Eighty-five years old, does not dislike a little controversy, which he has been engaged in for the greatest part of his life."[38]

An evident *hauteur*, often exhibited toward others, masked an overt sensitivity toward his status or reputation and, indeed, even his place in history. On innumerable occasions he went to great lengths to provide an alternative explanation or account if he was under any suspicion that he had been unfairly impugned or derelict in performing his duties. While many of these would be directed to the British ministry on such matters as land grants, the allocation of fees and payments while in office, and latterly the controversy surrounding appeals or his role in the Stamp Act crisis, the one that proved most enduring in its intensity was his response to a work written by the lawyer and historian, William Smith, Jr. [39]

As noted, William Smith, Jr., was a member of a legal triumvirate that also included William Livingston and John Morin Scott, a group that was to assume increasing prominence in the province after 1750. All three had received at least part of their legal education from William Smith, Sr., who had attended Yale College and studied law in England. The elder Smith did much to raise the standards and qualifications for legal education, and it was largely through such efforts that the professional status of lawyers was advanced in the colony.[40] He subsequently became attorney general of New York and a member of the provincial council.[41] Politically, he was part of the group that included Colden and James Alexander and, for a time, became Colden's close friend and political associate. While the son may have shared many of his father's political views, his relationship with Colden would prove decidedly more contentious.

The major work of William Smith, Jr., his *History of the Province of New York*, was published in London in 1757. It evolved out of a commission he had received, together with William Livingston, to edit the laws of New York dating back to 1691. Essentially, it became a digest of all laws passed in the province, including those that had been revoked or allowed to lapse. In this work, Smith particularly cited a law, which had been passed in 1699 and which had voided several large land grants; the original document pertaining to this law was now missing from the records. It was apparently intended that this information would be appended as a marginal note to the citation.

As it happened, Colden himself had purchased one of the vacated grants and now—fearful that this disclosure might jeopardize his claim—told Smith that he would use his influence with the governor to prevent Smith from being compensated for his work if the offending marginal note were not removed from the text. The threat had no effect. Smith would have regarded this suggestion not only as a personal affront, but also as an aspersion on his professional ethics. According to his account, at least, he promptly told Colden "he and the money might go to the Devil, and rushed from the room."[42] He was to become Colden's implacable foe, and thereafter resorted to using every opportunity he could to impugn Colden's reputation. The fact, of course, that Smith was also a member of that very "rank" or faction that Colden despised and held accountable for many of his enduring political problems only sustained their mutual antipathy. Colden, in turn, was not someone to mince words and did not hesitate to describe Smith as "a crafty, malicious smooth-tongued hypocrite."[43]

The publication of Smith's *History* set the stage for a lengthy diatribe by Colden, both in correspondence with Smith, who dismissed his criticisms, and thereafter in a series of lengthy letters Colden wrote to his son, Alexander, in which he took issue with the details and interpretations found in the *History*. These letters were to become a kind of commentary that was intended to provide an alternative account to that presented by Smith, or a kind of mini-history of its own. Smith's *History* also gave cause for others to complain as well. Samuel Johnson, president of King's College, particularly noted with displeasure Smith's denigration of the role of the Anglican Church and its missionary work in the colonies.[44]

Colden's review of Smith's *History* led him to complain of such particulars as that the work was more favorable to the Dutch than the English; that Smith had rated some governors higher than others and conversely, had not given enough credit to those that Colden particularly admired, such as Hunter and Burnet. Again, Colden argued that Smith remained too partial to the assembly in its relationship with various governors of the province. While these were general observations, Colden was to become particularly incensed because Smith—who had intended to cover the period up to 1732—had extended it specifically to include an incident that indirectly involved Colden in his role as surveyor general of the province in 1740.

Smith's version was that an offer of a land grant had been made to a Scottish promoter who had intended to settle Scottish families on the land, but who subsequently discovered that the amount of land he had initially expected had not materialized once he arrived in the colony with the settlers. For this unfortunate situation, Smith held Colden and other provincial officials responsible. According to Colden, the promoter knew that the land had already been allocated to others and that the settlers had no intention of becoming tenants; in any case, they were able to obtain land on their own once they arrived in the colonies. Various papers and official reports on this episode largely confirm Colden's account.[45] In short, Smith had shown a bias that obscured or ignored documentary evidence, but then historical objectivity was not always the primary consideration in such politically tainted accounts.

In other respects, too, Smith found the means to use his influence to provoke Colden while the latter was in office. When Robert Monckton arrived in the colony, he had yet to receive his commission and instructions for his government. On the day set aside for his inauguration, it was discovered that these were missing and, contrary to procedure, the event took place without the proper documents. Colden raised the issue of certain legalities, which led Smith to inform Monckton that Colden had certainly known of this situation all along and was only intent on preventing Monckton from taking his oath of office.[46]

Moreover, Smith used his influence in an attempt to place several new restrictions and conditions on the salary and fees that would accrue to Colden while he exercised the office of acting governor after Monckton had left on his military excursion to the West Indies. One plan proposed by Smith included the stipulation that Colden would receive nothing until Monckton's return, when the issue of the division of fees and perquisites would be decided; later, a less drastic proposal was made that would require Colden to take an oath—with a security payment and liability for any penalties—for failure to provide a strict account of income and expenses in the governor's absence.[47] While Monckton refrained from enforcing some of these terms and conditions on his return, Colden evidently would have known who had suggested such humiliating schemes merely to allow him to retain some of the basic emoluments of his office.

As a historian, Smith was also determined to leave for posterity an unflattering portrait of Colden that was intended to survive for all time. He had, as already mentioned, noted Colden's entry into the political affairs of the colony in 1760, but thereafter he was quick to note about this event: "the public soon after the session discovered Mr. Colden's late promotion to the rank of Lieutenant Governor was not the reward of merit, but the effort of low craft and condescension and fraud."[48] Even after Colden's death, he filled his diary at some considerable length in characterizing what he regarded as Colden's "Duplicity, Pride, Craft, Obstinacy, Vanity, Petulance, Ambition, vindictive Spirit and Avarice." Not satisfied even with this demeaning account, he went on to describe Colden as "quick and subtle, conceited and fond of Disputation, easily flattered, and anxious for preeminence in all Topics of Conversation, and rather disgustful than insinuating for he was hot, coarse, & assuming."[49]

If Colden's only enemies were public (as one witness contended) then Smith's campaign of vilification is certainly an example—even if an altogether exaggerated one—of the animosity, verging on outright hostility, that Colden could arouse toward his public *persona*. And if in private he only had friends, then it may be worth recalling that Franklin himself would, in the end, abandon him, deliberately failing to mention anything of their long association and the extensive correspondence they shared on scientific and various philosophical subjects, in his own *Autobiography,* this was due primarily to their identification with different political camps at the onset of the events leading to the American Revolution. Finally, Colden never achieved the recognition he sought above all for what was surely his most arduous scientific and intellectual endeavor, *The Principles of Action in Matter.* It was this work which he hoped and expected would put him in the "company of the great ones." Failing that, it was to be more his public than his private career, perhaps more his political than his scientific role, that was generally apt to draw the interest and attention of posterity.

In August 1776, now well into his eighty-eighth year, Colden drew up his last will and testament, providing for the division of his properties among his several heirs and stipulating that "his body be interred in a private manner with as little expense as with common decency may be." He died within a month, on September 20, 1776, and was buried in a small family plot located on the grounds of Spring Hill. His death marked the end of an era.

David, his son, remained as administrator of the estate until his political allegiances finally compelled him to migrate to England. As a loyalist, the estate that had been passed to him was seized as enemy property. Several years later, it was sold to a family and subsequently passed through various owners until it was eventually purchased by a cemetery association in the nineteenth century, complete with the house that Colden himself had built and occupied while serving as lieutenant governor of New York. As to his gravesite, no marker remains.

NOTES

1. Cadwallader Colden to Peter Collinson, *The Colden Letter Books,* 2 Vols., New-York Historical Society, *Collections* I, 28.

2. Cadwallader Colden to Thomas Pownall, August 22, 1760, in ibid., 13.

3. Patricia U. Bonomi, *A Factious People* (New York, 1971), 13.

4. Benjamin Franklin to Cadwallader Colden, October 11, 1750, *Colden Papers,* IV, 227.

5. Ibid., 176.

6. Ibid., 221.

7. Ibid., 155.

8. Bonomi, 155.

9. Alice M. Keys, *Cadwallader Colden: A Representative Eighteenth-Century Official* (New York, 1906), 184.

10. Ibid., 230.

11. Colden: "Memorandum" (May 6, 1752) appended to "The Lands of New York" (1732), Colden MSS, New-York Historical Society.

12. Cadwallader Colden, "State of the Province of New York," December 6, 1765, *Colden Letter Books,* II, 68–69.

13. Ibid., 69.

14. Ibid., 70.

15. Ibid.

16. E. Burrows and M. Wallace, *Gotham: A History of New York City* (New York, 1999), 179.

17. Milton M. Klein, *The Politics of Diversity* (Pt. Washington, N.Y., 1974), 161.

18. Colden, "State of the Province," 70.

19. Carole Shammas, "Cadwallader Colden and the Role of the King's Prerogative," *The New-York Historical Society Quarterly*, 53 (1969), 122.

20. Colden, "State of the Province," 73.

21. Keys, 309.

22. Cadwallader Colden to the Earl of Halifax, February 22, 1765, *Colden Letter Books*, I, 470–471.

23. Cadwallader Colden to the Lords Commissioners for Trade and Plantations, December 6, 1765, *Colden Letter Books*, II, 79.

24. "Notice served on Cadwallader Colden Concerning the Stamp Act," *Colden Papers*, VII, 85.

25. Lieutenant Governor Cadwallader Colden to the Lords of Trade, December 6, 1765, in E.B. O'Callaghan, *Documents Relating to the Colonial History of the State of New York*, 15 Vols. (Albany, N.Y., 1856–1857), VII, 792.

26. Ibid.

27. Secretary Conway to Cadwallader Colden, *Colden Letter Books*, II, 94–6.

28. James A. Wall, "Cadwallader Colden and His Homestead at Spring Hill, Flushing, Long Island," *The New-York Historical Society Quarterly*, 8 (1924), 12.

29. Ibid., 11.

30. Ibid., 16, 18.

31. James G. Wilson, *The Memorial History of the City of New York* (New York, 1892), 2 Vols., II, 400.

32. Ibid., 410.

33. Mrs. Anne Grant, *Memoirs of an American Lady with Sketches of Manners and Scenes in America as They Existed Previous to the Revolution* (New York, 1901), 6.

34. E.R. Purple, *Genealogical Notes of the Colden Family* (New York, 1873), 8.

35. Keys, 365.

36. Grant, *Memoirs*, 5. Another writer notes, "In stature he was small and high shouldered, of a dignified aspect, with a strong confirmation of body and a vigorous constitution." Purple, 8.

37. Cadwallader Colden to the Lords Commissioners For Trade and Plantations, January 22, 1765, *Colden Letter Books*, I, 45.

38. Quoted in Bonomi, 154.

39. Following the Stamp Act crisis, for example, Colden prepared and published a tract entitled "The Conduct of Cadwallader Colden, Esquire, Late lieutenant governor of New York, relating to the Judges Commissions, Appeals to the King and the Stamp Duty," *Colden Letter Books*, II, 429.

40. L.F.S. Upton, *The Loyal Whig: William Smith of New York and Quebec* (Toronto, 1969), 5.

41. William Smith, Jr., *The History of the Province of New York*, ed., Michael Kammen (Boston, 1972), 2 Vols., I, "Introduction," xviii.

42. Upton, 18–19.

43. Cadwallader Colden to John Pownall, November 26, 1761, *Colden Letter Books*, I, 137.

44. Ibid., 20.

45. William Smith, "Introduction," lxx.

46. Keys, 279.

47. Ibid., 280–283.

48. William Smith, 266.

49. Ibid., "Introduction," lxx.

SELECTED BIBLIOGRAPHY

COLDEN WORKS

Colden, Cadwallader. *An Abstract from DR. BERKELEY's Treatise on TAR WA-TER, with Some Reflexions Thereon, Adapted to Diseases frequent in America.* New York, 1745.

———. "Account of the Climate and Diseases of New York." *American Medical and Philosophical Register*, 1 (1811): 304–310.

———. "Annotationes in Physicam Generalem." University of Edinburgh Library.

———. *The Colden Letter Books.* 2 Vols. New York Historical Society. *Collections*, 9–10 (1876–1877).

———. "Copy Book of Letters on Subjects of Philosophy, Medicine, Friendship." Colden MSS, New-York Historical Society.

———. "The Cure of Cancers." *Gentleman's Magazine*, 21 (1751): 305–308; 22 (1752), 22.

———. *An Explication of the First Causes of Matter and of the Cause of Gravitation.* New York. 1745.

———. *An Explication of the First Causes of Matter and of the Cause of Gravitation.* London, 1746.

———. "Extract of a letter from Cadwallader Colden to Dr. Fothergill, concerning the Throat Distemper." *Medical Observations and Inquiries*, 1 (1763): 211–227.

———. *The History of the Five Indian Nations Depending on the Province of New York in America.* Ithaca, N.Y., 1964.

———. *The Letters and Papers of Cadwallader Colden.* 9 Vols. New-York Historical Society. *Collections*, 50–56 (1917–1923); 67–68 (1934–35).

————. *Letters on Smith's History of New York.* New York Historical Society. *Collections,* 1 (1868), 181–235.

————. "New Method of Printing." *American Medical and Philosophical Register,* 1 (1811): 439–445.

————. "Observations on the Fever which prevailed in the City of New York in 1741 and 2, written in 1743." *American Medical and Philosophical Register,* 4 (1814): 310–330.

————. "Observations on the YELLOW FEVER of Virginia, with some REMARKS on Dr. John Mitchell's Account of the Disease." *American Medical and Philosophical Register,* 4 (1814): 378–383.

————. "Of the First Principles of Morality or of the Actions of Intelligent Beings." Colden MS. The Rosenbach Museum and Library (Philadelphia).

[Colden, Cadwallader]. *PAPER Relating to an ACT of the ASSEMBLY of the Province of New York, For Encouragement of the Indian Trade, etc. and for Prohibiting the Selling of Indian Goods to the French, viz. of CANADA.* New York, 1724.

Colden, Cadwallader. *The Principles of Action in Matter, the Gravitation of Bodies, and the Motion of the Planets, explained from those Principles.* London, 1751.

————. *Unprinted Scientific and Political Papers.* New-York Historical Society.

Cadwallader Colden to Mrs. Elizabeth DeLancey (1737). DeLancey Papers. The Museum of the City of New York.

Letters to Cadwallader Colden from Dr. William Douglass. Massachusetts Historical Society. *Collections* (4th Series), 2 (1854), 164–189.

Letters to Cadwallader Colden from Benjamin Franklin, John Bartram, Samuel Johnson, Thomas Clap, Samuel Pike, John Fothergill, Robert Whytt. *Gratz Collection.* Historical Society of Pennsylvania.

BOOKS AND ARTICLES

Albert, E.M., T.C. Denise, and S.P. Paterfreund, eds. *Great Traditions in Ethics.* New York, 1953.

Aldridge, Albert O. *Benjamin Franklin: Philosopher and Man.* Philadelphia, 1965.

The America of 1750: Peter Kalm's Travels in North America. 2 Vols. New York, 1964.

Anderson, Paul R., and M. Fisch. *Philosophy in America: From the Puritans to James.* New York, 1939.

Andrade, E.N. da C. *Sir Isaac Newton.* New York, 1954.

Augustyn, Robert T., and Paul E. Cohen. *Manhattan in Maps, 1527–1995.* New York, 1997.

Axtell, James L. *The Educational Writings of John Locke.* Cambridge, 1968.

Ball, W.W. Rouse. *A Short Account of the History of Mathematics.* New York, 1960.

Barnes, Harry E. *A History of Historical Writing.* New York, 1962.

Barnes, S.B., and A.A. Skerpan. "Historiography under the Impact of Rationalism and Revolution." *Research Series 1,* 40 (1952). Kent State University, Kent, Ohio.

Baron, Margaret E. *The Origins of the Infinitesimal Calculus.* London, 1969.

Beck, John B. *Medicine in the American Colonies.* Albuquerque, N.Mex., 1966.

Becker, Carl. *History of the Political Parties in the Province of New York, 1760–1776.* Madison, Wis., 1960.

Bell, Arthur. *Newtonian Science.* London, 1961.

Bell, Whitfield J. "Medical Practice in Colonial America." *Bulletin of the History of Medicine*, 31 (1957): 442–453.

Bender, Thomas. *New York Intellect.* New York, 1987.

Berkeley, Edmund, and Dorothy Smith. *Dr. Alexander Garden of Charles Town.* Chapel Hill, N.C. 1969.

———. *Dr. John Mitchell: The Man Who Made the Map of North America.* Chapel Hill, N.C., 1974.

Berkeley, George. *Works.* 5 Vols. London, 1949–1955.

"Biographical Sketch of the late Honourable Cadwallader Colden, formerly Lieutenant-Governor of New York, with an account of his Writings." *The American Medical and Philosophical Register*, 1 (1814): 297–303.

Bissell, Benjamin. *The American Indian in English Literature of the Eighteenth Century.* New Haven, Conn., 1925.

Blake, John B. "Diseases and Medical Practice in Colonial Virginia." *International Record of Medicine*, 171 (1958): 350–363.

———. "Yellow Fever in Eighteenth Century America." *Bulletin of the New York Academy of Medicine*, 44, no. 6 (1968): 673–686.

Blewitt, George. *An Inquiry Whether a General Practice of Virtue Tends to the Wealth or Poverty, Benefit or Disadvantage of a People?* London, 1725.

Boas, Marie. "The Establishment of the Mechanical Philosophy." *Osiris*, 10 (1952): 412–541.

Boerhaave, Herman. *A Method of Studying Physic.* London, 1719.

Bolingbroke, Henry. *Letters on the Use and Study of History.* London, 1752.

Bonomi, Patricia U. *A Factious People.* New York, 1971.

Boorstin, Daniel J. *The Americans: The Colonial Experience.* New York, 1958.

Boyer, Carl B. *The History of the Calculus and Its Conceptual Development.* New York, 1959.

Brasch, Frederick E. "The Newtonian Epoch in the American Colonies (1680–1783)." *Proceedings of the American Antiquarian Society*, 48–49 (1939): 314–332.

———. "James Logan, a Colonial Mathematical Scholar and the First Copy of Newton's *Principia* to Arrive in the Colonies." *Proceedings of the American Philosophical Society*, 86 (1942), 3–12.

———. "The Royal Society of London and Its Influence upon Scientific Thought in the American Colonies." *The Scientific Monthly*, 33 (1931): 336–355.

Brett-James, Norman G. *The Life of Peter Collinson, F.R.S., F.S.A.* London, 1928.

Bridenbaugh, Carl. *Cities in Revolt: Urban Life in America, 1743–1776.* New York, 1955.

———. *Gentleman's Progress: The Itinerarium of Dr. Alexander Hamilton* (1744) Chapel Hill, N.C., 1948.

Britten, James. "Jane Colden and the Flora of New York." *The Journal of Botany, British and Foreign*, 33 (1895): 12–15.

Brown, Theodore M. "The Mechanical Philosophy and the 'Animal Oeconomy'–A Study in the Development of English Physiology in the Seventeenth and Early Eighteenth Century." Ph.D. Dissertation. Princeton University, 1968.

Buranelli, Vincent. "Colonial Philosophy." *William and Mary Quarterly*, 16 (1959): 343–363.

Burrows, Edwin, and Mike Wallace. *Gotham: A History of New York City*. New York, 1999.

Burtt, Edwin Arthur. *The Metaphysical Foundations of Modern Physical Science*. London, 1964.

Butterfield, Herbert. *The Origins of Modern Science, 1300–1800*. London, 1957.

"Cadwallader Colden." *The Historical Magazine*, 9 (1865): 9–13.

Cajori, Florian. *A History of Physics*. New York, 1962.

Calendar of New York Colonial Commissions, 1680–1770. New York, 1929.

Cassirer, Ernst. *The Philosophy of the Enlightenment*. Boston, 1961.

Castiglioni, Arturo. *A History of Medicine*. New York, 1958.

Caulfield, Ernst. "A History of the Terrible Epidemic Vulgarly Called the Throat Distemper, as it Occurred in his Majesty's New England Colonies Between 1735 and 1740." *Yale Journal of Biology and Medicine*, 11 (1938–1939): 219–272; 277–335.

Cohen, Paul R., and Robert T. Augustyn. *Manhattan In Maps, 1527–1995*. New York, 1997.

Collingwood, R.G. *The Idea of History*. New York, 1956.

Comrie, John D. *History of Scottish Medicine*. 2 Vols. London, 1932.

Conroy, Graham P. "Berkeley and Education in America." *Journal of the History of Ideas*, 21 (1960): 211–221.

Cragg, Gerald R. *Reason and Authority in the Eighteenth Century*. Cambridge, 1964.

Cremin, Lawrence A. *American Education: The Colonial Experience (1607–1783)*. New York, 1970.

Curti, Merle. *The Growth of American Thought*. New York, 1969.

Dalzel, Andrew. *History of the University of Edinburgh*. 2 Vols. Edinburgh, 1862.

Daniels, B.C., ed. *Power and Status: Office Holding in Colonial America*. Middleton, Conn. 1986.

Darlington, William. *Memorials of John Bartram and Humphrey Marshall*. New York, 1967.

Denny, Margaret. "Linnaeus and his Disciple in Carolina: Alexander Garden." *Isis*, 38 (1948): 161–174.

Diderot, M., ed. *Encyclopédie, ou Dictionnaire Raisonné Des Sciences, Des Arts et Des Métiers*. 36 Vols. Geneva, (1777–1779).

Diepgen, Paul. *Geschichte der Medizin*. 3 Vols. Berlin, 1949–1951.

Dijksterhuis, Eduard J. *The Mechanization of the World Picture*. Oxford, 1961.

Doren, Carl V. *Benjamin Franklin*. New York, 1938.

Duffy, John. *Epidemics in Colonial America*. Baton Rouge, La., 1953.

Edinburgh University Theses [Theses Philosophicae]. 1705.

Excell, A.W. "Two Eighteenth-Century American Naturalists: John and William Bartram." *Natural History Magazine*, 2 (1929–1930): 50–58.

Fairchild, Hoxie M. *The Noble Savage: A Study in Romantic Naturalism*. New York, 1928.

Flick, Alexander C., ed. *The Papers of William Johnson*. Albany, N.Y., 1925.

Forbes, Duncan. *Reflexions on the Sources of Incredulity with Regard to Religion*. London, 1750.

Foster, Michael. *Lectures on the History of Physiology during the Sixteenth, Seventeenth and Eighteenth Centuries*. Cambridge, 1924.

Fox, R. Hingston. *Dr. John Fothergill and His Friends: Chapters in Eighteenth Century Life*. London, 1919.

Franklin, Benjamin. *The Autobiography and Other Writings*. Jesse Lemisch, ed. New York, 1961.

Freke, John. *A Treatise on the Nature and Property of Fire*. London, 1752.

Garrison, Fielding H. *An Introduction to the History of Medicine*. Philadelphia, 1929.

Gasking, Elizabeth, B. *Investigations into Generation, 1651–1828*. Baltimore, 1967.

Gentilcore, Roxanne M. "The Classical Tradition and American Attitudes towards Nature in the 17th and 18th Centuries." Ph.D. Dissertation. Boston University, 1992.

Gilmour, John. *British Botanists*. London, 1944.

Gitin, Louis L. Cadwallader Colden as Scientist and Philosopher. *New York History*, 16 (1935): 168–177.

Gordon, Maurice Bear. *Aesculapius Comes to the Colonies*. Ventor, N.J., 1949.

Grant, Alexander. *The Story of the University of Edinburgh*. 2 Vols. London, 1884.

Grant, Anne. *Memoirs of an American Lady with Sketches of Manners and Scenes in America as They Existed Previous to the Revolution*. New York, 1901.

Graubard, Mark. *Circulation and Respiration: The Evolution of an Idea*. New York, 1964.

Greene, Jack P., ed. *Settlements to Society*. New York, 1966.

Greene, Robert. *The Principles of the Philosophy of the Expansive and Contractive Forces or an Inquiry into the Principles of the Modern Philosophy, That is, into the Several Chief Rational Sciences, which are Extant*. Cambridge, 1727.

Grummere, Richard M. *The American Colonial Mind and the Classical Tradition*. Cambridge, Mass., 1963.

Haley, Jacquetta M. "Farming on the Hudson Valley Frontier: Cadwallader Colden's Farm Journal, 1727–1736." *The Hudson Valley Regional Review*, 6, no. 1 (March, 1989): 1–34.

Hall, A. Rupert, and Marie Boas. "Newton's Theory of Matter." *Isis*, 50–51 (1959–1960): 131–144.

Hamlin, Paul M. "He Is Gone and Peace to His Shade." *The New-York Historical Society Quarterly*, 36 (1952): 161–174.

Hartley, David. *Observations on Man, His Frame, His Duty, and His Expectations*. Gainesville, Fla., 1966.

Harvey-Gibson, R.J. *Outlines of the History of Botany*. London, 1919.

Hawke, David, ed. *U.S. Colonial History—Readings and Documents*. New York, 1966.

Hazard, Paul. *European Thought in the Eighteenth Century*. Cleveland, Ohio, 1954.

Heaton, Claude E. "Medicine in New York during the English Colonial Period." *Bulletin of the History of Medicine*, 17 (1945): 9–37.

Hesse, Mary B. "Action at a Distance in Classical Physics." *Isis*, 46 (1955): 337–353.

Hindle, Brooke. "Cadwallader Colden's Extension of the Newtonian Principles." *William and Mary Quarterly*, 13 (1956): 459–475.

———. *The Pursuit of Science in Revolutionary America, 1735–1789*. Chapel Hill, N.C. 1956.

————. "The Quaker Background and Science in Colonial Philadelphia." *Isis*, 46 (1955): 243–250.

Hiscock, W.G. *David Gregory, Isaac Newton and Their Circle: Extracts from David Gregory's Memoranda*. Oxford, 1937.

Hoermann, Alfred R. "A Savant in the Wilderness: Cadwallader Colden of New York." *The New-York Historical Society Quarterly*, 62, no. 4 (1978): 271–288.

————. "Cadwallader Colden and the Mind-Body Problem." *Bulletin of the History of Medicine*, 50 (1976): 392–404.

Höffding, Harald. *A History of Modern Philosophy*. New York, 1955.

Hoffer, Peter Charles, ed. *An American Enlightenment*. New York, 1988.

Hornberger, Theodore. "Samuel Johnson of Yale and King's College." *The New England Quarterly*, 8 (1935): 378–397.

————. *Scientific Thought in the American Colleges, 1683–1800*. Austin, Tex., 1945.

Horne, George. *A Fair, Candid, and Impartial State of the Case between Isaac Newton and Mr. Hutchinson*. Oxford, 1753.

Humphrey, David C. "Urban Manners and Rural Morals: The Controversy over the Location of King's College." *New York History*, 54 (1973): 4–23.

Hunt, George T. *The Wars of the Iroquois*. Madison, Wis., 1980.

Hutcheson, Francis. *A System of Moral Philosophy*. London, 1755.

Hutchinson, John. *An Abstract from the Works of John Hutchinson, Esq. Being a Summary of his Discoveries in Philosophy and Divinity*. Edinburgh, 1753.

————. *Moses's Principia. Of The Invisible Parts of Matter; Of Motion; Of Visible Forms; And of Their Dissolution, and Reformation*. London, 1724.

Jarcho, Saul. "Biographical and Bibliographical Notes on Cadwallader Colden." *Bulletin of the History of Medicine*, 32 (1958): 322–334.

————. "Cadwallader Colden as a Student of Infectious Diseases." *Bulletin of the History of Medicine*, 29 (1956): 99–115.

————. "The Correspondence of Cadwallader Colden and Hugh Graham on Infectious Diseases (1716–1719)." *Bulletin of the History of Medicine*, 30 (1956): 195–212.

————. "The Therapeutic Use of Resin and of Tar Water by Bishop George Berkeley and Cadwallader Colden." *History of Medicine in New York State*, 55 (1955): 834–840.

Jones, William. *Memoirs of the Life, Studies and Writings of the Right Reverend George Horne, D.D.* London, 1799.

————. *Physiological Disquisitions; or, on the Natural Philosophy of the Elements*. London, 1781.

————. *The Theological, Philosophical and Miscellaneous Works*. 12 Vols. London, 1801.

Kammen, Michael. *Colonial New York*. White Plains, N.Y., 1987.

Kelly, Howard, A. *A Cyclopedia of American Medical Biography: From 1610–1910*. 2 Vols. Philadelphia, 1912.

Kennedy, Archibald. *The Importance of Gaining and Preserving the friendship of the Indians to the British interest, considered*. New York, 1751.

Keys, Alice M. *Cadwallader Colden: A Representative Eighteenth-Century Official*. New York, 1906.

King, Lester S. *The Growth of Medical Thought*. Chicago, 1963.

————. *The Medical World of the Eighteenth Century.* Chicago, 1958.

Klein, Milton M. "Politics and Personalities in Colonial New York." *New York History*, 47 (1966): 3–16.

Knight, Gowin. *An Attempt to Demonstrate, That all the Phenomena in Nature May be Explained by Two Simple Active Principles, Attraction and Repulsion; Where the Attractions of Cohesion, Gravity, and Magnetism, are shown to be one and the same; and the Phoenomena of the latter are more particularly explained.* London, 1748.

Koyré, Alexandre. *From the Closed World to the Infinite Universe.* Baltimore, 1957.

————. *Newtonian Studies.* London, 1965.

Kraus, Michael. *Atlantic Civilizations: Eighteenth-Century Origins.* Ithaca, N.Y., 1949.

————. "Scientific Relations between Europe and America in the Eighteenth Century." *The Scientific Monthly*, 50 (1942): 259–272.

Lach, Donald F. "China and the Era of the Enlightenment." *Journal of Modern History*, 14 (1942): 209–223.

Lamb, Martha J. *History of the City of New York: Its Origin, Rise and Progress.* 2 Vols. New York, 1877.

Lamprecht, Sterling P. *Locke: Selections.* New York, 1928.

Linnaeus and Jussieu; or, The Rise and Progress of Systematic Botany. London, 1844.

Locke, John. *An Essay Concerning Human Understanding.* 2 Vols. New York, 1959.

Lokken, Roy N. "Discussion on Newton's Infinitesimals in Eighteenth-Century Anglo America." *Historia Mathematica*, 7 (1980): 141–155.

Lucas, F.L. *The Search for Good Sense.* London, 1958.

Luce, Arthur A., and Thomas E. Jessop, eds. *The Works of George Berkeley, Bishop of Cloyne.* 5 Vols. London, 1949–1953.

Lustig, Mary Lou. *Robert Hunter, 1666–1734.* Syracuse, N.Y. 1983.

MacLean, Kenneth. *John Locke and English Literature of the Eighteenth Century.* New Haven, Conn., 1936.

McCutcheon, Roger P. *Eighteenth-Century English Literature.* London, 1958.

McManus, Edgar J. *A History of Negro Slavery in New York.* Syracuse, 1970.

McVicar, John. *A Domestic Narrative of the Life of Samuel Bard, M.D., L.L.D.* New York, 1822.

Middleton, William S. "John Bartram, Botanist." *The Scientific Monthly*, 21 (1925): 191–216.

Mitchell, John. "Account of the YELLOW FEVER which prevailed in VIRGINIA in the years 1737, 1741, and 1742, in a Letter to the late CADWALLADER COLDEN, Esq. In New York." *American Medical and Philosophical Register*, 4 (1814): 181–215; John Mitchell, "Additional Observations on the YELLOW FEVER of Virginia, addressed to Benjamin Franklin," in ibid., 383–387.

Morais, Herbert. *Deism in Eighteenth-Century America.* New York, 1934.

Morgan, Alexander, ed. *Charters, Statutes, and Acts of the Town Council and the Senatus, 1583–1858.* Edinburgh, 1937.

Newlin, Claude L. *Philosophy and Religion in Colonial America.* New York, 1961.

Newton, Isaac. *Mathematical Principles of Natural Philosophy.* Ed. Florian Cajori. Berkeley, Calif., 1946.

———. *OPTICKS, or a Treatise on the Reflections, Refractions, Inflections and Colours of Light.* 4th edition. New York, 1952.

New York: A Chronological and Documentary History, 1524–1970. Dobbs Ferry, N.Y., 1974.

O'Callaghan, E.B., ed. *The Documentary History of the State of New York.* 4 Vols. Albany, N.Y., 1849–1851.

———. E.B., ed. *Documents Relating to the Colonial History of the State of New York.* 15 Vols. Albany N.Y., 1856–1857.

Packard, Francis R. *History of Medicine in the United States.* 2 Vols. New York, 1931.

Pannekoek, Antonie. *A History of Astronomy.* New York, 1961.

Pemberton, Henry. *A View of Sir Isaac Newton's Philosophy.* Dublin, 1728.

Porterfield, William. *A Treatise on the Eye, the Manner and Phaenomenon of Vision.* 2 Vols. Edinburgh, 1759.

Postell, William. "Medical Education and Medical Schools in Colonial America." *International Record of Medicine,* 171 (1958): 364–379.

Priestley, Joseph. *Disquisitions Relating to Matter and Spirit.* 2 Vols. Birmingham, 1782.

———. *Lectures on History and General Policy; To Which is Prefixed, An Essay on a Course of Liberal Education For Civil and Active Life.* Birmingham, 1788.

Purple, E.R. *Genealogical Notes of the Colden Family.* New York, 1873.

Reed, Howard S. *A Short History of the Plant Sciences.* Waltham, Mass., 1942.

Reichwein, Adolf. *China and Europe: Intellectual and Artistic Contacts in the Eighteenth Century.* London, 1925.

Richards, Horace C. "Some Early American Physicists." *Proceedings of the American Philosophical Society,* 86 (1942): 22–28.

Rickett, J.W., ed. *Botanic Manuscript of Jane Colden, 1724–1766.* New York, 1963.

Robinson, Bryan. *A Short Treatise on the Animal Oeconomy.* Dublin, 1734.

Rush, Benjamin. *An Inquiry into the Influence of Physical Causes Upon the Moral Faculty.* Philadelphia, 1839.

Sachs, Julius von. *History of Botany (1530–1860).* Oxford, 1890.

Savelle, Max. *Seeds of Liberty: The Genesis of the American Mind.* Seattle, Wash., 1965.

Schargo, Nelly Noemie. *History in the Encyclopédie.* New York, 1947.

Schneider, Herbert. *A History of American Philosophy.* New York, 1963.

Schneider, Herbert, and Carol Schneider. *Samuel Johnson, President of King's College: His Career and Writings.* 4 Vols. New York, 1927–1929.

Selby-Bigge, L.A., ed. *British Moralists.* New York, 1965.

Shammas, Carole. "Cadwallader Colden and the Role of the King's Prerogative." *The New-York Historical Society Quarterly,* 53 (1969): 103–126.

Sher, Richard B., and Jeffrey R. Smitten. *Scotland and America in the Age of Enlightenment.* Princeton, N.J. 1990.

Shryock, Richard H. *Medicine and Society in America, 1660–1780.* New York, 1960.

Sidgwick, Henry. *Outlines of the History of Ethics for English Readers.* London, 1960.

Singleton, Esther. *Social New York under the Georges, 1714–1776.* New York, 1902.

Smallwood, William Martin. *Natural History and the American Mind.* New York, 1941.

Smith, James Edward. *Selections of the Correspondence of Linnaeus and other Naturalists.* 2 Vols. London, 1821.

Smith, Preserved. *The Enlightenment, 1687–1776*. New York, 1968.

Smith, William, Jr. *The History of the Province of New York*. Ed. Michael Kammen. 2 Vols. Boston, 1972.

Smollett, Tobias. *The Expedition of Humphrey Clinker*. Oxford, 1930.

Spearman, Robert. *An Enquiry after Philosophy and Theology*. Edinburgh, 1755.

Stanhope, Philip Dormer, Earl of Chesterfield. *The Elements of a Polite Education*. Boston, 1801.

Stephen, Leslie. *History of English Thought in the Eighteenth Century*. 2 Vols. New York. 1962.

Stern, Frederick. *The Growth of Medicine*. Springfield, Ill., 1967.

Stern, Fritz. *The Varieties of History*. New York, 1956.

Stokes, I.N. Phelps. *The Iconography of Manhattan Island, 1498–1909*. 6 Vols. New York, 1915–1928.

Stromberg, R.N. "History in the Eighteenth Century." *Journal of the History of Ideas*, 12 (1951): 49–83.

Strong, E.W. "Newtonian Explications of Natural Philosophy." *Journal of the History of Ideas*, 18 (1957): 49–83.

Suppes, Patrick. "Descartes and the Problem of Action at a Distance." *Journal of the History of Ideas*, 15 (1954): 146–152.

Swem, E.G. *Brothers of the Spade: Correspondence of Peter Collinson of London, and of John Curtis, of Williamsburg, Virginia, 1734–1746*. Barre, Vt., 1957.

Sydenham, Thomas. *Works*. 2 Vols. London, 1848.

Thatcher, Herbert. "Dr. John Mitchell, M.D., F.R.S., of Virginia." *The Virginia Magazine of History and Biography*, 40 (1932): 48–62, 97–110, 268–279; 104.

The Theological, Philosophical and Miscellaneous Works of the Reverend William Jones. London, 1801.

Tinker, Chaucey Brewster. *Nature's Simple Plan: A Phase of Radical Thought in the Mid-Eighteenth Century*. Princeton, N.J. 1922.

Tolles, Frederick B. *James Logan and the Culture of Provincial America*. Boston, 1957.

———. *Meeting House and Counting House: The Quaker Merchants of Colonial Philadelphia, 1682–1763*. New York, 1963.

———. "Philadelphia's First Scientist, James Logan." *Isis*, 47 (1956): 20–30.

Tucker, Louis L. "President Thomas Clap of Yale College: Another 'Founding Father' of American Science." *Isis*, 52 (1961): 55–77.

———. *Puritan Protagonist: President Thomas Clap of Yale College*. Chapel Hill, N.C. 1962.

Upton, L.F.S. *The Loyal Whig: William Smith of New York and Quebec*. Toronto, 1969.

Vail, Anna Murray. "Jane Colden, An Early New York Botanist." *Torreya*, 7 (1907): 21–34.

Wadsworth, Alice Colden. "Sketch of the Colden and Murray Families." Transcript, MS Division, New York Public Library, 1819.

Wall, James A. "Cadwallader Colden and His Homestead at Spring Hill, Flushing, Long Island." *The New-York Historical Society Quarterly*, 8 (1924): 11–20.

Wallace, Margaret V.S. "'BIG' Little Britain: Cadwallader Colden and His Canal." *Orange County Post*, February 20, 1967.

Wasserman, Earl R, ed. *Aspects of the Eighteenth Century.* Baltimore, 1965.

Weaver, George H. "Life and Writings of William Douglass, M.D. (1691–1752)." *Bulletin of the Society of Medical History of Chicago,* 2 (1917–1922): 229–259.

Weigley, Russell F., ed., *Philadelphia: A 300-Year History.* New York, 1982.

Weisinger, Herbert. "The Middle Ages and the Late Eighteenth-Century Historians." *Philological Quarterly,* 27 (1948): 63–70.

Werkmeister, William H. *A History of Philosophical Ideas in America.* New York, 1949.

Whitney, Lois. *Primitivism and the Idea of Progress in English Popular Literature of the Eighteenth Century.* New York, 1965.

Whittaker, Edmund. *A History of the Theories of Aether and Electricity.* 2 Vols. London, 1958.

Whytt, Robert. *The Works of Robert Whytt, M.D.* Edinburgh, 1768.

Wilson, James G. *The Memorial History of the City of New York.* 2 Vols. New York, 1892.

Wolf, Abraham. *A History of Science, Technology and Philosophy in the Eighteenth Century.* 2 Vols. New York, 1961.

Wright, Louis B. *The Cultural Life of the American Colonies, 1607–1763.* New York, 1962.

Wroth, Lawrence, C. *An American Bookshelf, 1755.* Philadelphia, 1934.

Yolton, John W. *Thinking Matter.* Minneapolis, 1983.

INDEX

Alexander James: associate of Colden, 12; criticism of Colden's natural philosophy, 87–88; interest in astronomy, 77–78

Barclay, Reverend Henry: Anglican missionary to the Indians, 165; blames European influence for Indians' "moral corruption," 165; supplies Colden with ethnographic details relating to the Indians, 165

Bartram, John: creates first botanical garden in the American Colonies, 25–26; describes Colden, 25; international botanical reputation, 26; publications relating to natural history, 24

Burnet, Governor William, 11

Chrystie, Alice (Mrs. Cadwallader Colden): marriage to Cadwallader Colden, 5; role in managing Coldengham, 17

Colden, Cadwallader: adopts a philosophical dualism relating to the activities of matter and intelligence, 136;

attacks legal profession in New York, 178–179; attempts to reform large land grants in the province, 177; birth in Ireland, 2; botanical achievements, 19; classifies social rankings in New York, 177–178; corresponds with Dr. Fothergill on the throat distemper, 55–56; critical attitude to excess emotionalism or "enthusiasm" in religion, 125, to "enthusiasm" in history, 126–127; critical response to William Smith, Jr.'s *History of the Province of New York*, 186; death in September 1776, 188; discusses educational precepts for women, 156–158; discusses Franklin's *Proposals Relating to the Education of Youth in Pennsylvania*, 153; discusses the nature of ideas, 114–115; discusses the role of the Intelligent Being, 132–133; discusses several operations of the mind, 130; discusses theories contained in his *Principles of Action in Matter*, 82–83; dismisses the charge of implicit atheism directed at his natural philosophy, 119–120; ed-

About the Author

ALFRED R. HOERMANN is an independent researcher. After completing graduate work in the history of ideas, he has taught courses at several universities and, more extensively, at a visual arts and design institution. He currently resides in Long Island, New York.